NO LIMITS
My Autobiography

NO LIMITS
My Autobiography

IAN POULTER

Quercus

First published in Great Britain in 2014 by

Quercus Editions Ltd
55 Baker Street
Seventh Floor, South Block
London
W1U 8EW

PICTURE CREDITS
(plates numbered in order of appearance)
Getty Images 11, 12, 13, 15, 16, 17, 18, 19, 26, 28, 30, 31, 32, 33, 34, 35, 36, 37, 38
Action Images/Reuters 29
© *Ben Van Hook* 43, 45
Mike Egerton/PA Images 46
All other images provided by Ian Poulter

A CIP catalogue record for this book is available
from the British Library

HB ISBN 978 1 78206 688 0
EBOOK ISBN 978 1 78206 690 3
TPB ISBN 978 1 78206 689 7

10 9 8 7 6

Typeset by Jouve (UK), Milton Keynes

Plates designed by Rich Carr

Printed and bound in Great Britain by Clays Ltd, St Ives plc

I would like to dedicate this book to my darling Katie, my wife and love of my life, as well as to my four proudest accomplishments, my children: Aimee, Luke, Lilly and Joshua. I love you all.

Contents

CONTENTS

INTRODUCTION

'An autobiography? Why would I write an autobiography? I don't read books, and I haven't finished with my career yet. No. Absolutely not. Tell them all no.'

That was Ian's visceral reaction to the flood of book offers we had received post 2012 Ryder Cup, now dubbed the 'Miracle at Medinah'. My business partner of six years, Paul Dunkley, and I fielded phone calls from both sides of the Pond – him in the UK and me in the US. We were both surprised at the somewhat sudden intensity of interest in Ian Poulter.

And to be fair, neither Paul nor I were initially in favour of a book, either. After all, Ian was right: he was nowhere near retirement and ready to recap on his comprehensive playing career. But, the more Paul and I talked about Ian as the person we both know so well (Paul for nineteen years and me for almost seven), the more we thought perhaps it merited further exploration.

Ian is always intense, always raw and always emotional. In a sport where many of his colleagues were 'groomed' to be professional golfers from an early age, Ian willed himself to rise to the top. He has an insatiable appetite to compete at whatever the game may be: golf first and foremost, but snooker, table tennis, darts, or even aiming rubbish at a bin. Whatever the game, Ian wants to beat you at it, for no other reason than to beat you at it.

He's self-confident and decisive. He never views anything or any goal as outside of his grasp. He's easily distracted, but never loses sight of what he wants to achieve or own. He operates most effectively when he's backed into a corner. The higher the pressure, the greater the likelihood of his success.

Paul and I aim to balance Ian's ultra-competitive nature, which often comes with knee-jerk reactions (like the opening comment of this Introduction), with a more objective and analytical approach. Paul deals with on-course mindset and mentoring, and I manage all the Poulter off-course business. It's a balance that works well. It's a balance that ultimately resulted in this book being written.

After a month of convincing conversations, Ian finally agreed to do the book on a couple conditions:

1. That it would not be written or viewed as an end to his story, but more of a beginning.

2. That he could say what he really felt, and when you're around Ian you realise that happens pretty frequently anyway.

And so based on those conditions, this book came into being.

I don't think Ian fully comprehended the amount of work it would take to author something so real and honest. It's easier to manufacture fiction. Truth can be hard, and Ian does not particularly like to let people really 'in'. There are a few of us, very few, who see the other side to the Ryder Cup ninja. The majority of what people see from Ian, on course and through his obsession with Twitter, is when the curtain goes and up and the stage is lit. Paul and I have encouraged Ian to share some of the backstage side. There's a reason Ian likes beautifully made cars and clothing and houses. There's a reason he avoids sad movies.

From my vantage point, I will share this: if you are someone Ian cares about, he will protect and defend you ferociously. If you needed something, anything, he would be offended if he wasn't your first phone call to ask for help. He doesn't only want the best of everything for himself, but he wants it for you too. He's completely generous with his time and possessions.

Ian does all things to the extreme – when he cooks (very well, I might add) he is not shy with the herbs and wine. When he orders champagne, it is routinely a choice vintage. He dons vibrant colours and bold patterns. His watches exhibit complex movements, and his cars are all very fast and loud. But, all these things that Ian surrounds himself with, all these accumulations and toys do not truly fulfil Ian. In truth, they merely explain him. They evidence a journey of a young man from working-class England, an aspiring and obscure athlete who fanatically and tenaciously created this life for himself. It is a life he now deeply appreciates, thoroughly enjoys and always lives with *No Limits*.

R.J. Nemer, September 2014

CHAPTER I

Gary Is No Longer With Us

Gary was thirteen when he died. He was six months younger than me. He always bought some sherbet lemons before school and, at morning registration one day, he was leaning back on his chair in the classroom. The stool tipped too far and he fell backwards. Gary inhaled the sweet. Nobody knew what had happened straight away. The teacher didn't know what to do. I don't think she even knew he'd been sucking a sweet. By the time they got him to hospital, Gary had died.

My mum came to get me from my school. I was at a different school to Gary. I was in a French lesson and the teacher came to the classroom and said I needed to be excused. I saw the emotion on my mum's face and I knew something was wrong. We started to walk back to my nan's house.

'Gary's no longer with us,' Mum said.

I didn't really know how to take it. At that age, I didn't really understand death.

'Can't they bring him back?' I said.

It was a ten-minute walk. I can remember every step of it. Nobody close to me had died before. If only someone knew he had the sweet. If only the teacher had somehow realised he was choking. This kind of grief, which I was about to see in other people, well, it just wasn't something I had ever experienced. Gary was my cousin. He was my uncle Phil's son. He was my mate. I didn't understand what it meant. I played with him most days, every Friday night, every Thursday night, Saturday and Sunday.

And then, suddenly, he was gone.

We were a very close family. There was my dad and his brothers, my uncle Phil and my uncle Ray. Uncle Phil had two kids, Gary and Emma. Uncle Ray's kids were Stuart and Michael. My dad and his brothers were the anchor of our family. Every Friday and Saturday night, we went round to my nan's house in Sish Lane in Stevenage and my mum and dad and my uncles all went down to the Prince of Wales to have a drink and play in the local crib and darts leagues.

Like a lot of working-class families, our free time revolved around sport. My dad and both his brothers played football. Every week was based around my dad's sport at the weekend, and the pub. My mum and dad had met in a pub, the Dun Cow in Stevenage. She worked there for a while behind the bar while she was at college. Back then, in the late seventies and early eighties, what else was there, apart from the pub and sport? There was crap on TV. And, because of my dad's job, we had access to some of the best sports facilities in the area.

My dad worked for British Aerospace and they had an amazing sports ground right next to Stevenage Golf Club. My dad played football there on Saturdays, and my cousins and I would spend all our time down there, playing football or messing around with the arcade games in the clubhouse, while my dad was at his match. They had several rugby fields, football fields – lots of acreage. Table tennis tables, snooker, pool. They were our Saturdays.

My nan had a lovely big back garden and so Gary, his elder sister Emma my brother Danny, who is two years older than me, and I used to play football there. My granddad had died quite young but he had been fantastic at green bowls and the club he had played at was just over the fence. There was a putting green there, too, and for years and years, we used to sneak on to that putting green.

It had those old, painted stainless steel flagpoles with a triangular hoop on the top and numbers on them from one to eighteen. The guy who was manning the hut at the front couldn't see us putting round the back. We used to do that on Friday nights and then, on Saturdays, I snuck off with my brother into the golf club to go out searching for lost balls.

We were a happy little crew until Gary died and my mum came to take me out of school to tell me the news. She picked my brother up at the same time and the three of us walked back to my nan's. Everyone was gathering there. It was a really emotional day and a really emotional year. I took it very badly. I've never really been able to talk about it until now.

So I have blotted it out for a long time. For more than twenty years. Since Gary died, I've become good at putting things in a box and putting the box on a shelf and leaving it there and never going back to it. I don't like to think about unhappy things. I don't want anyone diving too deep into what's inside my mind. I suppose that's why I've never really talked about Gary.

7

It affected my uncle Phil and his wife at the time very badly. They are no longer together. We don't talk about it. I never have talked about it to my uncle Phil because it's very difficult. I don't deal with that kind of stuff that well. I just kind of deal with it myself.

It's not that I want to block it out of my memory, but it is something that was tragic enough . . . I don't like those things. It still upsets me. I don't like seeing people hurting like that. It was a huge shock to the family. You never get over something like that. My uncle Phil will never get over it. There's a hole in the family that can never be filled.

It took me a while to comprehend it – the funeral, all of that. Gary's bedroom was the same for a long time. My uncle Phil never touched anything in his room. He still lives in the same house. It was twenty-five years ago. Unfortunately, it took several weeks to find out properly what had happened. When the post-mortem was being done, there was a lot of speculation as to the cause of his death. In the end, they found the sweet in his throat.

It was agonising. It was an avoidable death. If the teacher had realised he was choking, she could have done the Heimlich manoeuvre and dislodged the sweet. When the stool he was sitting on started to fall over, Gary must have gasped and inhaled the sweet. It seems such a small thing. You're fit and healthy and you pass away because you are eating a fricking sweet.

How has it affected me? Well, because of Gary's death, I tend to hold my emotions in. Emotions on the golf course are different. I can express myself on the golf course and be me. That's me doing what I love to do. But when it comes to personal emotions, I don't want them to affect anybody else. I think I can deal with them my way.

I'm stubborn and my dad's stubborn. I don't like to share my feelings with anybody. Someone took my mate away and there was nothing I could do. I have a really tough time with watching people struggle. I really don't like it. I don't like poverty, either.

I get a lot of pleasure helping people with the Dream-flight charity, which has become a passion of mine. But I find it upsetting to see kids in wheelchairs, to see people suffering from illnesses. It upsets me and I don't like crying. I don't like watching people suffer. I like to see people happy.

I don't think I have ever got over Gary's death. I have never really talked about it properly, or even considered talking about it with anybody in an in-depth way, and when I do it upsets me. I don't see psychologists for that reason. I don't want them digging around. It's my problem and I will deal with it.

There are people in my life I do talk to, who I can open up to, but it's fewer than a handful. If I went to a psychologist, I worry that it would bring stuff to the surface that I don't want to deal with. I choose to block a lot of stuff, and generally that is not the nice stuff. The things that have been difficult, I shove them to one side and mentally move them out of the way so I can do what it is I enjoy doing.

I never want to forget Gary but I don't like dwelling on anything sad. I am a confident person. I am someone who has always been really positive in everything I have ever done. I think that is something which is a strength and not a weakness, so I try not to dwell on things too long. I try to get over them and move on.

I have tried to push the trauma of Gary's death away. I wanted to forget the trauma of it because of the pain I saw it cause. So I try to block stuff and if I can't block something, I move away. That's what my family does. We tend to keep things under. I know I do. I know my dad does. I guess it's an old-school thing, in a way. I'm sure my granddad passing was traumatic for my dad but he never talks about him. I have got to be honest, I was less than two years old so I barely know anything about my Grandad Ron and I think my dad probably doesn't want to talk about him because it's emotional.

I never mentioned Gary to my uncle after the day he died. Not once. I didn't know how to approach the subject. It's something a twelve-year-old can't really deal with. For a while, I could see the pain, so I didn't want to bring it back up. It never got discussed.

My mum and dad split up not long after – maybe a year or so. That wasn't very helpful. My uncle Phil and his wife split at a similar time; the same with my uncle Ray and his wife. I don't know why. I don't know if it was Gary's death. It wasn't going to help. I didn't see any signs of the break-ups, not even with Mum and Dad, to be honest. There was the odd argument in the house, which most people have in their upbringing. Silly little things. My early teenage years, if I look back, they were . . . well, there was a lot of upheaval.

It was tough for a long time. I found my parents' divorce difficult, obviously. Dad was moving out. There were arguments. There was stuff that wasn't right, but if people split up, they split up. It's just not meant to be. I didn't favour sides. I never have and I never will. What happened, happened. I had to deal with that myself. Through those years, there were a lot of unhappy thoughts spinning round in my mind.

When I was sixteen, my dad met somebody else. He was happy and my mum seemed happy and settled. My mum had met a guy called Mark Wall just after the split. He was a teaching pro at the Jack O'Legs Golf club. My dad's girlfriend, Maz – she was lovely. But she was found to have ovarian cancer. She had a full hysterectomy and, in the aftermath of the operation, they found that it had spread. She was young. She was only thirty-three or thirty-four. She passed away when I was nineteen. My dad was devastated.

Everything was a mess. Maz passed very quickly, which affected my dad badly. I went to stay with him over in Letchworth because I was worried about his state of mind. But the girl I was going out with at the time, she was ten years older than me, she had just got divorced, and she became very angry when I told her I was going to stay with my dad for a little while. She wanted me to live at her place.

I told her I needed to spend a lot of time with my dad and she couldn't rationalise that. She wasn't invited to Maz's funeral but after it was over and we had all gone back to my nan's house in Sish Lane, she came round anyway and caused a scene.

I was talking to somebody else, which made her angry, and she slapped me. It was chaos for half an hour. She left after a bit of screaming and shouting and everyone was incredibly upset. A little while later, I decided I'd drive my dad back to Letchworth and the next thing I knew, she was alongside us in her car, trying to drive us off the road.

She was trying to kill us. We were side by side, she was trying to sideswipe my car, I was taking roundabout after roundabout at breakneck speed. It was like a car-chase scene in a film. It was as emotional as it gets to see my dad so unhappy and then have Psycho Woman try to drive us off the road. I drove to the police station and jumped out of the car, with her following me. She jumped out and started telling the police I had been drinking.

I went back to live with my dad and stayed with him for a while. I had to get a court order against her because she came up to Chesfield Downs, the golf club where I was working, and caused another big scene up there.

It was all a little crazy. I found it very hard to deal with. It felt like a lot of big things were happening, all before I had even grown up.

CHAPTER 2
The Stall

Until Gary died, everything had been normal. There had been lots of normality. I only ever lived in one house throughout my entire childhood: 405 Canterbury Way, on a drab, modern estate on the outskirts of Stevenage, in roundabout land and dual-carriageway country, in a suburb called St Nicholas.

It was a little house in a terrace of fourteen, part of the New Town that had been built after the Second World War. Our view out front was of a row of twelve garages with three flats above them. The garage doors were bright blue. They were the only splash of colour around. It wasn't picturesque but it was all I knew.

I went back there recently to show my kids where I'd lived and pulled up outside our old house in my Rolls Royce. A woman leaned out of one of the windows and I told her why I was there. She looked around at the rubbish bags that were clogging up some of the raggedy front gardens and at the state some of the houses were in. 'You want to be glad you don't live here now,' she said. 'It's a shit hole.'

I never thought of it that way. I didn't know any different. When you grow up in that environment, you take it for what it is. It was my normality and I was happy. It's everything that's around me today that isn't normal: my Ferraris in the garage, my house in a gated community in Florida. All that kind of stuff. I know it's not normal but I've earned it and I'm proud of it.

All my mates back in Stevenage lived within walking distance. I'd just go round and knock on their doors. We'd play football against a wall. Yes, I broke a neighbour's window. Didn't everybody, once? We'd get chalk out and draw a goal on the wall and play until the woman who lived there got home from work in the evening.

We didn't have much money. My dad worked in engineering for British Aerospace, programming precision milling machines that cut blocks of steel and metals. I didn't really know too much about what the work entailed, but I did know it got us access to BAe's great sports ground. I would have jumped at any chance to go to watch Arsenal play now and again, but we couldn't afford it.

We didn't go on too many holidays, either. Mum and Dad would have loved to sit on the beach every summer, but we didn't have the money. The first holiday we had, I was probably eight or nine and Grandma and Grandad White paid for us all to go to Lanzarote together. A year later they took us all to Gran Canaria. We only had a couple of holidays where we went on an aeroplane. Some years, Mum and Dad just hired a sunbed so it looked like they had been on holiday.

My mum worked several jobs to help pay the bills. She worked in the Dorothy Perkins store in Stevenage for a long time and then got promoted to being the store manager of the shop in Letchworth, a few miles away to the north.

My mum and dad were always very excited when they changed cars but they could never afford to buy a new car. I think they had a blue Austin Allegro and my dad's favourite was a VW Scirocco. It had plenty of rust, but he covered it up. Dad always tinkered with his cars, sanded them down and sprayed them so they looked good. But there was always rust underneath.

At quite a young age, I decided that, if we didn't have any money, I'd go out and earn some. My brother and my friend, Paul Clarke, had got jobs working on stalls at Stevenage open-air market in town and one day Paul told me that the guy who ran the stall next door, Alan, needed someone to help him out. It was a clothes stall. Menswear. It measured thirty-six feet by twelve feet. I signed up. The pay was fifteen pounds for a Saturday shift.

People talk a lot about how I didn't exactly follow a conventional path towards becoming a professional golfer and I suppose you could count this among the kind of things they mean. Putting up a stall before dawn. Packing it away after dusk. Selling shell-suits and T-shirts. But actually, it helps to explain what drove me on.

I was only eleven. I wanted to go to work early because I didn't want to ask Mum and Dad for anything because I knew they weren't in a position to give anything to me. I was always getting my brother's hand-me-downs and I didn't like it. I wanted nice stuff. That's ingrained in me. It made me work harder and want better things. It meant so much to be able to go out there and fend for myself.

I was a shit-hot salesman, too. I loved it. I loved everything about working on the market stall: setting up at five in the morning every Saturday, getting all the metal bars laid out and putting it all together. I think of everything in my life as a game, as something competitive, so I kept asking myself how I could set that stall up more quickly or more efficiently. I did it in twenty-two minutes once, so that was always my target. Then, at the end of the day, it was all about how quickly I could pack the stall away into the back of Alan's van.

I did all the merchandising. If Alan had new product in, he wanted me to display it in a certain way. If he had a new style of shirt or tracksuit, we hung it in a certain way, colour-coded everything. There were probably twelve different colours in every size of piqué T-shirt, so I had to get out all the shirts in the right size order, then hang them and put them on a rail in size order. The hangers had to be round the same way.

It was very regimented so it was easier for us to sell, rather than searching through stuff. Alan went on holiday once when I was thirteen and left me in charge. He gave my dad the van, but I set the stall up and I was the boss. I had the money bag and ran the stall. My dad helped out. I loved it.

I wasn't a fruit salesman, so I wasn't out there screaming, 'Five bananas for a nicker!' but that was happening all around me. I understood that if the stall looked nice, it would pull people in to buy the merchandise. If it looked drab, it wouldn't. There was competition between stalls about whose displays were the best because we all knew that would affect sales. Who has got the posh stand? Who has got the posh red-and-white canopy that goes over the stand?

All that order, all that organisation – it suited me down

to the ground. It's in me. I love organising things. Can't have it any other way. I've got Obsessive Compulsive Disorder. I'm a classic case. I've got a big closet at my house in Orlando; when you walk in, it has to be relaxing on the brain. Colour-coded. Everything colour-coded. The tie drawers are all dead neat, hangers the right way round. There's no stress on the mind.

It's the same when you walk into a pound store or Louis Vuitton. You walk into a pound store, it's chaotic, it's stressful, you sense panic in there. You walk into a Louis Vuitton store, it's relaxing on the brain, it's attractive to the eye, it makes you want to spend money. That's the power of branding. When you walk down the aisle at a supermarket, Kelloggs' products are at eye level. They pay more money to be at eye level. That's where people will see them.

So I started earning money. And I saved every penny. With the first eighty pounds, I bought a purple Raleigh bike – the first bike I'd ever owned. I was proud to spend every penny I'd saved on a brand new bike. With the second eighty pounds, I bought a lovely pair of brand new orange, red and white Nike trainers. I've had a shoe fetish ever since. I was so proud I could walk into a shop and pay eighty pounds of my own money for a pair of trainers. They were the best trainers anyone could buy. Hardly anyone else had them.

I wore those new trainers to school. Some dickhead who was jealous decided to stamp on them and make them filthy dirty and I was so angry. He didn't know. He didn't know I had earned the money myself to buy those shoes. Maybe it wouldn't have made any difference to him if he had known. If I had been big enough, I would have slapped him black and blue.

All of that stuff meant so much to me. Mum and Dad couldn't have afforded to buy those trainers for me. That made the reward of buying them even better. I feel exactly the same today. I have earned the right to build a beautiful house for the whole family to enjoy. I get the same kick out of buying something I can afford, be it a Ferrari or a holiday home. The feeling is identical. I have earned the right.

I was precocious in strange ways as a kid. Every Sunday morning, when I was eight or nine, I got up and cooked Mum and Dad breakfast and nipped up the shops to get the newspapers for them. When I say breakfast, I mean the works: beans on toast with egg for my mum and a full fry-up for my dad. I loved cooking. I loved being in charge in the kitchen. Still do.

And then there was Danny. I always looked up to my brother. Danny was close enough to me in age that life was a competition.

Danny can ride a bike, so I need to ride a bike.

Danny can kick a football, so I need to kick a football.

Danny can climb a fence. I need to climb that fence.

So I could ride Danny's old bike without stabilisers when I was twenty months old. I had to do it because I could see him doing it. He was everything that I wanted to be. And that attitude filtered into sport.

I wasn't one of the cool kids at school. I went to the Barclay School in the Old Town area of Stevenage and I wasn't one of the kids sneaking off round the back of the bike sheds for a smoke. In some ways, I was a bit of a loner. All I was interested in was sport. If I had any spare time at all between lessons, I headed for the school field, playing football or hitting golf balls.

My school reports are shocking, in some respects, in that I really didn't concentrate on anything other than my sport. I wasn't really any good at anything at school. I struggled in English because I never spent any time reading books. My English teacher, Mr Wallace, who was one of the teachers I respected, tried to get me to read magazines, just so I'd be reading something.

I started reading some poetry books. I didn't mind reading poems. The reason I can't read books is I can't store the information. I can't remember what I've read five pages ago because my brain's so all over the place with other stuff. I'm looking at a book and my mind's dancing about somewhere else.

Art was the only thing I was good at, at school. I paid attention in art and graphic design, and maybe English because I liked Mr Wallace. And of course, I liked my PE teachers, Mr Green and Mr Smith. And there was a great PE teacher called Merv Smith, who had a big influence on me as well.

The only academic subject I wasn't too bad at was maths. I found that a challenge. I would compete with myself to try to do the sum as quickly as I possibly could. I found it fun to try to work out the equation. History? Boring. Science? Boring. Burning stuff in test tubes didn't float my boat. Anything where I could be competitive, that switched my brain on.

Socialising didn't bother me, either. I just wanted to compete.

I played for all the athletics teams, I was county pole-vaulting champion, and I played basketball for the school. I was on the cricket team. I wasn't overly popular with the girls because I couldn't give a monkey's about girls back then. There was one other kid like me, Jamie Robertson, and in the last couple of years at senior school, I spent a bit of time with him.

He was a member of Knebworth Golf Club, but I couldn't afford to go and play there. We sat next to each other in the classroom, designing golf courses in our science lessons and then comparing notes at the end. We designed par threes and par fives with water hazards. I thought that was fun stuff.

John Sanders was my best mate at school in the last few years I was there. He was the rich kid in the class. His dad ran a trading floor at Barclays de Zoete Wedd in the City, and one year we both did our work experience there. It was great fun.

I was interested in golf because my dad played it now and again, but I wanted to be a footballer. And the Barclay School was a football school. It had a reputation for having the best team in the area and there was real kudos attached to being in the team. They read the results of the weekend matches out in Monday morning assembly and if you had scored a goal or played particularly well, you got a round of applause.

Being an Arsenal fan, I guess Ian Wright was my hero and, later, Dennis Bergkamp, but I didn't get to watch them that much, even on television. It wasn't like now, with Sky, where you can watch pretty much every single game. I see more games now, sitting in my cinema room several thousand miles away in Florida, than I did when I lived an hour's drive away from Highbury.

My dad wasn't pushy. But he was good at football and golf, and my whole upbringing was all about competing. All I knew was playing football and golf with my older brother.

My dad was vocal on the football sidelines. He had been a decent player himself, in his youth. He had had trials for Brentford, but the school hadn't let him take it any further. Maybe he hoped I'd go a step further. He wanted me to perform all the time. He wanted me scoring goals, taking free kicks and getting stuck in. Getting stuck in was important. So I got stuck in.

Mr Wallace's son, Sam, is the chief football writer for the *Independent* now. He was already writing match reports when we were kids. He was in the same year as me and he usually played right back when I was at right midfield.

He told a friend of mine recently that one of his memories of those games is trying to grab hold of me to drag me away from confrontations with other players. I wasn't averse to the odd altercation with the referee, either, which was very much frowned upon by the school. I did not have a great deal of respect for authority.

I got a mention in one of Sam's match reports (which they still have pinned up on a wall at school) because my tackling was so aggressive. I was a tall kid back then. I didn't take any prisoners. I think a few parents of opposing players were not overly happy with some of the challenges I used to make.

My dad wouldn't be too amused if I was substituted.

Not too pleased with the manager. I wouldn't say he was forceful, but he instilled this winning mentality in me. My dad is not a very good loser. I have seen him walk off golf courses numerous times when he has been having a bad day. He didn't like having bad days.

My dad worked hard all week and he enjoyed his weekends a lot. When he played football, he loved to play well and if it didn't happen, it really pissed him off. So when I played, I wanted to perform for him because I knew it would make him proud. I could see his mood change if I had a good game or a bad game. I could see that frustration in him, which I can relate to.

My dad's the type of guy who will turn around and say, 'Arsenal are going to win five-nil today.' He will still send me a text message saying, 'Go and shoot 59 today.' It is unrealistic in some ways, but it is nice. There's always a chance of something special happening, in my dad's mind.

He has always had that mentality. He hasn't deviated from that. When I was a kid, it was, 'Go and score five goals today.' His mindset is that anything is possible. He never said, 'Let's win one-nil and then shut up shop.' Parts of my career have actually fulfilled some of those extreme ambitions. Other parts haven't.

As well as playing for the school, I turned out for a club called Fairlands Youth in Stevenage, which was one of the best in the area. I trained on Wednesday nights and played for them on Sundays. My dad came with me. He used to roll the sides of my shorts up before I went out on to the pitch, as for some reason I didn't like long shorts. I loved football.

I was a decent player. I played right midfield for the school, but I played centre back at Fairlands. I took the corners. I took the free kicks. And no one got past me at the back. I'd clout people all over the place. I was desperate to make it as a footballer and I thought my big break had come when I was invited for a trial, by Spurs.

I had been getting a bit of attention from scouts from a few clubs and this was a big deal for me. I was thirteen or fourteen and this was my opportunity. I travelled down with a mate who had also been invited and got ready to give it my best shot.

But it didn't happen for me. I felt like I was never given a proper chance. There were too many kids and I barely touched the ball. I didn't get the opportunity to show what I was capable of. Maybe that's just the way it has to be with so many boys competing for places, but it was ruthless. It all happened so quickly, I wasn't given any real time and, before I knew it, somebody was taking me to one side.

'Unfortunately, you haven't been selected to go forward,' he said. That was it.

It was demoralising. Sport was what I was all about and I found the rejection hard to take. The lad I had travelled down with had got through to the next stage, which made it worse. One kid is going home with a bag of sweets and the other kid has got none. I felt incredibly dejected.

It was a turning point for me. After Spurs rejected me, it took all of two hours for me to process that in my brain and move all my commitment to golf. The disappointment, the rejection, the emotion of someone telling me I wasn't good enough, without even giving me a chance to prove myself, flicked a switch. I made a crossover by saying, 'Okay, fuck you, I'll do it myself. I'm going to play golf because then I'll be in control.'

With golf, I knew I would be my own master. I knew I would not be putting myself in a position where somebody was going to tell me whether I was good enough or not. Nobody would be able to judge me. My scores would be the only judge.

I knew that, if I worked hard, I would be good enough to go and do great things in golf. I turned one switch off and flicked another one on. So I stopped playing football, stopped playing for Fairlands, stopped playing for the school team, stopped working on the market stall and poured everything I had into golf.

CHAPTER 3
Mars Bars and Pringle Sweaters

Football was my first love but I wasn't a stranger to golf during my childhood. When the football season was over and Dad didn't have a game at the weekend, occasionally he and my uncle Phil played a round at Stevenage Golf Club and my brother and I used to walk around with them.

It was a very busy municipal course so they had to be pretty dedicated in order to get a tee-off time. Usually, one of the four ball would sleep in his car in the golf club car park on the Friday night so he could be right there when the pro shop opened at 6 a.m. to book their tee time. They took it in turns for the sleeping-in-the-car shift and did it for a number of years.

I was bugging my dad to let me play all the time. My dad was a decent golfer. He had a single digit handicap and he let me mess about with an old three-wood he had customised for me. It was a laminated, black head, red insert three-wood, which he took the soleplate off. Then he dug out the lead weight in the bottom of the club so that it was really light. He wrapped some tape around the shaft of the club where he had cut it down, and that was my club.

So, one Saturday when I was six or seven, I bugged him all the way round the golf course to let me have a shot. By the time we got to the back nine, I'd finally worn him down. We were on the first par-three on the back nine, which was about 125 yards downhill to the pin. So I pegged the ball up off the men's tee and Dad and his mates stood back and let me hit it.

There were four guys on the green, but no one thought I'd get it anywhere near them. I don't think Dad thought I'd get it off the tee. But I absolutely flushed this ball. Someone said, 'Holy shit, he's nailed it!' and there were a few shouts of 'Fore!' The ball landed on the green, right in the middle of this group of four blokes.

Maybe my dad was impressed, but he was embarrassed, too. The guys on the green were startled. My dad sent me down there to apologise to all of them. I walked towards them, crying my eyes out. It was humiliating for me back then. My first shot on a golf course and I had nearly killed one of four grown men. Still, Dad encouraged me to play after that.

I started going out, hitting balls on the football field near my junior school at Wellfield Wood. And my brother and I went down there for an hour or two at weekends. We took ten golf balls. I stood in one penalty area and my brother stood in the other and we tried to get the ball through the other's goal. He'd hit it at me and I'd hit it at him.

One Christmas, when I was thirteen, we got a full set of Wilson Patty Berg irons which my Dad had bought second-hand. My brother got the odd numbers and I got the even. He got three, five, seven, nine, sand iron and I got four, six, eight, wedge. I wanted what he had because he got the extra club in the bag. But it didn't matter because that present is still shaping some of my habits now. When I warm up before a day's play, I only practise three, five, seven, nine, sand iron – the clubs I didn't have as a kid.

Once we got those clubs, we were off down the park for hours, hitting balls. Those football pitches at Wellfield Wood aren't there anymore. They've built a housing estate on them.

So, when I was rejected by Spurs, I turned straight to golf and decided to pour all my energies and all my commitment into that. I gave up my job on the market stall and started to spend as much time as I could up at a new golf course that had been opened on the outskirts of Stevenage. It was called Jack O'Legs, after the legend of a giant who was supposed to have lived in Hertfordshire in medieval times.

I really wasn't a decent schoolboy golfer at all, but my brother was better than me and he had got a part-time job up there. Nick Faldo opened the Jack O'Legs golf centre in 1991 and that was one of the seminal events of my life. I was fifteen years old and Faldo pulled up in this big car and started hitting balls down the range. It was unbelievably impressive.

He was the world number one at the time and he crushed ball after ball down the range. The crowd was massed on both sides so that he really only had a narrow tunnel to hit down. As I marvelled at his skill, part of me was thinking that, if he shanked one, he might kill somebody.

This is my game and this is what I want to do, I thought as I stood watching him, transfixed.

Faldo signed a golf ball for me that day, which I still have. It is sitting in my trophy cabinet at home in Lake Nona. Not everybody liked him back then. Not everybody likes him now. He was dedicated, driven and he would do anything he could to win, and that's what I admired about him.

I was desperate to get a job up at Jack O'Legs like my brother. Danny was seventeen by now and he wanted to become a professional golfer. He was trying to get his handicap down low enough that he could become an assistant pro. He led the way for both of us.

I never had any golf lessons. We didn't have the money for me to join a club of any sort, so I never got involved in amateur golf. I don't have any amateur record. I came up a very different way to people like Justin Rose and Luke Donald.

I couldn't even tell you the name of any big amateur tournaments in the UK. They just weren't on my radar because there was never any possibility of me playing in them. That's not a sob story, by the way. I didn't feel sorry for myself about it. It's just the way it was.

Jack O'Legs was up towards Hitchin, about ten minutes' drive from my house, and when I was fifteen, I got a part-time job up there, working in the golf shop. I spent all my time there. All my time. I tried to work the hours which enabled me to get access to the course so I could play and hit balls on the driving range in my free time. Money was very tight, but balls on the range were free because I worked there.

I hit balls there for hours and hours and hours. I left school that summer, just before I was sixteen, before I took my GCSEs, although I still went back to sit the exams. I had lined myself up a position to work at the golf shop full time once I left school, so I didn't do any revision for my exams. I didn't even go down to pick up my results. I had no interest. I didn't care whether I passed or failed.

My mum picked up the results, but I was never going back. I didn't enjoy those last years at school because I didn't feel they were any use to me at all. I just wanted to play sport, so why should I be concerned about history or geography?

Even before I left school, I was throwing everything into golf. My mum would drop me off in the morning near school and, now and again, I would wait for her to drive off and then nip down the cut-through and hop on the bus to go up to the golf club. I was caught out at least once. One day, I went into school and handed in my absence note, which I had forged in what I thought looked like Mum's handwriting. Mr Parry, my head of year, read the note then stared at me.

'You looked okay yesterday when you were walking up to Jack O'Legs with your golf clubs on your back,' he said.

My mum was working in Letchworth by then and the golf course was on her way to work, so she dropped me off at 8 a.m. and I hit balls for an hour before I started my shift in the club shop. I was paid £3.20 an hour and I usually worked about a fifty-hour week.

Reporters always write that I was selling Mars Bars and tee pegs. Well, that's true, but I was doing other stuff, too.

That pro shop held £200,000 of stock. It was an enormous shop. We used to have all the major brands, all the major clothing companies, on display there. People would come in from a long way away to buy the new stock. Every new season we would have the best, including cashmere

Pringle sweaters, and it was always the same customers who bought those jumpers.

So, as I say, it wasn't just selling Mars Bars. It was moving the stock, Hoovering, dusting, selling, doing club repairs, cutting off grips, re-gripping – everything a big shop would require. The Mars-Bar-and-tee-peg seller – that's your private golf club. It's a tiny little pro shop at an old quirky golf course, which has £10,000 of stock which it doesn't rotate that often. So all you are really doing is taking a green fee and selling a Mars Bar and a packet of tees to a member who doesn't buy much stock.

At places like that, it's only when a member brings a guest to go and play golf that you've got a chance of selling a shirt with a logo on it. Some of these members at these old private clubs have had the same set of clubs and the same shoes for forty years. When it comes to the pro shop, they tend not to be big spenders.

What I was doing was hard graft. I didn't waste a minute of the day. The boss walked round all the time, making sure he'd piss you off somehow. I was always on my toes, dusting off the clubs. It was a nine-to-five job and I was a hard worker. I was always merchandising the shop. I didn't just stay behind the counter. I wanted to get stuck in. I wanted to pull the displays apart. I wanted to make sure the shop was looking really good. I was always one of the top salesmen. We got paid a tiny bonus if we reached targets, and I was good at hitting mine.

Jack O'Legs went bust in the mid-nineties and a new group bought it and renamed it Chesfield Downs. It sounded much more Home Counties. The new owners hired this guy, Paul McCullough, to run the show and I don't think he liked me. I certainly didn't like him. I guess that made it a personality clash.

I always wanted to better myself. I wanted to become an assistant pro. I knew that if I could get my handicap down to four, I'd be able to turn pro. I was totally self-taught. I read magazines and books and looked at the pictures of golf swings in coaching manuals. I bought a golf magazine that came out every week and I referred to that as my tuition book.

I measured my progress by scores and handicap. When I was fourteen, I was a junior member at Stevenage and occasionally I handed my cards in there, like you would in a monthly medal, to get my handicap down. When I got to Chesfield Downs at fifteen, I played in monthly medals. I played the Letchworth Open once and won Best Net. I played the *Daily Telegraph* competition at Chesfield Downs. I think I won that. My handicap wasn't even single figures then.

I don't have an amateur record. Just these competitions at Chesfield Downs, a small club on the outskirts of Hitchin that no one has heard of. That's it. Once I started working full time in the shop, I only had time to play the odd monthly medal at the club and any other competition the club hosted. By the age of seventeen, I had got my handicap down to four, but I stopped playing competitions between seventeen and nineteen because Paul McCullough wanted to charge me to play golf.

If I played in a medal, I'd have to pay my medal fee and a green fee, and I couldn't afford it. I didn't have fifteen pounds to go and play golf. It was too much money. I stopped playing golf in terms of paying for green fees. I played when I could, but not in competitions. I played after hours and went on the par-three course and practised on the driving range.

My brother turned assistant pro. He had been working at the club full time, going through his PGA exams. After a while, he bought a car and took a job at a club called Panshanger in Welwyn Garden City, Nick Faldo's home-town. I was left working at Chesfield Downs and feeling increasingly isolated because of the clash between me and my boss.

In May 1995, when I was nineteen, I turned assistant pro off a handicap of four. It's not that unusual to do that. Once you got down to a four handicap, it allowed you to apply to be an assistant pro. I was in charge of the handicap committee at Chesfield Downs at that stage, so, whenever a monthly medal was done, I collated the cards and processed everyone's handicaps and put the new handicaps up on the board.

I hadn't played a competition for two years, so, theoretic-ally, I probably didn't even have a handicap. Jane Fearnley was the lady club pro at the time, so I wrote her name on the handicap sheet and sent it into the PGA, and so it hap-pened that I was accepted as a PGA member, as an assistant.

I played my first competition as a pro soon afterwards at Panshanger. The first day, I shot 66. I was unaware of it at the time, but I was eight under through fifteen holes. I knew I was making lots of birdies, but I only checked when there was a hold-up on the sixteenth tee. I have always written my score on the scorecard the same way since I was a kid: I circle a birdie and underline a bogey.

So I found out I was eight under through fifteen.

Holy shit, I thought. Surely that's leading.

Then I got nervous. I hit a bad tee shot off sixteen, which was a par five. I hit a tree forty yards away with my tee shot and made a bogey. At the seventeenth, I drove it straight down the middle of the fairway, then hit it in the front bunker, didn't get up and down, and recorded another bogey.

The last hole was a par five. I hit a lovely drive straight down the middle of the fairway, seven-iron into the middle of the green and then three-putted for a par. So I had gone bogey, bogey, three-putt, par, and I handed my card in and I had a two-shot lead. I had been eight under par through fifteen holes, and thought I could birdie the last three. Instead, I made a mess of them, but I was still leading by two.

It was my first professional tournament.

This is all right, I thought.

I felt at home very, very quickly.

I'd developed asthma by that point in my teenage years and I had a flare-up that night. It got so bad that I went to the Lister Hospital in Stevenage in the middle of the night because I was struggling to breathe. They put me on a nebuliser for a couple of hours and that calmed everything down.

I'm actually allergic to grass, trees, moss, mould and pine, all of which is slightly inconvenient if you're a golfer. I try to control the allergies from March through to September, taking tablets and nasal spray and eye drops and an injection to try to settle it down. I have something before the Masters because it's particularly bad at Augusta.

I don't know what brought on the asthma at Panshanger, but I got a couple of hours' sleep when I got back from the hospital, went out later that day and shot another 66 to win the tournament by two.

Everyone knew Danny because he had been playing for two years. But no one really knew Danny's little brother. And I went out in my first tournament and shot twelve under par and took all the money at the Panshanger Classic. That was my introduction to professional golf.

I won something like £1,200 for that event. I was earning £120 a week, so that was almost three months' wages in two days. There would always be one guy at regional level who would clean up on the local order of merit. There are good players in the regions and, every single tournament, you see the same guy shooting good scores and taking the pot. They were usually local club pros who played every pro-am in the region and every possible event. You could make a nice little extra income from playing those events. My brother Danny does that now.

I took the trophy back to the pro shop at Chesfield Downs after I won at Panshanger and put it on the counter. I was proud of my trophy and the members were proud. I had got to know a lot of them really well and I thought it was something that would bolster the image of the club and help its reputation in a small way.

Paul McCullough disagreed. He told me he didn't want the trophy in the club shop. He told me to take it home. I don't know why. I thought that was pathetic and disrespectful. The guy was a prick, basically. I don't think he even played golf. I certainly never saw him play if he did. He didn't have any feel for the game. He wasn't fun to work for. In fact, I found it very stressful to work for him.

At the end of 1995, I had another clash with him and I decided I'd had enough. I bought a new car to replace the green Vauxhall Astra rust bucket that I'd paid £300 for when I was seventeen. Then I went in to see him and told him to poke his job.

CHAPTER 4
A Trial at a Tea Party

I went for an interview at Leighton Buzzard golf club. I was nineteen. The head pro was a guy called Lee Scarbrow, who was a terrific coach then and is still one of the best in the country. I knew he was a Tottenham fan so I kept quiet about my Arsenal allegiances. He saw something in me and I got the job. I'd like to think he recognised my golfing talent, but in a newspaper piece a couple of years ago, he said I was 'world class at folding shirts'.

I was on £120 a week, but I got to keep my teaching money, too. The shop wasn't nearly as big as it had been at Chesfield Downs and so it took up a lot less of my time. I taught a group of juniors on Saturday mornings and built up a decent junior programme with the other assistant pro, Phil Abbott. The classes comprised about fifty or sixty kids, split into groups of eight to ten which we shared out and we charged them a pound each for a group lesson. If a kid wanted a private lesson on the practice ground, down to the left of the eighth hole, it would be fifteen pounds for an hour.

I liked teaching. I had a good level of understanding of the golf swing, the kids were usually receptive to what I was saying and, of course, it was decent extra money. Lee Scarbrow was a good example to me as well. He was busy from nine to five with private lessons because he had such a good reputation.

Lee was a stickler for making sure every lesson was filmed and whoever his pupil was always got a copy of his lesson on video. He coached me, too, when the opportunity arose. Now and then, I'd video my swing and ask him to have a look at it and give me advice.

When I was working at Chesfield Downs, we had a camera set up in the old clubhouse so we could video golf swings for teaching and coaching purposes. It was a dingy, damp, small place that we were using while the new clubhouse was being built. One day, when I obviously had a little bit too much time on my hands, I thought I'd go down there and play a trick on Lee Scarbrow, who was away for the afternoon. So I set up the camera, stripped down to my underpants, pulled them right up the crack of my backside and then smashed a drive down the imaginary fairway. I left a note for Lee saying that I thought I had made some improvements to my swing and that I had recorded the evidence on camera. I left the sequence number so he could find it easily. When he got in the next day, he switched the machine on and got a great view of my arse cheeks.

I hadn't lost any of my bravado. The first tournament I played after I arrived at Leighton Buzzard, I spent most of the day before telling Lee and Phil that I was going to win it. It was part of the Jimmy Thomson Tour where all of the pros in the East region got together on a Monday and paid twenty pounds entry fee and the money was divided into a prize fund. Lee said in that interview that he was listening to me boasting about how I was going to win and thinking, Yeah, right, Ian. But I went and won that, as well.

I was doing everything I could to make ends meet. I even moonlighted as a chauffeur for a while for a guy called Mark Litton, who was the touring pro at Chesfield Downs. Mark played on the Challenge Tour and European Tour and he's a rules official on the European Tour now, so we often reminisce about old times.

When he was playing a tournament abroad, I drove him to Heathrow on the Tuesday morning before it began and picked him up on the Sunday night. He didn't actually pay me cash; I got a dozen balls for every job. They were Titleist professional nineties. I only realised later that Mark was given balls when he played on the European Tour!

I went to his flat in Hitchin once to pick him up and, when he was packing his suitcase, he opened up his wardrobe. I saw inside it and nearly fell over. There must have been sixty dozen balls stored in there. I said, 'Holy shit! How on earth have you got all these balls?' Mark just smiled. He was always pretty frugal. Paying me with golf balls was a good deal for him, but I learned a lot from talking to him and being in his company, so it was a deal that I was more than happy with.

This was Mark Litton, European Tour golfer, and it was a big deal for me to be able to talk to him and measure myself against him. We played at Chesfield Downs now and again and it was a benchmark for me to try to perform against someone who was much better than I was. One round, I was eight under after twelve holes and we had to come off because there was a huge storm coming. I was so mad. I so wanted to finish that round of golf, but we never did get back out.

I was always late for work at Leighton Buzzard. It wasn't that I was a party animal – far from it. It's just that I have always loved sleeping. I had every single excuse in the book. I exhausted them over the years, to the point where it just made Lee laugh. One of my staples was rubbing my hands on the brake dust on the wheels of my car and telling Lee I'd had to change a flat tyre on the journey into work. I was a master of bullshit.

It was about a thirty-mile journey into the golf club, which was normally about forty-five minutes. I managed to get it down to about twenty-eight minutes on a really good run. I'd got rid of that Astra, which was a heap of shit. I bought a Vauxhall Nova with the money I earned from winning the Panshanger Classic. Soon after I took the job at Leighton Buzzard, I fell in love with a Ford Fiesta XR2i. It was older than my Nova but it was way cooler. I had to have it.

I was proud of that car because that thing was fast. It meant I could get an extra ten minutes in bed before I set out for work, for a start. I got alloy rims on it, the works. I was quite the little boy-racer back then. And, obviously, it wasn't that long before I smashed it up.

I went the back way into work, along the country lanes, hopping over the M1 and heading due west. I'd got about halfway to Leighton Buzzard one morning and was in the area around Barton-le-Clay. I went round a bend too quickly, hit some black ice and lost control. My lovely XR2i slid for a hundred yards or so down the road and smashed into a car coming the other way.

The impact tore the front end of my car off and blew the bonnet 200 yards down the road. It was a right mess. I banged my knee, but it was just a bruise and, apart from that, I was okay. The other guy was okay, too. I thought he was going to beat the living crap out of me when he got out of the car, but he just about managed to hold it together.

While we were dealing with the shock of what had happened, some army guys on a route march stumbled across us. They came over to make sure we were both okay and then ten guys picked my car up and dragged it into a lay-by. I had to get a truck to come and pick the car up and take it back to my house. At least I had a real excuse for Lee Scarbrow for being late that day, but that was the end of my XR2i.

I tried to salvage what I could. I got the exhaust system off it, removed the spare alloys and stripped the interior out. Then I bought a clapped-out Ford Fiesta for £150 and put my XR2i interior and my XR2i steering wheel on it. I drove that for about six months before it blew up.

I loved it at Leighton Buzzard, though. Lee was brilliant with me and I started to get more and more opportunities to play. During my first year there, sometime in 1996, I even got my first chance to play abroad. Lee had broken his collarbone and so I substituted for him at a Lombard top club trophy qualifier and we won it. That meant we went to play San Lorenzo in the Algarve. We didn't win, but my horizons were starting to widen.

I was studying for my PGA exams while I was at Leighton Buzzard, so that I could become fully qualified.

The way I approached my PGA coursework was a mirror image of how I had treated schoolwork. Whether it was one page, ten pages or a hundred pages, I did it the night before. It was always lastminute.com. I handed in my coursework late at the end of the first year in 1996 and made my excuses by saying it must have been delayed because of a postal strike.

The PGA didn't buy it and Lee got a letter notifying us that I had been called up for disciplinary action. I was mortified. I had to go up to the Belfry for a hearing chaired by the PGA's executive secretary, David Wright, and attended by one of the PGA's directors, Brian White.

It was an intimidating set-up. They had lawyers sitting down one side of this big boardroom table, taking notes, to scare you. I was sitting at the end. They asked what my excuse was for the coursework being late and I trotted out the stuff about the postal strike.

Then Brian White intervened.

'Where do you see yourself three years from now?' he said.

'Winning European Tour events,' I told him.

Well, he flipped. He smashed his hand down on the table so hard he nearly knocked over his coffee cup.

'We're not running a blasted tea party here,' he shouted at me. 'This isn't some Mickey Mouse operation, you know. You're in the wrong position if you think you're going to be winning tournaments.'

I was taken aback. The guy had asked me a question and I'd answered it.

Maybe he wanted me to say how much I respected the PGA and that it was the limit of my ambition to become a fully qualified and thoroughly upstanding PGA pro. But I didn't say that. My goal was to become fully qualified and then move on and win golf tournaments on the European Tour. I didn't realise that that wasn't the route most guys on tour took and that it might appear I was being insolent.

I just thought that was the way it happened. I didn't have an amateur background or an amateur upbringing. I thought guys got their qualifications and then went and played golf. Or, if they were really, really good, they just got their Tour card. I thought I was answering the question sensibly.

I didn't realise then that the way I was trying to become a leading golfer was unconventional. It was the only route open to me. It wasn't like I had any choice. I didn't go to private school or have the money to join a private golf club and play amateur tournaments when I was a kid. I did what I could. Simple as that.

I don't know how many of my peers took the same route. Maybe Robert Rock. But there are really not very many. The vast majority of leading English Tour players these days had a decent amateur career. They got their handicap down playing regularly for their clubs and then they were selected to play for their county or for England.

I'm guessing most of them came from an affluent enough background that they didn't have to work. If they did work, they probably didn't work in a pro shop. Good luck to them. I would have done it that way, if I could. I'm sure a lot of them are thankful they didn't have to go down the PGA route.

I might be in a minority in terms of how I forced my way into the sport, but I have never felt discriminated against or looked down upon. People talk about snobbery in golf but I have never really experienced it. I think things have changed a lot since the days when you had to be rich or privileged to play. I'm proof of that.

CHAPTER 5
Brothers

I have never been scared of pushing myself forward. So, at the end of 1996, when I was twenty, I went to the first stage of qualifying school to try to gain my European Tour card. The entrance fee was £1,500 back then. My brother had paid his money. So I did, too. I thought I'd give it a go. The first stage was pre-qualifying at a course called Five Lakes at Maldon, in Essex, and I got through that.

The second round of pre-qualifying was at a course called Pals, up the coast to the north of Barcelona. I was going for one of nine places that would take me to the final Q School. I started well, but I hit 76 on the final day and bogeyed the last, which cost me dearly. I finished fifteenth. My chance was gone.

I tried the same the following year; didn't do any better. I kept working at Leighton Buzzard, entering regional tournaments, hitting balls for hours and hours on the practice range, constantly striving to get better. I won the East Anglian Open in 1997, which was a decent chunk of money, and, in 1998, I joined the Hippo Tour.

The Hippo Tour was a UK-based tour that was a rung below the Challenge Tour. I paid the £150 entry fee, like everyone else, and then played to try and win it back – and win everyone else's entry fee, too. There were seventeen

Hippo Tour events in a year and I could only play a max-
imum of half of them because the other assistant pro at
Leighton Buzzard wanted to play the tour, too, and we had
to take it in turns to have our weeks off.

I got my first sponsor that year. I couldn't have played
the Hippo Tour without one. He was a local guy called
Barry Jones, who owned a company called Merley Paper,
which made till rolls and paper rolls for garages and businesses. He was a member at Chesfield Downs and I'd got
to know him there and played in his company golf day.

He used to come over for lessons. One day, I just asked
him if he would think about sponsoring me. I wrote down
a list of the tournaments I wanted to play throughout the
year and how much it would cost in terms of entry fees
and accommodation. I was still earning just £120 a week at
Leighton Buzzard, so the Hippo Tour would have been a
non-starter for me if I hadn't got help.

Barry agreed to pay my entry fees and accommodation
for the year. I played seven tournaments out of the seventeen on the Hippo Tour schedule in 1997 and stayed in the
cheapest possible hotels. Often, I'd share a room, which
made the expenses light. In return, Barry put his company
name on my golf bag and got some logos made up and
had them stitched on my shirts. It was a real boost to know
I could plan for a series of events without wondering
whether I'd be able to afford to play in them.

Andy Day also helped me out. Andy used to have lessons at Chesfield Downs and one day he asked me how
things were going. I was struggling a bit at that time and he
asked me if £1,500 would help. Andy worked in IT. He
wasn't a rich guy but he wanted to try to help me out. That

meant an incredible amount to me and I have never forgotten it. Andy's been to every Ryder Cup I've played in and I've taken him out to the US Open. It was an unbelievable gesture from him.

I played Branston in Staffordshire, Cumberwell Park in Wiltshire, Bowood in Wiltshire, Duke's Dene in Surrey, Hever Castle in Kent, the Warwickshire near Warwick and Pleasington in Lancashire.

Even though I played fewer than half the events, I was near the top of the Order of Merit for most of the season. I was up against a decent player called David Ray, who took part in most of the tournaments on the tour, and in the first six events I played, I finished fifth, first, first, twenty-first, twelfth and third.

I needed a good finish in the final event at Pleasington and, even though I finished second, losing by one stroke, it was enough for me to win the Order of Merit by £253. I shot 66 in the final round. If I had shot 67, I would have lost out to David Ray in the Order of Merit. When I totted it up, I had won £11,301.25 in prize money that year.

At the end of that Hippo Tour season, I launched myself back into another attempt to get my European Tour card and at least make it through to the final Q School. My brother caddied for me at Pals this time and, even though I struggled in my final round, when I stood on the eighteenth tee, I thought that, if I could make par, I had a decent chance of getting through.

It was a par five and I hit a block cut into the right-hand trees off the tee. I left myself with no shot, so I had to chip it out on to the fairway. I had my back against the wall now.

I had 228 yards to go. Danny and I talked it over. I said to him I had to take the shot on and try to hit it in the middle of the green.

'It's a risky shot,' he said. He didn't mean it in a way that was discouraging, just that I'd have to make it perfect.

'I think I can pull it off,' I told him.

I drilled this low-drawing two-iron round some over-hanging cork trees and the ball rolled to within fifteen feet of the pin. I two-putted it and got the last of the eight spots to go to final Q School. I had a European Tour card in my sights. It was like glimpsing the pot of gold at the end of the rainbow.

So, at the end of November 1998, I went to final Q School with 180 other players, all competing for thirty-five cards – thirty-five golden tickets. Everything you've heard about Q School, everything you've been told about how nerve-racking, how gut-wrenching, how heartbreaking, how exhilarating it can be, is all true.

Q School is ruthless. It's horrific. It's absolutely awful. You play four rounds of golf to try to make the cut and then two more rounds to try to get your card. When I was competing, it was held on two courses, San Roque and Sotogrande, near Gibraltar. Two days of practice, six days of competition, eight days of nail-biting hell where the stakes are the highest they've ever been.

It's big pressure. It's your livelihood that you're playing for. That's your job. At the end of it, you're either going to go and play for a lot of money or you're going to be cast back into a world of scratching a living.

I stayed in the local apartment complex in the Sotogrande area. It's hard not to be aware of the dramas that are playing out around you. There are guys that have lost their card and are trying to get it back, guys that are starting out and trying to make their name. It can be heartbreaking. There are guys in tears, guys bogeying the last to miss their Tour card, doubling the last to miss their Tour card, three-putting from four feet to miss their Tour card. It all happened and I was now there to witness it.

I fell somewhere in between those extremes of emotion. I hit rounds of 74, 73, 73 and 73. I made the cut. I knew I was really close now. But I played poorly over the weekend, shot 77 and 78, and never really got near to challenging for one of those thirty-five treasured cards. But there was a silver lining of sorts: everyone who had made the cut got a Challenge Tour card, the level below the European Tour. I took it up, obviously. And I ran with it.

1998 was my last full year in the pro shop at Leighton Buzzard. I stayed on for a few months at the beginning of 1999, then I told Lee Scarbrow I was going on the Challenge Tour. I had a blip when I failed my PGA exams. I did well in Rules and Club Repairs but I failed the Commercial Studies part of the paper. That meant I had to do a resit, which was a bit of a bind. I did the retakes with my brother and we both scraped through. We were now both qualified as PGA pros.

There is something a little bit poignant about that moment for me, because that is really where our careers diverged. I went off on the Challenge Tour and Danny stayed as an assistant pro at Panshanger. The thing is, he was a more talented golfer than me. He beat me a number of times as an assistant. But I don't think he had the drive to work really, really hard and, to me at least, that's a shame.

If he had had that drive, there is no question he could have done exactly what I have done. He could still be doing it. Instead, he stayed at Panshanger for a while and then moved around a few different golf-club jobs. He went to Welwyn Garden driving range. He moved over to another course in Wheathampstead. He played assistant's golf. He did a lot of teaching.

He played in all the regional events that I used to play in. When I look back now through my own records, I see his name everywhere in the lists of top finishers. He just didn't work hard enough to make it as a pro.

It is such an interesting dynamic, the older brother/younger brother thing. It had a fundamental effect on me. I was always chasing him. Whatever it was I was doing, I was always second best. That applied to things like clothes, too. I was the younger brother so I got the hand-me-downs. I just detested being . . . not that I was second best in the family . . . but I didn't like being the younger brother.

We shared a room for a number of years when we lived in Canterbury Way. It was cosy. Then, a little later on, he managed to get the big bedroom at the front and I got the tiny bedroom at the back, until he moved out.

Not that I had a chip on my shoulder, but, after playing second fiddle all my life, I just wanted to go out and get better and to win. I had that want-to-win mentality. That has been a theme in everything I have ever done.

One year, when I was about twelve, my dad played in a pool tournament for British Aerospace down at the club-house at their sports ground. I went up there with my mum and Danny to watch Dad play in a tournament. My dad's team was one short because someone hadn't turned up, so one of his mates told him to put Danny in.

Danny got beaten, but my dad went through to the next round. Then it turned out there was another vacancy in the team, so they decided to give me a go. I won my match. Then I won my next match. Then I won my quarter-final. Then I won my semi-final. My dad got knocked out in the semis, which really annoyed him, and there I was in the final.

I was shaking with nerves. There was a ring of people around the pool table watching me. I had a dead-straight pot on the black to win and I said to my mum, 'I can't do this.' She told me not to be ridiculous, so I stepped forward and potted it. I beat the guy. I won the trophy. I couldn't bear to be beaten, even then. It was a fantastic trophy. It had been made in the shape of a rack of balls, spray painted and expertly milled by someone at BAe. It was a really valuable prize and I thought I was going to get it. But they decided that because I didn't work for BAe, they couldn't award it to me even when I won the tournament. They didn't give it to anyone in the end.

Danny is still in the golf environment. He still plays pro-ams, still picks up okay money. Still shoots 66 now and then and wins £1,500. It is the same old Danny from twenty years ago. His name still figures on the pro-am lists and the same sheets that I have as keepsakes from 1996. All the pro-ams that we entered then, well, he is doing the same thing now.

I don't know whether it's difficult for him having a

younger brother who's a well-known golfer. Maybe. Everybody wants more, so there might be that little niggle in his brain that tells him he could have gone for it. If he had worked his balls off, and proven himself to get sponsorship, I think he would have made it.

He is still Danny. He has got two lovely kids and a wife and they wouldn't love him any more than they already love him if he was out on tour. I get on well with him. We have had our moments, but he's my brother. It's a shame he and his family are so far away because I'd like to see them more.

Some people have a drive to keep getting better. Some people are happy just ticking over and I think Danny falls into the ticking-over category. And I feel he has got more in him than that. I really do. It's not a case of disapproval. I'm not looking down on him – the opposite, actually. I have a very high opinion of him. He's my big brother.

I couldn't have achieved what I have achieved without the belief that I can keep trying to better myself. The majority of people are happy ticking over and going on holiday once a year and being in the jobs that they are doing and that's their life and that's what makes the world go round.

On the other hand, people that have a slightly different mindset and a slightly different drive are the guys that take the chance to run their own businesses and put stuff on the line. If it goes well, great, and if it doesn't they are going to be back to square one and they'll have to work hard again.

Danny got himself in that ticking-over mindset and I

think he can get himself out of it and still do something to better himself. I believe that. The guy goes without practice for three months and then shoots 66 in a pro-am and picks up £1,500.

If he goes and does that in one day, what would he be capable of if he were to practise every day and spend five hours a day on the driving range, working? It blows my mind. He turned forty recently and he is the type of person that, if he pushed himself, he could go and play some seniors golf if he wanted to, because he is that good. He could make an extra living.

CHAPTER 6
Boys On Tour

The Challenge Tour was a stepping stone. It was halfway to the big league. It was packed with players desperate not to slide any further down the ladder and others, like me, scrabbling to get their hands on the top rung and pull themselves up. I realised straight away I was competing against players I could beat. I was in a league where I felt I could win.

There were some very good players on the tour, sure. The Welshman, Bradley Dredge, Carl Suneson, from Spain, who won the Challenge Tour Order of Merit that year, Niclas Fasth, from Sweden, David Lynn and Simon Hurd. It was a great year. We had a lot of fun. We travelled a lot and it was the first time I'd experienced the camaraderie of being in a group of players on the move.

Merley Paper still sponsored me and I had got McCann Homes involved as well. The Challenge Tour was a whole new level in terms of travelling and accommodation costs, and, together, those two companies contributed about £20,000 to keeping me going that season. I counted myself very lucky to have their backing.

I missed the cut by three shots at the first event in Kenya. I made a share of twenty-second at the second event in Spain and won €645 in prize money. The next event was the Ivory Coast Open at the Ivoire Golf Club outside the capital, Abidjan. This was eye-opening stuff for me. I'd played in the tournament in Kenya a few weeks earlier, but this felt like a taste of the real Africa. I was very sheltered, in terms of travelling, and I was taken aback by the poverty.

I shared a room with David Lynn that week, at the Intercontinental Hotel in Abidjan. It was enormous. I was like a kid in a sweet shop. This kind of thing was all new to me. I was a bit giddy. I signed for food all over the place to lots of different rooms, which was naughty but very funny.

I saw the economic flip-side when I got to the course, though. The caddies were paid fifty pounds a round, which was a lot for them, and it was clear that there was a lot of competition for the work. There was a crowd of them jostling for the bags. My guy was a Rastafarian with dreadlocks and a Rasta hat. We played the whole four days singing Bob Marley songs as we went.

By the last round, we had a number of these little local kids following us round, singing along with us. It seemed to do wonders for my game. I shot 69 in the first round, which put me in second, and I stayed in contention all the way through the tournament. I had a share of the lead at the end of the second round and I was two shots clear going into the final day. I managed to hold off Sébastien Delagrange and David Park, and won by two shots.

I got a cheque for €11,370.45. It all felt surreal. I had just won my first big tournament and I was in this alien environment a long way away from home, with caddies crowding round to congratulate me. My caddie was treated like a celebrity because he had been on the winning bag. I sent him a cheque for £1,500 and made double sure he had got it. He told me that amount of money would change his life.

The win was a massive boost to my confidence, but I didn't handle the aftermath of it very well. I hung on to it for way too long. I basked in it a bit. I have been guilty of that at other times in my career, too. I really should have kicked on. It wasn't that I got lazy, but it might have all happened a bit too soon. I didn't get over it quickly enough to press on, and I missed a lot of cuts.

But I did have some fun. I accept that some of it was pretty childish stuff, but that's what happens when you get lads on tour. At the Rolex Trophy in Geneva in the middle of July, a group of us came off the eighteenth at the end of the first day and started to head for the bus that was going to take us back to the hotel. Simon Wakefield was a few yards behind and he asked if we would hold the bus for him while he went to change out of his golf shoes.

We told the driver to leave for the city straight away. Simon was stuck there with no way of getting into town. When we got back to the hotel, I went down to Simon's room on the floor below and filled his keyhole up with some superglue. When he eventually got back to the hotel, he tried his key in the lock and couldn't get in.

Hurd, Lynn and I were like the Three Musketeers back then and we had to walk past Simon's room on our way out for the evening. There was a task force of people outside it by then, trying to force their way in. Simon asked us if we knew anything about it and we just about managed to keep straight faces as we rushed past.

We went for a pizza round the corner and came back to

reception and Wakefield was still there in his golf clothes. There was a locksmith at his door, trying to hammer the barrel out of the lock. It got to about 10 p.m. and we could hear people shouting down the corridors, 'Shut up! We've got to get up in the morning to play golf!' And Wakefield still wasn't in his room.

The following morning, we got down to breakfast and he was still in the same clothes. They had called the fire brigade out to get a ladder up the outside of the hotel, and they'd taken the window out to access his room. It was an old-fashioned hotel with steel doors, so there was no other way of getting in.

For some reason, the finger of suspicion was pointed at me, Hurd and Lynn. All three of us were called into the office of Alain de Soultrait, the director of the Challenge Tour. Before we went in, we each swore not to rat the others out. We were given a bollocking but none of us spilled the beans. De Soultrait said if he found out which one of us it was, he would suspend us.

I told you it was childish.

Most of it was Lynn's fault. I drove my own car to one of the events in Wales. My number plate back then was 1AN P. One night, Lynn changed the *1* to a *T* and the *N* to an *M* and added *A* and *X* on the end. TAM PAX. Practical jokes were played on everybody. People got out on the course, pulled their driver out of their bag and found the cover had been superglued to it. Superglue was a bit of a theme.

I missed a couple of weeks of the Tour because of some of these high jinks. Not long after I won in Ivory Coast, Lynn and I had dashed back to our hotel room at the end of the Luxembourg Open to get our stuff together and head off to catch an 8 p.m. flight back to England. The doorbell rang and I went to answer it. I tried to jump over the golf bags which we had left strewn by the door but my foot got caught in one of the bag handles and I went down in a heap.

I sprained my ankle and I was screaming in pain. The guys ran some freezing cold water in the bath but, when I put my foot in it, I passed out with the pain. Lynn thought I had swallowed my tongue. The boys said I pissed my pants. I don't remember. I'm sure they just made that up, or one of them threw a cup of water over me. To this day, Lynn insists I wet myself and I insist it's bollocks.

It wasn't all laughs. In fact, I was disappointed with myself at the end of the season. I hadn't claimed one of the top fifteen places in the Order of Merit, which I needed to do to retain my Tour card automatically. I'd made €21,000 in prize money. Scotland's Greig Hutcheon, who claimed the last of the fifteen spots, had made more than €31,000. I wasn't even close. That meant I had to go back through the ordeal of Q School to try and get my card back.

A week before I flew to Spain, though, I lost my sponsor. Barry Jones phoned me and said he wasn't going to be able to provide me with funding anymore. It was a massive blow. He had given me £10,000 for my costs in that Challenger Tour year and now I wasn't sure I was going to have enough money to play the following season, whatever happened at Q School. I was incredibly grateful for what Barry had done for me, but that call was not the best timing.

Then I got lucky. I had become friendly with a bloke called Paul Dunkley who owned a company called Camden Motors. He had lessons with Lee Scarbrow at Leighton Buzzard and Lee drove a car with Paul's company name emblazoned on the side of it. I saw him in the club shop just after I'd taken the call from Barry, and Paul invited me to come to his office and tell him what my business plan was.

I took him a proposal and he told me that, if I got my Tour card, he would cover all my expenses. The deal was that if I made the cut at an event, I paid my own expenses. If I didn't, Paul would take care of it. It was a huge relief. It lifted a real weight off my shoulders. I could go and play golf, knowing I had everything covered for the following year.

That was the beginning of a friendship and a business relationship with Paul that is still going to this day. In the short term, it meant I could go to Q School in Sotogrande and play with a certain amount of freedom. It was the same deal: six rounds of golf and European Tour cards for the top thirty-five finishers at the end of it. Make the cut and you are back on the Challenger Tour for another year.

My scores were all very steady. I was always fairly well in control of my game. I was never out of it. I played really nicely and made the cut and then I played steadily over the weekend, too, to close it all out. I got the twenty-first card. So, in 2000, I was going to be playing on the European Tour. I was what they called a category-eleven player, with automatic entry to a lot of top events with decent prize money.

I phoned home and told them I was going to be mixing it with the big boys. I felt like I had finally cracked it. I knew I was going to have the opportunity now to earn the kind of money I had only ever dreamed about earning before, the kind of money that was going to change my life and the lives of some of those around me.

I was engaged by then. A few years earlier, sometime in January 1996, I'd been for a night out in Luton with Lee Scarbrow and we ended up at a seedy, dingy little joint called Legends, having a few drinks and a laugh. A girl came over and said she thought she knew Lee. It turned out she didn't, but I got chatting to her mate, Katie, and we talked for the rest of the evening. I got her number before she left.

I called her three weeks later. I know, I know. That was quite a long time to leave it. Bit of a risk. But I asked her to come round on Valentine's Day and I told her I'd cook dinner. She was a nurse at Addenbrooke's Hospital in Cambridge. She arrived in this old banger that looked like a Chevette. I'd cooked a sweet-and-sour chicken stir-fry and afterwards we had strawberries and champagne. That was our first date. We never looked back.

I was only twenty and she was living in nurses' accommodation in Cambridge, but the following Christmas, I asked her to marry me. She asked me if I'd asked her dad. I hadn't. She told me I needed to. I was pretty nervous about that. I finally plucked up the courage to ask him when we were standing in the kitchen at his house.

'I'm going to ask Katie to marry me,' I said. 'Is that going to be all right?'

He started throwing questions at me. He wanted to

know what I was going to be, how I was going to earn money.

'I'm going to be a famous golfer,' I told him.

'That'll be fine,' he said.

So I went in to see Katie and she said I needed to get down on one knee. So I did that as well. And then she said, 'Yes'. I bought a ring with a tiny pinprick of a diamond on the top. It still cost me about a month's salary. And then we moved into our first house, a maisonette at 10 Brimfield Close, in Luton, which cost us £29,500.

We're still together now, although I made her wait eleven years before I married her. I always said I wanted a big wedding, and I wanted Katie to have a big wedding, so we had to wait until we could afford it. We got married at Woburn Abbey in September 2007 and it was the day we'd always dreamed of.

We're as happy now, with our four wonderful kids and living in Orlando, as we were when we first met and I was working in the golf shop at Leighton Buzzard as an assistant pro. She's the person who's made me the player I am today. It feels like we've travelled a long way together to a point where we can provide for our kids in a way we never imagined possible.

It is not always easy because I'm away from home for long periods of time, but we've seen it all together. I was earning very little when we got together. Then the money came quickly. I'm lucky I found my soulmate when I did because I think it must be difficult to be in the public eye and to be single.

Back when we bought the maisonette in Luton, Katie paid the mortgage out of her wages and the house was in her name. My contribution was paying the food bill each week. Now and again, for a treat, we'd have a Chinese or an Indian takeaway. We didn't have any spare cash and I'd do any odd jobs I could to earn some extra money.

At the end of 1998, after I'd finished my season on the Hippo Tour, Katie's dad asked me to decorate his hallway and offered me £300 for it. He had quite a big stairwell with a high ceiling, so it was an awkward task, with a couple of tricky spots, high up. I didn't want to fall off the stepladder, but I didn't want to screw it up, either. It was Katie's dad, after all.

Before I finished, I signed a bit of the wall. A couple of years ago, someone else decorated the house and stripped away the wallpaper. They found what I'd written and posted it on Twitter.

The inscription went like this:

29.1.1999
Ian James Poulter, European Tour Star To Be.
Decorating in Spare Time With Style xxx.
And Katie's Help.

There you go. European Tour star to be. A year later, I was ready to try to make that boast a reality.

CHAPTER 7
Darkness at the Edge of Golf

I made my debut as a holder of a full European Tour card at the Alfred Dunhill Championship in Johannesburg in the middle of January 2000. A lot of the big European stars didn't make the trip, but there were still some names in the field that made me realise I had made a step up. Retief Goosen was one of them. He won the US Open the following year.

I did okay. I finished just outside the top twenty and won a cheque for more than €7,000. That was a decent start. It gave me a bit of confidence but it still took me a while to find my feet. I was playing in a different league now. I could feel that.

Soon, I found myself playing in tournaments alongside people like Lee Westwood, Colin Montgomerie and Darren Clarke, the guys that had played the Ryder Cups and were contending for Majors. I didn't feel comfortable around them to begin with because they had an aura about them. I knew I would have to raise my game to get close to them.

There was an intimidation factor on the golf course when you played with Monty, Clarkey, Westwood or José María Olazábal. It felt different. It took a while to feel accepted.

I was in awe of some of those guys. Early on in my career, a friend of mine asked me to get Darren Clarke's autograph on a glove for him. I was at a tournament at Hanbury Manor in Hertfordshire where Clarkey was playing and I felt anxious about going to do it.

In the end, I saw him sitting on the clubhouse balcony after he'd finished his round and I seized my chance. He was fine about it, but I was a bag of nerves. It was a big deal for me. I had never spoken to him before.

You had to earn your place to be able to go and sit at the same table for lunch or an evening meal with the top players. All those famous golfers, they hung around together. They dined together in the Players' Lounge. I was nervous about putting my plate down there and having dinner with those boys. The same thing happens now, I suppose, except I'm one of the established ones. I dine with Justin Rose and the other well-known players. So if it's someone's first year and they have just graduated, I guess they'd think twice before they came to sit with us.

Justin and I soon became friends on the tour. I got to know him a little bit at the French Open in 1999 when I was a reserve and doing a lot of hanging around. He was on the putting green and I went over and started to talk to him. He is a quiet, thoughtful, respectful guy. And I'm not, which is probably why we hit it off so well.

Rosie was in that spell of bad tournaments at the time, when he was still trying to fulfil his talent after his emergence at the Open at Royal Birkdale in 1998. He missed the cut in twenty-one straight tournaments when he turned professional. I felt for him because it was obvious he was a seriously talented golfer, but he had all this pressure on him about how he was supposed to be the next great English hope, and it was weighing him down.

I liked him straight away. I liked his work ethic and the fact he was courteous and quiet and studious. He had come into the game a very different way from me and his father was an incredibly important influence on him. I hung out with him and Simon Hurd that first year on the European Tour and Rosie and I often shared a room.

I shared up to the point when I felt like I needed to have my own space. Money stopped becoming an issue, which was a real novelty for me. That first year, I earned €447,000 in prize money, which was a significant amount of money. At the end of 2000, I got a three-year deal to use Taylor-Made equipment and shoes. That was good money, too. It was life changing.

McCann Homes, my sponsor, was building new houses and so Katie and I moved up the property ladder. We had already moved out of Brimfield Close into a place in Milton Keynes that we had bought for £365,000, now that I was doing okay on the European Tour. The new house had five-bedrooms and was overlooking a little lake in Milton Keynes. Everything was changing fast.

It was a good first year on the Tour for me – really good. I had come second at the Morocco Open in Marrakech in April, finishing four shots behind the winner, Jamie Spence. I won €50,000 for that, nearly five times more than anything I'd made at a single tournament before. It was an indication of the opportunity I'd earned.

My form was uneven, however. I'd play well and challenge, then I'd miss a cut. But when I got to the final tournament of the season – the Italian Open in Sardinia, at the end of October – I was still in with a chance of winning the European Tour Rookie of the Year award. Alastair Forsyth was ahead of me, but I was desperate to win it.

I felt under pressure because you only get one chance to win Rookie of the Year and I wanted to grab that chance with both hands. I slowly got myself in position that week. I got a hole-in-one at one point and I went into the final day leading the field. Alastair Forsyth missed the cut.

It was a close finish. Gordon Brand Jnr made a real charge in the final round and shot 66 to take the clubhouse lead. But I made a birdie on seventeen and then hit a great drive down the middle of the eighteenth fairway. I needed par to win the tournament.

I hit a six-iron from 184 yards for my approach shot and, as it sailed away, I was shouting, 'Come on!' at it. It came to rest fifteen feet from the pin and I two-putted it to get my first win on the European Tour and the first prize of €166,000. The money was good. The prestige was better. It was huge to get that win, huge to get Rookie of the Year and pip Alastair Forsyth. He didn't take that very well. I could see in the locker room how annoyed he was.

I didn't blame him. Winning the Italian Open gave me a two-year exemption, which meant my place on the European Tour was guaranteed. That was a great feeling. It lifted a lot of pressure. It meant I could try and improve my game without worrying all the time about the short term. I finished thirty-first on the Order of Merit.

I felt like I'd arrived. I felt like I was part of the gang. I felt like I was a proper player and that I could aim higher and higher. Another part of that process was playing in the Open.

The Open was at St Andrews in 2000. I had never played in the Open and I had never even seen St Andrews. I had tried to get into the Open through regional qualifying in previous years but had always fallen short. Now that I had a European Tour card, it meant I was automatically entitled to go through to the final stage of qualifying, which was at Ladybank Golf Club.

Ladybank is only about fifteen miles from St Andrews and, by then, we knew that all the grandstands would have been erected ready for the tournament. Some of my friends went over there the day before to check it out and get a feel of the place. They wanted me to go with them, but I refused. I didn't want to see St Andrews and then not qualify.

What was the point of getting excited about playing one of the most famous courses in golf and then having to deal with the crushing disappointment if I didn't get through? I didn't want to see it unless I was playing it. The mystery could stay a mystery for a bit longer.

At the end of qualifying, I found myself in a play-off. There were eight players for the last three spots. The first extra hole was a par three, so I went on the range and warmed up with a seven iron. The pin on the range was pretty much the exact same yardage as the pin on the course. I hit a shot on the practice ground and holed it. Then I hit another one to within a foot. Then I hit another one and I holed it again.

I got called up for the first extra play-off hole and I hit the seven-iron to a foot. I was in the first group, walked up to the green, tapped it in and that was me done. I walked to the office to pick up my credentials for the Open and then I drove straight to St Andrews, parked up, hopped over the fence and wandered on to the Road Hole.

I walked out on to the seventeenth green and thought, Holy crap, how can these be greens? They look like fairway! I didn't know then how perfectly they ran. I walked a number of holes, stuck in a state of disbelief. It was absolutely magical. I couldn't wait to play. My first Open Championship was going to be at the Home of Golf.

The day before play started, there was an event that brought past champions together to play a four-hole loop at the course. A lot of the greats were playing: Sam Snead, Jack Nicklaus, Arnold Palmer. I sat on the steps of the clubhouse with Paul Dunkley, who had become my manager by then, watching these guys come and go and savouring the moment.

When I was on the practice range, I realised at one point that Slammin' Sam was warming up next to me. I couldn't believe that Sam Snead had put a bag of balls down next to me. After he'd finished, I got one of the balls out of my bag and said, 'Mr Snead, is there any way you would sign a golf ball?' He signed it and I wrapped it up in a glove and put in the side pocket of my golf bag. I've always treasured that golf ball. I've got it in my trophy cabinet at home.

As for being in proximity to Nicklaus and Palmer, well, that was special, too. They're both iconic players, and both successful businessmen. What they did for golf was remarkable. I would love to have been able to see them playing their best golf. But I do know that they complemented each other, Palmer as the crowd pleaser, Nicklaus as the winning machine.

The Open at St Andrews was also the first time I encountered Tiger Woods. Everybody was in awe of him in 2000. I had been watching television in the pro shop at Leighton Buzzard when he battered Augusta into submission and won his first Major at the Masters in 1997. Now he was demolishing fields and looking like he would win every tournament he entered.

A month before he arrived at St Andrews, he had won the US Open at Pebble Beach by fifteen shots. He was redefining golf. What he was doing was phenomenal. When he walked on the range at St Andrews, people stopped to take notice. You knew when he was coming because you could hear it above the silence of the crowd.

It's like when a football team starts coming down the tunnel. You knew when Tiger Woods was coming to the driving range because you could hear the pitter-patter of feet rushing to try to get in position to see him hit a ball. That still happens today. He demands that respect on the golf course. I tried to watch him as much as I could that year at St Andrews. You want to learn from the best players in the game, so you do want to take note of how he is swinging his clubs and how he is hitting the ball. I wanted to emulate what he was capable of doing. The only way of improving is to watch people who are better at their job than you.

I was nervous when I finally got to stand on the first tee on Thursday afternoon to begin my first round. It's the widest fairway in golf, but a couple of people have still managed to hit the ball out of bounds with their drive. And, even though the fairway is so wide, you still can't stop yourself having a quick look right and left. Somehow, there is a millisecond where you have a little look and think about how embarrassing it would be if you hit it out of bounds.

So, the nerves were there and the adrenaline was pumping. It was my first Open. I was proud to be there. My family were up there in the stand. Paul, my manager, was watching. I wanted to go out there and win the tournament. Or at the very least I wanted to make the cut and be there for the weekend, and all that stuff.

What spoiled it slightly was that I was in the final group to go out. We teed off about 4.20 p.m. The last of the big TV groups had gone out by 2 p.m. so the end of their rounds would get a big television audience. I was among the afterthoughts. I wasn't TV group material back then. I was a long way from being TV group material.

I got off to an okay start. Nothing special. I got to the fifth hole, the par five, and there were four groups waiting on the tee. I couldn't get my head round that. I know now that the fifth green is doubled up with another green on the back nine so it always backs up there. But, as I got to the tee, I realised I was going to have a forty-five minute wait.

By the time we got out to the ninth and tenth, the furthest point away from the clubhouse, there was nobody there. Most of the spectators had gone home and the ones that hadn't had absolutely no interest in following my group. It had taken nearly three hours to get to that point, it was half past seven at night and you could hear the lorries coming in to empty all the bins and that bleeping noise they make when they go into reverse.

The volunteers were sweeping away all the rubbish that

had built up during the day in the grandstands and the noise of chairs being stacked up echoed around the links. I have to be honest: it felt shit. It was a massive disappointment. It wasn't very nice. The adrenaline I had had on the first tee? That had gone.

I had to get my head back together and remind myself that, if I started playing well, there was a chance that, one year in the future, I might be playing in a TV group and not working my way around the course at dusk. Actually, forget dusk. By the time I got to the seventeenth, it was dark. It was overcast; clouds had rolled in. I was in the middle of the fairway and I called the referee because I couldn't see the pin.

I was quite a distance back and it's a long par four. The referee just said, 'You have to finish.' It was clear from his tone that there was not much point in prolonging the conversation. And who am I to stand there and argue my case in my first Open? So I played to a pin that I couldn't see, which was interesting.

The last hole was better. It's a short par four and I drove it far enough up the fairway that I could just about see the flag. I only had a sixty-yard approach shot, as opposed to the 180 yards I had had on the Road Hole. It was dark enough that the floodlights were on on the outside of the clubhouse. I finished out last of the group. It was 10 p.m. At least I made it on to the ten o'clock news that night; they showed the last putt of the day in their report. Then I went to have dinner.

I shot 74 in my first round. I knew I was going to have to play very well to make the cut. And, on Friday, I went out in the middle of the day and caught some of the buzz you expect to feel at the Open. I felt like I was really part of it this time. I responded well to that, played one of the best rounds of anyone in the field that day and shot 69 to squeeze above the cut line.

Tiger Woods won the tournament by eight strokes from his nearest challenger. I shot 73 and 75 over the weekend, but I finished on the same score as Lee Westwood, who went on to win the Order of Merit that year. He probably wasn't particularly pleased about his finishing position, but for me it was a satisfying end to a weekend that let me rub shoulders with the best players in the world and begin to take aim at them.

CHAPTER 8
Tales from the Caddyshack

By the time I had played my first Open at St Andrews, I had already added something else to my game that made me feel like I was in the big time: I had my own caddy. On the Hippo Tour, you carry your own bag. On the Challenge Tour, you pick up local caddies week-by-week. But now I was on the European Tour and so by my side walked Edinburgh Jimmy.

James Rae was a Scotsman. A real Scotsman. He had a broad Scottish accent and a fondness for a bevvy or two. He was the most hard-nosed Scot I'd ever met. He didn't care what he said or who he said it to. He was utterly ruthless when he was taking people down with his quips. I've seen famous golfers wince when they realised they were going to have to walk past Edinburgh Jimmy.

He used to rip it out of Colin Montgomerie, in particular. He'd make observations about his weight as he marched past on the driving range. Darren Clarke, Thomas Bjørn, Ernie Els – they all got it from Edinburgh Jimmy. If somebody had been leading a tournament and had fallen away in the last round, he'd be on at them about how they'd choked. Anything he could make a joke about, any weakness he detected in a player, he went for the jugular and tore them to pieces.

But he was still a great caddy. A lot of players recommended him to me when I was starting out and he caddied for me the second time I was at the Qualifying School, and then stayed with me for the European Tour. He had caddied for Mark Roe before I picked him up and he is still caddying now, for Paul McGinley.

What makes a good caddy? Well, he or she has to know what you are thinking in terms of shot-making, has to know your capabilities so they are not going to ask you to hit a shot you're not capable of, and has to be able to add up and take away and not make any mistakes. You have to accept that they will sometimes make mistakes (because we all do) and for that reason, I have always carried two yardage books.

Your caddy has to be able to pull the right club out of the bag and know how you are going to hit the shot and exactly how far it is going to go. If they tell you that you need a five iron, you have to be confident that they're right. Oh, and this is important, too: your caddy has to know what to say at the right time. And that was not Jimmy's strong point.

He was so ruthless that he pissed me off on a reasonably regular basis. Let me give you a sample of our interaction. We discussed what club to hit, he advised me, I selected the club he had suggested, I hit the ball with the club and the ball sailed over the back of the green. I looked for a bit of sympathy, maybe even a bit of contrition, perhaps some puzzlement. Jimmy did not respond in that way.

'Here,' he'd say in that broad Scottish whine, 'you've flushed that one.'

No, I didn't flush it. It was the wrong fucking club.

It was never his fault. His logic was that it was the right club. It was just that I had hit it too hard.

I wasn't blaming him. I just wanted an acknowledgement that we had selected the wrong club.

But Jimmy was never going to keep his gob shut. You can't shut him up. You can't outwit the guy. He has got an answer for everything. If it comes up short, you hit it heavy. No, no, no. If I have chosen the wrong club, that's fine and I will take responsibility. I'm just making it known that it's probably the wrong club we've hit and we probably should avoid hitting the wrong club again because it's going to get expensive. But I never made any headway with that. It was never, ever Jimmy's fault.

Caddies are a breed of their own. They are funny people. Most of them have a great sense of humour and it is humour that makes weeks away on tour such good fun. Jimmy was old school. He liked a drink, he never lost an argument, he was never wrong. And you are not going to shut him up and you are not going to stop him drinking.

You have to like your caddy, and I liked Jimmy. He was on the bag for my first three years on the European Tour and he is probably the most generous, kind-hearted person I have ever met. He'd give you his last ten pounds. That's why people love him. I've had a fiery relationship with all my caddies, in terms of argumentative banter. It is never malicious, even though it can seem quite aggressive. Jimmy's one of those guys they'll write a book about one day. People laugh about his sayings all the time.

In that first year on the European Tour, I was playing with Adam Scott in the final round of the Moroccan Open and we were both challenging near the top of the leader board. We were on the eighteenth, a par five. We were in the middle of the fairway. Adam hit a massive drive thirty yards past us, so he was standing parallel with us as I took my second shot. There was water all around the right-hand side of the green and I hit this unbelievable three-wood, with thirty yards of cut, to try to get at the pin, which was tucked right by the edge of the green, next to the water.

I hit the shot to within six feet of the hole.

'What a shot!' Adam said, congratulating me. 'The crowd will love that.'

Edinburgh Jimmy turned to him with a sneer.

'Here,' he said, 'we're not here to make friends, we're here to make cash.'

Adam still laughs about that to this day. That was typical Jimmy. He would say something cutting, laugh to himself and then walk off.

I didn't like it when Jimmy turned up for work reeking of booze and I'd tell him so, but he would still do a great job and I couldn't really find too many faults with him.

He told me a story once about how he had been a tearaway as a youth and had got into trouble after a row in a pub that had ended with him breaking windows. He had to go to court and the judge offered him the choice of paying a £600 fine or spending thirty days in jail.

'I'll take jail,' Jimmy had told him.

He knew he'd get fed in jail. And that it would be a roof over his head for a month.

Things have changed a lot now. The caddy lifestyle is different. It has to be, really. There is so much at stake for them now, so many rewards. I don't drink the night before a tournament and I don't really want my caddy to drink, either, because I want him as alert as I am going to be. You need to be a team to be able to perform.

Back when I first joined the European Tour in 2000, there was an older group of caddies who would still roll into the course in the morning after a heavy session the night before. That was the mentality. For a lot of them, the weekly wage just paid their bar bill. They lived off the percentages their player paid them, depending on his success.

I had Jimmy on five per cent if I made the cut, seven per cent if I finished in the top ten and ten per cent if I won. I paid him £500 a week basic and contributed to his airfare when there was long-haul travel involved. I made sure he wasn't out of pocket for that. The wages have gone up significantly since then, of course. A lot of caddies wear corporate hats now and some of them have shirts with the odd logo on them, which they are being paid to display.

I have changed a few things in the way I pay my caddy now. I have done away with the five per cent and there is no alteration in the basic percentage if I finish in the top ten. I pay an across-the-board number and a higher percentage if I win. A caddy can earn serious money now. Henrik Stenson would have had one happy caddy at the end of 2013.

When Stenson won ten million dollars for winning the FedEx Cup, his caddy would probably have got a million-dollar bonus. And he would have got his regular percentage for the tournament win, which would probably have been worth $140,000. So, in one week, he pocketed $1.14 million.

A lot of the caddies are doing very well, so you expect them to be professional. Most of them are. They're not stupid. They know they have an awful lot to lose.

In the end, Jimmy and I were just having too many arguments. I got to a stage where I was progressing and asking more and more of myself and I didn't think there was any extra commitment level from him. He lived for the day. He was such a lovely bloke and he always had my best interests at heart, but I needed to get away from the old-school caddy mentality. I had had enough. Late in my third year on the European Tour, I decided it was time to move on.

Simon Dyson had injured his arm and was going to be out for a few weeks, so his caddy, Mick Donaghy, was available. I said I'd take him for the week and he was on my bag for the Italian Open in Rome at the end of the 2002 season. I won. That often seems to happen in golf when you throw a new partnership together, so I kept him on and Dyson picked up another caddy when he recovered from his injury.

I felt guilty at the time, taking someone else's caddy. Dyson might have been a bit upset, I'm not really sure. But I wasn't a Premier League player at that stage and it wasn't as if I was nicking one of the top caddies off someone. Mick wasn't working that week and that was it. Stuff like that happens. Players and caddies chop and change all the time.

Mick was a great caddy. Another Scotsman. Another caddy who loved the booze. Not that I knew that when I took him. We had some good times but it was a relationship that was similar, in some ways, to the one I had had with Jimmy. Mick was ridiculously stubborn and he was never wrong, either. He would tut and roll his eyes if I hit a bad shot.

He didn't make many mistakes, it has to be said. But again, his massive downfall was the alcohol. He was so good on the golf course that I didn't mind him having a drink at night. For the first couple of years, he was always there on time, but late in our partnership, we had a number of incidents that were unacceptable, as far as I was concerned.

At a PGA Tour event in New Orleans in 2005, which was a big deal to me because I was still finding my feet on the American circuit, it got to within an hour of my 1 p.m. tee-off time and there was still no sign of Mick. I needed to head off to the driving range to start warming up, so I asked some of the other caddies if they knew where he was.

A few of the lads who had been out with him the night before said he had had a heavy one, but they had got separated from him at the end of the evening. I called him, but his phone was switched off and it got to a point where I had to ask around for someone else. Stephen Leaney had missed the cut and so I was able to get Mark Fulcher, who now caddies for Justin Rose, on my bag for that round.

So I had a caddy I didn't really know on the bag. He didn't know my yardages. He was a good caddy but it was all alien to both of us. I was trying to win a golf tournament worth a million dollars and loads of world-ranking points, and I didn't have my caddy. When I finished the round, there was still no sign of Mick.

I asked one of the policemen at the course if he could find out if a Mick Donaghy had been taken in for some reason the previous evening. After my round, the copper came up to me and said Mick had been jaywalking the night before and had had an altercation with a police officer about it. They had thrown him in a cell for the night and didn't release him in time for him to make it up to the course.

The thing was, Mick never apologised. It was just one of those things. It wasn't his fault that he had been thrown in jail, he said. I should have fired him then, but I kept him on for a while longer. It was my third year with him by then and I had never stopped being impressed with how good he was on the course. But at the end of that year, we had another falling out and I decided enough was enough.

We were at the HSBC event in Shanghai and they always hold a caddy awards evening that week. The free bar ends at 9 p.m., so the hope is that your caddy won't get completely and utterly sloshed. It's always a great night; it's behind closed doors and there is an amazing amount of banter being thrown around.

This particular night, Mick stayed at the bar and then fell asleep in the hotel corridor at 5 a.m. I was on the tee on the Saturday morning and there was no sign of Mick, so I had to get this local Chinese caddy to come and carry my bag. I was really pissed off. I got back to the hotel and sent him a text: *Where the hell are you?*

I got a short response.

Oh, I forgot, Mick texted back. *Caddies aren't allowed to be sick, are they?*

He wasn't sick. He was hungover. I sacked him at the end of that week.

For 99.9999 per cent of the time, caddies are great fun;

they are brilliant professionals who do a great job of getting us round the golf course; they are good company and there is an amazing bond between them and the players. It is just that, occasionally, things happen and you have to move on.

Mick caddies for Jamie Donaldson now. He picks up good players because he's a good caddy. But, as I've already said, the culture is changing among the caddies who work for the best players in the world. And, by the best players, I mean probably the top one hundred players, who have fairly high demands about what they want from their caddy.

So, for a start, the top caddies are all a lot fitter than they were. It's a lot more professional. Players are not going to put up with guys turning up stinking of booze anymore. That culture is in the past. The rewards are so great for all of us that you have to be at your absolute best as a team when you get out on the course.

I've had experience of a couple of other caddies. Nick Faldo's long-time caddy, Fanny Sunesson, caddied for me at the Masters one year because Mick was at home for the birth of his son. It was great for me to have her on the bag, but I'm not sure how it was for her. I hit two shanks in the first two days. My second shot on the seventh ended up on the seventeenth fairway. She must have wondered what the hell she had got herself into.

Since I split with Mick, I have been with Terry Mundy. Terry had worked mainly on the women's tour before, and I knew he had a good reputation. Terry's part of the new breed of caddy I'm talking about. He adopts the same

attitude to professionalism that I do. It's still a sparky relationship. We still have animated discussions and dis-
agreements, but we think the same way about the game.

After I sacked Mick in 2005, I got about twenty text
messages from caddies asking for the job. I was a top-fifty
player by then and I was earning a significant amount of
money, so I was an attractive proposition. Terry was the
only one who called me and asked if he could come in and
have a face-to-face chat about the job.

I found it strange that the other guys thought I might
give them a job that was potentially worth half a million
dollars a year on the back of a ten pence text message.
Terry lived near to me, in Bedford, so I told him to come
for an interview at Paul Dunkley's office in Northampton.
We discussed a number of things: things I like, things I
don't like, things I would expect from him, things he would
expect from me.

I had never had that kind of conversation with Jimmy
or Mick before either of them became my caddy. I should
have done. This time, I made it clear that I didn't want my
caddy turning up for work smelling of booze. The conversation went well and I said we'd do a trial for three months
and see how it went. That trial is now nine years and count-
ing and our working relationship has gone from strength
to strength.

Terry and I are very similar personalities. He is always
laughing and joking, always taking the piss. Some people
think it's a volatile relationship, but it's not. Everybody
works differently. Phil Mickelson and his caddy, Bones, will
have a very detailed conversation about their approach to

a round or to an individual shot. Ours will be a bit more fiery and piss-takey, but, essentially, we will discuss the same things.

I like Terry's company, basically, and that's a good start when it comes to having a decent relationship as golfer and caddie. He follows the same thought processes as me and he has the same work ethic. The more he knows about any given course, the more knowledge he has at his disposal about a hole, the more he can step in and be confident enough to say if he thinks I might be about to do the wrong thing.

One other thing about Terry: he is absolutely not a 'yes man'. I don't have 'yes men' on my bag. If there is one thing that the three men who have caddied for me have in common, it is that they have all been strong characters. Terry is not afraid to voice an opinion and sometimes it might appear that we are being aggressive with each other. We're not. We're just exchanging views.

Sometimes, if there's a gap in tournaments, I might not see him for three weeks, but Terry now lives five minutes away from me in Orlando and fifteen minutes from my base when I'm back in the UK. We have become good mates. I almost spend more time with him than I do with Katie.

It was also Terry who made me aware of the Dreamflight charity, which is something I will always be grateful to him for. Every year for the last twenty-eight years, a wonderful, inspirational lady called Pat Pearce MBE has raised the money to organise a ten-day trip to Orlando for nearly 200 very poorly children. They go to every park and, on the last day, they take these kids, many of whom are wheelchair-bound, to Discovery Cove, where they swim with dolphins.

Pat's philosophy is based on a belief that fun and joy are just as important as medical research and equipment, especially for children who may not be able to wait long enough for the breakthrough they need.

But it's a huge undertaking. Dreamflight book out an entire hotel in Orlando, they have to charter a BA plane, pay for the fuel, arrange for nearly fifty American helpers to meet them at the airport when they arrive in the US and stay with them for the duration of the trip. They pay for entry to all the parks, pay for food for 200 kids for ten days, pay for ice cream for 200 kids.

But what Pat has achieved is wonderful to see. I have been to Orlando airport to welcome the plane when it touches down, and it's amazing. First of all, two fire trucks come out to meet the plane, which gives the kids a great thrill straight away. Then twenty police bikes zoom up and start circling the aircraft. The kids' faces are priceless. I don't know how Pat has managed to arrange this, but the police then give the kids' coaches an escort to the hotel.

When I first got to know about Dreamflight, I sat down with some of these kids and I found it hard to keep it together. They all have inspirational stories. Some of the stories make you want to cry, but they are such brave, bright kids that they make you laugh, too. And Dreamflight does wonderful things for them. The kids get inspired by feeling normal again. That trip to Orlando has changed the lives of some of them. A couple have gone on to win gold medals in the Paralympics.

I said before that I don't like seeing suffering, and that

stands, but I find it rewarding being around these kids. So many of them have got an amazing mindset. They are mentally strong because they have to be. They are so upbeat about life, despite their problems. In fact, they don't see them as problems because it's their reality.

I've tried to do as much as I can to help Pat with the funding. I started off by signing stuff for auctions and things like that, but then Pat asked me to become the charity's patron and it was great to get more involved. I have a fund-raising day at Woburn every year after the Open and, in March, I stage the Ian Poulter Charity Classic at Lake Nona. In 2014, we raised $254,000 and one particularly generous donor, Miles Nadal, guaranteed $50,000 each year for the next ten years to the charity.

That was amazing. It takes a bit of the pressure off Pat, knowing that that money will be there. But I'd like to do more. One of my ambitions is to raise enough through my charity days to fund the annual trip to Orlando entirely. I have been fortunate in many areas of my life and getting involved with Dreamflight is certainly one of them.

I'm also a patron of the Willow Foundation, which was set up by former Arsenal goalkeeper Bob Wilson and his wife Megs in memory of their daughter, Anna, who died of cancer when she was just 31. I was approached to help because I'm an Arsenal fan and it's always been a privilege to be involved. The charity helps provide special days for seriously ill people between the ages of 16 and 40 and so over the years I've offered to play rounds of golf that have been auctioned off by the charity to raise money. Bob and his wife are lovely people and they're doing tremendous work.

CHAPTER 9
Ferrari

After I won the Italian Open at the end of my debut year on the European Tour, I set myself a target. The target was not to rest on my laurels in the way I had done when I won for the first time on the Challenge Tour. And to make my target finite, I told myself that, if I met it and if I kept excelling, I would reward myself with something I had always dreamed of. The next time I won a tournament, I promised myself, I would buy a Ferrari.

I've always loved cars. It started from just being a boy, I suppose. And from reading the odd car magazine and thinking, Wow! Wouldn't it be nice to have a proper car one day? My dad loved cars, but he could never afford a nice one, so he always bought rust buckets and tried to turn them into the car he dreamed of.

My uncle Phil was in a different financial position. He always had fast cars. He had the Sierra Cosworth when that first came out, with the massive ironing board as a spoiler on the back. He bought an Escort RS 2000 and the 2.8 injection Capri. Then he bought himself a Porsche. I always loved cars and speed, and my cousin Gary and I would sit in the back of Uncle Phil's car, giggling when he put his foot down.

Gary and I always talked about cars. They were the

dream things. I had a poster of the Ferrari F40 on my bedroom wall. My dad often worked on his latest banger in the street outside our house, bleeding the brakes, touching up the paintwork, spraying them, filling them, sanding them, painting them, tinkering with the engine. I was always fascinated and would watch him at work.

When I was a kid, I knew I wanted a quick car when I grew up. It's that boy-racer thing. I had friends with nice cars and I wanted one. I didn't want a clapped-out banger. If you want something badly enough, you are going to work hard to get it, but owning a Ferrari had always seemed like the embodiment of an impossible dream to me.

I had to work my way towards one. Paul Dunkley got me a nice little car in 2000. He had negotiated a brand new Vauxhall Corsa for me as part of a sponsorship deal and, at the end of 2001, he got me a deal with Nissan which meant that, in exchange for putting Nissan branding on my golf bag, I got a nice silver Nissan Primera.

Soon after that, Paul convinced Nissan to give me a Nissan GTR, which was the boy racer's real deal. It was an R34 in bright blue, which was their show-car colour. It had a top speed of 185 miles per hour and I knew it could do nought to sixty in under four seconds. Paul gave me the keys on the condition that, if I got myself into trouble with it, he would take it away.

I collected it from Paul's car dealership with my brother and Paul's son, James, and set off for my house. We got on the dual carriageway at Milton Keynes. I wanted to test the acceleration, so I did a bit of a cheeky overtaking manoeuvre and whipped round the outside of the guy in front.

The guy in the car I had overtaken wasn't impressed. He

followed me all the way back to my house. When we pulled up, he leapt out and started giving me a bollocking. I was having a real tear-up with this bloke when Paul arrived. He had been following us all the way. I calmed the guy down but, as soon as he left, I got an even bigger bollocking from Paul. I did manage to hang on to the car, though. Just.

As I dreamed of that Ferrari in 2001, I entered a new phase of my career. I was trying to make sense of having the two-year exemption that came with winning the Italian Open the previous season, trying to work out what it meant to be a winner, what it meant to be Rookie of the Year, and trying to move forward to win bigger and better tournaments.

I was aiming for the WGC tournaments now and automatic qualification for entry into the Majors. I had to get my head around the science of world-ranking points and start scheduling events more carefully, as well as processing a lot more organisational information.

Every box I could imagine had been ticked in that first year on the European Tour and the second year was the start of being more ambitious. I believed now that I could compete with the top guys, that I could challenge in the biggest tournaments, that I could look towards contention for a place on the 2001 European Ryder Cup team and that I could compete in Majors.

I felt more accepted in the top group once I had got that win in Italy and picked up the Rookie of the Year award. That put me in good company when I looked down the list of previous winners. Sergio García, Colin Montgomerie, Nick Faldo, Sandy Lyle: they were all on it. I felt more comfortable around the top players now that I had served my apprenticeship. It was time to move onwards and upwards.

I began to force open some doors. I won at Rabat in Morocco in April 2001, holding off my old mate David Lynn down the stretch and winning by two strokes. It was great to get another win on my résumé. It also meant I pushed myself into contention for the Ryder Cup and qualified for the WGC tournament in St Louis in September 2001.

At that stage, I was ahead of Montgomerie, Langer and García in the rankings as we tried to qualify for Sam Torrance's European team to play against the United States at the Belfry that September. But in the next five tournaments, I only made the cut once and my chances of making the team began to fall away.

I was still desperate to play, though, and I thought I might just have done enough to persuade Torrance that I was worth a wild card. I thought maybe he'd see how much progress I'd made and how much potential I had and give me a shot. I guess everybody who isn't an automatic pick is thinking like that and it turned out I was deluding myself. Torrance went for García and Jesper Parnevik as his captain's picks.

He did ring me. It was a horrible phone call to take. I wasn't really expecting a pick, but you are hoping and praying that the captain wants you on the side. I was very upset after the phone call. Sam just said he couldn't pick me, but he would like me to be his first reserve. I didn't know how to take that, really. It's not like you are going to go there and hang around hoping someone is going to get injured.

The following week, I played the Omega European Masters at Crans-sur-Sierre in Switzerland. And guess who I was paired with in the first round? Yep: Sam Torrance. I had nothing against Sam. I knew it must have been a hard phone call for him to make, but my emotions were pretty low.

Sam mentioned the Ryder Cup again when we met up at the tournament, but there was nothing he could really say to make me feel any better. I was a bit of a mess, to be honest. I probably should have withdrawn before the start and not even turned up. As it was, I went out on the course and I was nine over for the first nine holes.

I had to get out of there. I had to leave. I was not emotionally ready for that. I couldn't rationalise anything. I couldn't concentrate, my head was spinning, I didn't want to be there and I was getting frustrated on that front nine. I told the guys I needed to go home. I gave them my scorecard, packed my clubs and got out of there. That had never happened to me before, but I couldn't deal with it at the time. It was best I excused myself.

I got my head together and, a few days later, I arrived at Bellerive in St Louis for the WGC American Express Championship. I was driving to the golf course for a practice round when I heard some chatter on the radio about a plane hitting the World Trade Center in New York. There was still a lot of confusion about what had happened and it was only when I got to the clubhouse, wandered into the locker room, stared up at the television and saw the second plane hit that the enormity of what was happening became apparent.

Everybody panicked. I phoned Katie. I think everybody

had the same instinct on 9/11: try to speak to your loved ones, no matter how far apart you might be. When both buildings collapsed, it started to feel like the end of the world. Everything unravelled very quickly. Every plane was grounded and was going to be grounded for a good number of days.

We all had the same worries as everyone else. Were there going to be further attacks? When were we going to be able to get home? When would we see our families again? Did we want to get on an aeroplane after what had happened? It was a desperate time. Some of the companies that were sponsoring the tournament in St Louis had lost a lot of employees in the attack. It was awful.

I just wanted to go home. I was worried. I was panicking. No one hit another ball in St Louis, obviously. Everyone congregated in the bar and stared at the news tickers on the television screens. After a couple of days, we were told that the Tour had managed to charter the Phoenix Suns' corporate plane and that we were going to fly back to Europe in it. The players picked up the tab and we got all the caddies and European Tour officials on board, too. It was such a relief to get home.

It was hard to get back to golf for a while after that. Sport didn't seem important. I didn't play for nearly a month. The Ryder Cup at the Belfry was cancelled. The American team didn't want to get on a plane to fly across the Atlantic; no one wanted to fly around that time, so it was hard to blame them. Their country was still in mourning. In fact, everyone was still trying to come to terms with what had happened.

It was absolutely the right decision to cancel the Ryder Cup, although it was a big blow for the sport. It was so close to the event that all the temporary grandstands had been erected. They came down. To all intents and purposes, that was the end of the golfing year.

I had another slightly uneven year in 2002, but it was still another year of progress. There were even some suggestions I might be handed a Ryder Cup reprieve. The competition had been rescheduled for September 2002 and both teams had kept to the original line-ups, but Monty, Thomas Bjørn and Lee Westwood were all suffering from various injuries and for a while it looked like I might get a call-up. It didn't happen. They shook the injuries off and played their part in beating the Americans at the Belfry in another memorable competition.

I got over the disappointment of not being involved in the best possible way. A month after the Ryder Cup, I was playing in the Italian Open again. I shot 61 in the first round and, in the final round, Paul Lawrie tied me for the lead with two holes to play. Then I three-putted the seventeenth to go one down with one to play. We were standing on the eighteenth tee – par four, slight dog-leg, right to left – and Paul hit his drive straight out of bounds.

I knew I had to seize my chance. He made six and I made a birdie, so I beat him by two shots. It was great to win again and I was fairly stoked. I did not try to hide my excitement, put it that way. Paul said in his autobiography that he was disappointed with my celebration. He said I was 'disrespectful', 'rude' and 'unprofessional'. He spoke to me about it before the Ryder Cup at Medinah many years later and basically said he'd been misquoted in his own book. I felt for him, but I was there to win a golf tournament.

After I won in Italy, I said to Paul Dunkley that I thought I finally had enough money to buy myself a Ferrari. I asked him to go and select a Ferrari 360 Modena for me, so he went to the Maranello dealership in Surrey and picked out a red-and-cream model that came with a £117,000 price tag. I got back home and there she was, waiting in my drive.

It was a symbol of something for me. It had seemed like an impossible dream when I was a kid and now it was real. When you are a kid and you do something good and your mum takes you down the shop to get a packet of sweets, you feel good, don't you?

I have got more Ferraris now. In fact, I've got a small collection of them. Some people get offended by the fact I take pleasure in owning nice cars. But a huge percentage are very happy for me because they know where I have come from and how hard I have worked to be able to provide for my family and to enjoy nice things in life.

My cars are my art. To me, owning them is like owning paintings. I cherish them and I make sure they are gleaming. I take great pleasure from looking at them as well as from driving them. Actually, I don't drive the supercars that I have bought that much because they are investment pieces and, as a general rule, the more you drive them, the less they appreciate in value.

I've had my Ferrari 288 GTO for eighteen months and I've done fewer than fifty miles in it. I've had the F40 for sixteen months and I've done fewer than forty miles in it. I've had the F50 for seven months and driven it a hundred yards. It's only got 230 miles on the clock. I've done maybe 300 miles in the Enzo. That's the one I've driven the most.

My Ferrari 275 GTB/4 is the most valuable of all of them. It's got 67,000 kilometres on the clock and I have probably only driven that for about thirty kilometres. I have just sent it away for an eighteen-month restoration that is going to cost me about $300,000. It's probably the most beautiful Ferrari ever made. It's worth about three and a half million dollars.

I know it all sounds extravagant, but I've earned my money and I'm spending it how I want. I'd rather have it embodied in beautiful cars than in stocks and shares. I'd rather be able to see it and enjoy it. There was a time not very long ago when I could only dream about owning a Ferrari. I dreamed and I dreamed and now the dream is a reality.

CHAPTER 10
A Twenty-Eight-Goal Football Match

I won two tournaments in 2003: the Wales Open at Celtic Manor in June, and the Nordic Open in Copenhagen in August. In 2004, I was invited to play in the Masters for the first time. They were important milestones for me, but they were stages on a journey to what I considered the most important goal so far: representing Europe in the 2004 Ryder Cup at Oakland Hills.

Part of the reason it had hurt so much to miss out in 2001 and again in 2002 (the competition was moved on a year because of 9/11) was that the Ryder Cup was the event that had done the most to inspire me to become a professional golfer. I went to the Belfry as a fan in 1993 and watched golf being played like I'd never seen it played before.

I was seventeen and had started full-time work at Chesfield Downs when Bernard Gallacher's European team, which included Nick Faldo, Seve Ballesteros, José María Olazábal and a young Colin Montgomerie, took on Tom Watson's USA side, which had its own share of greats like Fred Couples, Payne Stewart and Ray Floyd.

I was working in the pro shop at the club, which was managed by a guy called David Dennier. He and the pro, Mike Isaacs, said they could get tickets for the Belfry and so we decided the three of us would go up there to watch.

We took the week off work, drove up to the Midlands on the Wednesday afternoon before play started on the Friday, and tried to find somewhere to stay.

We hadn't booked anywhere. We had assumed that we would be able to camp, but when we arrived at the campsite, it was full. The old lady who was in charge could see how disappointed we were and she took pity on us. She lived nearby and she said we could pitch our tent at the end of her garden.

A tent's a tent. It didn't make any difference to us whether we pitched it in the official campsite or in a back garden. So we agreed to pay her three pounds a night for the week and she said that we could use her kitchen. We were eating tinned food, but each night it was my job to go and knock on the old lady's back door and go in to wash the plates and the cutlery.

I think she felt a bit sorry for us because she gave us a bottle of wine each night. So, for three pounds a night, we stayed in her back garden and got a bottle of wine. We'd polish that off and fall asleep and then, about three o'clock every morning, I'd get a smack on the head because I was snoring horrendously. Three guys, living on canned food and sleeping in a very small tent in someone's back garden was not a great recipe for a quiet night – but it was brilliant.

We had an absolutely amazing week. I had been to Wentworth and Woburn with my dad before, but this was the first really big golf event I had attended and nothing had prepared me for the atmosphere of the Ryder Cup. We were walking up to the thirteenth hole when Nick Faldo got a hole-in-one on the fourteenth during his singles match against Paul Azinger on Sunday and the noise from the crowd was the loudest roar I had ever heard. I was still being converted from football to golf and this was louder than anything I'd ever experienced at a football match. The hairs on the back of my neck were standing up on end and I was thinking, Holy shit, this is unbelievable. It was the first time I'd really felt like that at a sporting event.

The noise, the electricity, the buzz, the excitement, the atmosphere between the USA and Europe: it was intense. As the two sets of fans go, it is the closest you are ever going to get to the atmosphere at a big football match. Every shot that gets hit, every putt that gets missed, it's almost identical to the ebb and flow of emotion at a football match.

There's the team dynamic, too. That has always been what I have missed in most of the golf I play: not being with your teammates, not having anyone to share the highs and lows with. But the Ryder Cup's different. I realised that straight away at the Belfry in 1993. The emotional rollercoaster is amazing from start to finish. It's the whole buzz. It's played over three days but it's up and down the entire time. It's a long football match, is what it is. It's a twenty-eight-goal football match.

That was the beginning of my long love affair with the Ryder Cup. Watching Seve and Olly express themselves on a course in a way I'd never seen them behave in any normal tournament was startling. It was like watching different players. It was like watching men transformed. The Ryder Cup does that.

That week at the Belfry changed everything for me. That was the point which was the real kicker for me. I said to myself that this was exactly what I wanted to do with my life. This was what I wanted to be. These were the people I wanted to emulate. This was what I wanted to be involved in. This was what I wanted to achieve. This was what I was going to strive for.

The dream of playing in the Ryder Cup came a lot closer for me in 2003. It was great to win at Celtic Manor because Mum and Dad and a lot of my family and friends were there. I played solidly all week and won by three shots. I had a lot of support and it was the first time I had won a big tournament on home soil, which made it special.

Winning in Denmark later in the year was probably more satisfying, though. Mainly, that was because I went head to head with Monty for the last couple of days and came from behind to beat him. To have a player as good as him pushing me all the way, and to be able to deal with it and shoot final rounds of 65 and 66 to win by a stroke was huge for my confidence. Monty, who finished with rounds of 64 and 68, was a big scalp.

So I was feeling chipper as we went into Ryder Cup year, in 2004. I was in the top fifty in the world and at the beginning of January a letter came through my door telling me that I had been invited to play at Augusta National between 8 April and 11 April. Every young golfer wants to play Augusta. It was another dream come true.

I was like a kid in a candy store from the moment I was picked up from the airport and driven to the gates at the end of Magnolia Lane, which leads down to the clubhouse. The police guard asked for my name and I saw him check his list and find it. He put a tick against my name and we were cleared to drive down the famous Magnolia Lane.

The smallest things were a thrill for me: seeing the driving range, getting my credentials, seeing Tiger Woods and Mark O'Meara practising, strolling down the hill and seeing Amen Corner for the first time. I took photos constantly, like a tourist, a wide-eyed golfer at a place where legends were made.

I didn't want anybody close to me to miss out on this. Katie couldn't travel at the time as she was heavily pregnant with Luke, who was born about five weeks, later. I rented a house about fifteen minutes from the course and Dad and his second wife Sue, Mum and Mark, my brother Danny, Uncle Phil, manager Paul and his son James, and my friend Andy, all stayed with me. I am lucky that Mum and Dad get on fine after their divorce, so we were all able to stay together in the same house and enjoy the week.

I played one practice round with Ian Woosnam, who had won the Masters in 1991. And I played another with Justin Rose and Adam Scott. As we played our way around the course, it felt like we had all come a long way since our days together on the Challenger Tour.

Paul Dunkley caddied for me at the par-three tournament that is always held the day before the Masters begins. Rosie's mum caddied for him. That whetted the appetite for the real thing and, before I left the course that night, I saw armies of mowers heading down the first fairway in formation, putting the final touches to the preparations for the next day.

I did okay that first year at Augusta. I made the cut, anyway. I shot 75 in the first round, the same as Woods and Jack Nicklaus. I was in the middle of the field. Rosie was leading. I played better in the second round and shot 73, so I was there for the weekend while the reigning champion, Mike Weir, was going home.

Phil Mickelson won the tournament that year. I finished tied for thirty-first. I could have done even better, but I had a few putts that shaved the hole. I was just delighted that I was going to get two more days of experience of the course. I loved everything about playing there: the tight grass, the short game that is required, the fast, sloping greens. I have always played well around that type of course.

My season was going okay, but everything was about qualifying for the Ryder Cup team and impressing the European captain, Bernhard Langer. I finished sixth at the Italian Open, tied for twentieth at the British Masters at the Forest of Arden, and then headed over to Heidelberg in Germany for the Deutsche Bank SAP Open TPC of Europe.

There was a complication. My first child, Aimee-Leigh, had been born in 2002 and now Katie was heavily pregnant again. The baby's due date was the Sunday of the Deutsche Bank, but Aimee had been two weeks late and Katie said she felt it was going to be the same with this one.

I was keen to play. It was a big tournament. I was honest with Katie about it. It was Ryder Cup year, I was doing quite nicely and I was desperate to push myself into an automatic qualification spot for the team. But I was also desperate to be at the birth of my child. I had been there for Aimee's birth and I didn't want to miss this one, either.

Katie told me to go and play in the tournament. I decided that's what I'd do on the proviso that, if she went into labour, I would withdraw from the tournament immediately and come home. I had joined a scheme called

NetJets, which was like a credit card that allows you to rent private planes. I had bought twenty-five hours' worth of flights and, if something happened with Katie, I thought I'd be able to get home very quickly.

I made the cut on the mark in Heidelberg. My tee-off time for the third round was early Saturday morning. But in the middle of the night, my phone started ringing. I was in that confused state you get in when you're woken in the early hours and at first I thought it was my alarm going off to get me up and out for the start of my round.

But it was Katie calling me from home, saying her waters had broken. I thought, Oh shit, I've got to get home. I looked at my watch. It was 3 a.m. I called NetJets and asked them if they had a plane sitting in Germany that could get me home. They said the earliest they could get a plane scrambled to me was 8 a.m. I called British Airways and they had a really early flight out of Frankfurt that was due to get back to London about 8 a.m. That was my best chance.

I still thought I might make it. I kept thinking about the fact that Aimee had been late. I got a message to the tournament organisers that I was pulling out, drove to Frankfurt and checked in. I had just gone through security when my phone rang. It was Katie. 'It's a boy,' she said.

It had all happened so fast that Katie said she thought she was going to give birth to our son in the car while her sister was driving her to the hospital in Milton Keynes. It was only a few minutes away, but they still only just made it in time. I got there a few hours later and there he was, our lovely little boy, Luke. I was gutted I'd missed it, but

Katie and Luke were happy and healthy, so I couldn't feel too disappointed. Actually, I felt blessed, and I'm pleased to say I was there for the births of Lilly-Mai in 2009 and Joshua in 2012.

And I pressed on with my pursuit of that prized place in the European Ryder Cup team. I had got so close the last time that I was desperate not to miss out again, but when I arrived at the final qualifying tournament of the year, the BMW International Open, in Munich, my place was still in doubt. I needed to finish in the top forty-five to be sure of making the team.

Thomas Levet, Padraig Harrington, Sergio García, Miguel Ángel Jiménez, Darren Clarke and Lee Westwood had already sealed their berths on the team, Colin Montgomerie and Luke Donald were the favourites to get Bernhard Langer's two wild-card spots, and Paul Casey, David Howell and Paul McGinley were in strong positions.

I made the cut with no problems but, as the final round began to unfold, it became clear that the struggle for the final place on the team was going to be between me and Fredrik Jacobson. Jacobson needed to finish fourth to earn a spot and, for most of Sunday, that's exactly where he was.

I didn't have any margin for error but, on the tenth hole, I made a couple of big ones. I hit two shots into the water and made quadruple bogey. Now I was right down in forty-fifth place, absolutely the lowest position I could afford to be in, and my mind was spinning. I was worried my dream of playing in the Ryder Cup was about to be ruined again. I knew I had to dig deep. I was having a horrendous round.

I was playing with Darren Clarke. As we walked to the eleventh tee, he tried to reassure me. He told me to try not to worry, to go out and make a ton of birdies on the back nine. 'You're going to be fine,' he said. 'You're going to make it.' That helped me. It was nice to have someone like him supporting me in those final few holes.

I responded, too. I went on a real charge and picked up six shots in the last eight holes. As I moved back up the leader board, Jacobson dropped a shot on the fifteenth. I started to feel more confident. In the end, I finished in twenty-fifth place. For a little while, I found it hard to grasp the reality of what had happened. I had qualified. I was going to go to Oakland Hills, just outside Detroit, Michigan, to play for Europe against America. I was going to play in a Ryder Cup.

CHAPTER 11
Easy Ryder

I walk out to the first tee at Oakland Hills on Friday morning. Bernhard Langer has told me I am going to sit out on the first day, but he wants me to watch the action and feel the atmosphere.

'You need to know what it's going to be like,' Langer says, with an air of slight foreboding.

I think I know what it's going to be like. I went to the Belfry in 1993. I know it will be loud and I realise there are going to be some nerves among my teammates. But I am totally unprepared for what I am about to witness.

I am disappointed I'm not going to play on Friday. I want to play. I want to get going. But I'm fine with Langer's decision. He wants to win the competition and he needs to put the team out there that is going to get the job done. If that means I'm going to rest, I'm going to rest.

So I stroll down to the first tee with David Howell, who is also sitting out, and try to take it all in. The crowd is loud. Very loud. Patriotic. Oakland Hills is just outside Detroit. These are noisy fans. Blue collar. They want to make themselves heard. A lot of them have had a few drinks. They are roaring their heads off, screaming, 'USA! USA!'

There are helicopters overhead, there are television

cameras everywhere, there are European supporters doing their bit, there are the team captains, there are players' wives, there are celebrities. I start to realise this is going to be very different to anything I have experienced before as a player.

I stand a few feet away from Luke Donald as he prepares to take his first tee shot in his morning four ball. The crowd is screaming and yelling as he bends down and I see Luke's hand shake as he tries to put his ball on the tee peg. That blows my mind. I think, Oh shit. I know I am going to have to do that the next morning. Now I am properly nervous.

Anyone who says they are not ridiculously nervous on the first tee at a Ryder Cup is lying. It is the most daunting tee shot you will ever play in your life. I don't care if it's the Sunday of a Major. I don't care what tournament it is. Nothing compares to that. The Sunday of a Major is not a patch on the Ryder Cup. It affects everyone.

The American captain, Hal Sutton, has decided to pair Tiger Woods with Phil Mickelson. It is a bold strategy. He chooses to ignore all the stories about the chemistry between the two of them being awkward. He decides to send out his best two players in the first match and blitz the opposition. He wants them to set the tone.

I am out there on the first tee to watch them, too. Mickelson hits his tee shot fifty yards left and Tiger hits his fifty yards right. I feel a bit better then. If it can happen to Woods and Mickelson, I think, it's okay if it happens to me, too. If nerves can do that to the best players in the world, they can do it to anyone.

It's the Ryder Cup. It does strange things to people. The

pressure is crippling. At the opening ceremony, Hal Sutton makes a speech and forgets how many kids he has. He thanks his wife for providing him with three children. She just smiles and holds up four fingers.

What's the Ryder Cup doing to you if you forget one of your kids? Making a speech like that, knowing that all of golf is watching, knowing that it's going out to millions – it turns you to jelly. It really does. It puts you in a stir. You can't put your ball on a tee peg; you can't hit it within fifty yards of the fairway. It's something you can't explain. It puts people under the most obscene pressure they have ever felt.

A lot of people aren't used to the pressure of being in a team, for a start. I had never played Walker Cup or a team event of that magnitude. In that Ryder Cup week, you learn more about players and their personalities than you do in months and months of travelling the tour with them. You start to become friends, not just rivals, and that makes you even more determined not to let anybody down.

The other thing about the Ryder Cup is the history. You get in a Ryder Cup team and you feel the weight of history on your shoulders. You think about all the great players who have played in the Ryder Cup before you: people you have respected and followed as a fan, people who have helped inspire you to become a player, people who have carved out their legends at the Ryder Cup.

When I arrive at Oakland Hills, I think back to Seve, Olly, Monty, Faldo, Woosnam, Lyle. I think of how they gave everything they had for the team and how much it meant to them to strive to get their hands on that little trophy. I think about what it meant way back when you played for Great Britain and it was such an unequal contest against the USA.

You owe it to those players to play the Ryder Cup in the spirit in which they played it, to give everything. You give exactly what they gave. You don't put a price on it. It's not about money. What you are doing is honouring the spirit of golf and doing what you feel is right and trying to create moments of magic the fans will treasure alongside all the rest.

I can reel off a whole list of personal favourites, even by the time I get to Oakland Hills. Costantino Rocca beating Tiger Woods in the singles at Valderrama in 1997, or Philip Walton closing it out in 1995 at Oak Hill, or Howard Clark making that hole-in-one the same year, or Faldo's hole-in-one at the Belfry, or David Gilford over the back of a green in his match, trying to chip it with a five iron and Seve having a full flap.

I've got plenty more memories, don't worry. At Valderrama, where Monty's got that little wedge shot into the seventeenth and Seve is coming in to interfere, to try to tell Monty how to play a shot, and Monty is basically telling him to piss off and leave him alone. I remember all of them. Phil Price on that sixteenth green at the Belfry in 2002, when he beat Phil Mickelson and he was fist-pumping in a way you have never seen Phil Price fist-pump before.

Or Christy O'Connor's two-iron into the eighteenth green at the Belfry in 1989, or Paul Azinger holing his bunker shot at the same hole in 2002. Can you remember that many shots from other tournaments down the years? You just don't. You have got all that in your memory and you have got all the displays of emotion from all those great players in your memory, too. And that's why it is the competition it is today. It is the biggest spectacle in golf for that reason.

There is the build-up, too. I find that incredibly draining. I have been measured for my outfits before I even know whether I have qualified for the team or not. Then there is the excitement of my travel outfit arriving in the post. Never mind the first tee, I feel the nerves kick in as soon as I get to Heathrow and mill around with the other players and their families for the flight to the States. My mum and dad come with us on the team plane, as well as Paul Dunkley and, of course, Katie and Luke.

Luke is only a couple of months old. It isn't really the done thing to take kids to the Ryder Cup, but Katie is still nursing Luke and can't bear to be parted from him. The truth is, I don't see that much of them when we get to the States. It is so busy from start to finish at the Ryder Cup that you hardly spend any time with your family.

I get up at 5 a.m. every day and I do not have a spare minute until I fall into bed. Having breakfast, being stretched, getting to the golf course, playing practice rounds, coming back, the opening ceremony, the gala dinner, press conferences, team meetings, more press conferences. That's how it goes.

I get to my room at the team hotel and all my outfits for the week are there in day order. They are all laid out on the bed. That really gives me goosebumps. My shoes are all lined up and colour co-ordinated. I swap my clubs over from my own golf bag to the special Ryder Cup bag with my name on it, which has also arrived. Then there is my suit for the gala dinner and my jacket for the opening ceremony.

This is for real now and this is a big deal. This is a huge week. I am starting to get anxious. The nerves are building. I sense the level of importance. I sense how long and intense the week is going to be.

Langer is very quiet and thoughtful in his planning. He is very regimented in his team meetings. It is all very exact. So when he says a team meeting starts at 7 p.m., it starts at 7 p.m. on the nose. Everyone is in the room and then the door closes. No one else is in the room – just him and the players. It is very boardroom-ish. Very businesslike. It is a quiet, measured conversation.

That is Langer's style. That is his personality. He isn't larger than life, like Seve. Langer is very quiet. He asks one-on-one what you are thinking and what your pairing preferences are. He also tells me I'll be sitting out the first day.

I understand. There are always going to be guys sitting out in the first couple of days. I am a rookie. I'm certainly not expecting to play five matches at Oakland Hills. You accept whatever decision your captain makes and respect his wishes.

There is nothing to reproach Langer for. We get off to a flying start at Oakland Hills. I can see Hal Sutton's logic in pairing Woods with Mickelson, but it just doesn't work. And instead of giving the US team a huge confidence boost by winning that first four ball against Monty and Padraig Harrington, their defeat deals them a body blow.

Langer has been very methodical about everything. The

crowd is noisy, certainly, but not hostile. Langer has made sure we do everything we can to win the fans over early in the week. He tells us that the US players are refusing to sign autographs during the practice rounds, so we sign every single bit of paper thrust our way. Our practice rounds take a hell of a lot longer, but the autograph policy wins us plenty of friends.

Langer never stops analysing stuff like that. There is not one moment of Ryder Cup week that is chit-chat. It all feels meaningful. Even though you're relaxing in the evening, trying not to think about it too much, there are always people coming up to you, asking questions.

How are you feeling?

Were you happy with your round?

Would you be comfortable being paired with so-and-so?

How did so-and-so feel when you were out on the course with him?

How do you think you'd react to playing twice today?

How's so-and-so hitting it?

It is endless. Whatever is being asked is always for the benefit of the team. Usually, it is one of the vice-captains asking the questions. They are working non-stop, trying to find out every single last detail about everybody in the team to make sure they're feeling all right and to find out any extra information. You're under the magnifying glass the whole time.

I walk the course a lot on Friday and I see the body language of Woods and Mickelson at first hand. It is poor. I am standing on the eighteenth tee when Mickelson carves his drive way, way left. It hits the out-of-bounds fence and stays in. I look at Tiger and there is an expression of pure disgust on his face that he simply cannot disguise.

They look awkward together. Everyone knows they haven't been best mates over the years. There is a rivalry there, which is no secret. There is bound to be. It's probably healthy on a week-to-week basis when they are bringing the best out of each other because they are competing. But this is a Ryder Cup and they can't get to grips with the fact they are playing on the same side.

Mickelson has just changed club manufacturers. He is paired with Tiger, using a golf ball he has never hit before with a club he has barely swung before. It is a recipe for problems before you even take their rivalry into account. And the Ryder Cup is not the format best suited to Tiger's strengths.

For the vast majority of the year, when Tiger plays, it's about Tiger. He is unbelievably ruthless, probably the most ruthless golfer I have ever seen: the way he practises, the way he strides on to the range, the way he goes about his business, the way he disappears at the end of play, the way he doesn't allow anybody or anything to get in the way of him playing and practising.

I don't think the Ryder Cup allows him to be him. That's the key. He has to abide by the rules and regulations of what the Ryder Cup stands for and wear the team uniform and go to the opening ceremony. He is not his own man. It is not just about him for that week. It's about the whole team.

I'm not saying that he's too selfish to play in a Ryder Cup, or anything like that. I'm just saying that being selfish or single-minded or dedicated or ruthless, or whatever you want to call it, is an incredible asset for most of a golfer's year. It just doesn't work for him in that Ryder Cup format because he can't be himself.

He is not in control that week. There is a captain in control. There are eleven other guys that have to be looked after and that Tiger has to think about and help and take into consideration. That's what it looks like to me. Maybe he doesn't get the time he needs alone – or in the gym, or wherever – to get his mind right. I don't know.

He and Mickelson lose that first match against Harrington and Montgomerie, and the European team never looks back. Mickelson and Woods lose again in the afternoon and, by the end of that first day, we are leading 6½–1½. I still haven't hit a ball in anger.

I get my chance the next morning. Langer pairs me with Darren Clarke, a classic combination of experienced pro with rookie. And, as a treat for my Ryder Cup debut, we are drawn against Chris Riley and Tiger Woods. I am shitting myself as I walk to the first tee. My legs feel like jelly.

Darren gives me some fairly basic advice.

'Stand up and hit it as hard as you can,' he says. 'I don't care where it's going to go, but I will stride down the middle of the fairway right behind you, wherever it ends up.'

My main concern at that point is not where the ball is going to go but whether I am actually going to make any kind of contact with it at all. That first tee becomes a kind of out-of-body experience for me. All these people are standing around the tee box, screaming and roaring, and you have got to send your drive down the fairway. Tiger is standing a few feet away, staring me down.

My first shot's a blur. I don't remember it. Some stuff in the Ryder Cup is like fog.

I do make contact, I know that, but Darren and I don't play well. That applies to me, in particular. It just doesn't work. We are 1down after the first hole and 2down after the second. We never get back into the match. I make a birdie on the fourteenth, but that still leaves them 3up and they close out a 4&3 victory on the fifteenth.

Tiger plays extremely well that morning. And we can't give him and Riley a game. I find it really hard to take. I have looked forward to this moment for so long and now I am part of a pairing that has been seriously beaten. I am gutted I have lost the first point I have played for. I try not to show it, but I take it badly. We are still well ahead in the competition, but I feel I have let the team down.

I am 'rested' again for the afternoon session on Saturday, so I know I have to go out in the singles and get stuck in. I don't want to have gone all that way and not put a point on the board. I am desperate to avoid that. I have worked myself up so much to make the side, having missed out in 2002, and I know that if I don't win my singles now, it will feel as if I am not really part of the victory we are heading towards.

We have a commanding 11-5 lead at the start of the singles and Langer puts me out in tenth place in the line-up. Paul Casey goes out first and loses to Tiger, but Sergio García is out second and beats Mickelson. Luke Donald loses heavily to Chad Campbell, but we never have anything less than a comfortable advantage as a team.

I have been drawn against Chris Riley again. It feels like everything is on the line. I go out with a raging need to win. If my fourballs was disappointing, my singles match is an amazing experience. I go 1up on the first and, although Riley brings it all square on the next hole, I go back into the lead on the seventh and never relinquish it.

I go 2up on the fourteenth and, as we get to the fifteenth green, I study the scoreboard and realise the team only needs another half a point to reach fourteen points. Because we are the holders, that will be enough for us to retain the Ryder Cup. I don't pay too much attention to that because I know Monty is in the final throes of his match with David Toms and is 1up, playing the last.

I have hit a nice shot into the fifteenth and I hole my putt for a birdie. That puts me 3up with three to play, so I am dormy. That means we are guaranteed at least half a point from my game and that is enough to put us over the line. I don't celebrate at that stage because I want to win my match and I haven't done that yet. But I know what it means.

A few seconds later, I hear this amazing roar coming from up ahead. I guess it is Monty closing things out on the eighteenth. That is an incredible feeling. It is beyond doubt now. We have not just retained the Ryder Cup. We have won it in the USA.

I have been asked from time to time whether I believe I hit the putt that won the Ryder Cup. Well, the answer is that it doesn't matter. It is neither here nor there. There is no extra reward for holing the winning putt and it is fitting that history should record that it was a great player like Monty who holed it on the last hole in front of a big crowd, rather than some rookie out on the fifteenth green.

I wouldn't have liked to be the man to tell Monty it wasn't actually his putt that won the Cup.

I am aware my putt takes us over the points tally, sure, and yes, I feel a great sense of elation when it drops, but some people have pointed out, correctly, that, even though I was then dormy, it was still technically possible that I could have been disqualified during the course of the last three holes. The scoreboard and the records of the tournament only take account of concluded matches.

I feel excited as I dash to the party which is taking place by the side of the eighteenth green. I realise the Ryder Cup is everything. To win that match against Chris Riley and to be able to celebrate it with the team and with my friends and family is a special experience. You don't get to do that too often. It is an amazing feeling.

To get a point is a job well done for me. I have done my bit. I have made my contribution to the winning score and added something I am going to be proud of. I have a fifty-per-cent success rate and on my Ryder Cup debut as part of a triumphant team; I am happy to take that.

It is a critical moment in my career. Oakland Hills confirms everything I want to be true about the Ryder Cup. It makes it real. It gets me totally and utterly hooked. It cements friendships for me, too. Even if you think you are good mates with someone, being part of a team with them and facing that kind of pressure together makes you bond more.

After we get back to the hotel, we go to an Irish bar across the road. Langer stays behind, but most of the rest of the team go to the bar. The place is packed with fans and, before I know what is happening, Lee Westwood climbs up on the bar. He begins to introduce us one by one in a very theatrical kind of style and each time a new name is called out, another member of the team clambers up on the bar beside him.

In the end, we are all up there, leading the rest of the bar in a sing-song, having drinks handed to us and generally having a hell of a time. That lasts for an hour or so and then we head back to the hotel to rejoin our families and continue with the party.

A few of us don't bother going to bed. We go straight from the bar to the airport. Everyone gets on the plane, has a couple more drinks and falls asleep. Luke is cuddled up with me and he falls asleep as well. When I wake up, Luke is still slumbering, so I get the Ryder Cup, put it in the spot where I have been lying and nestle it next to my young son. The Cup and Luke are about the same size.

Sergio García comes to have a look at what is going on because everyone is cooing over Luke. Sergio leans over and the lid falls off the trophy, smacks Luke on the noggin and wakes him up. Now everyone on the plane has a sore head.

CHAPTER 12
A Fashion Statement

Some people talk about the clothes I wear and say I'm an attention seeker. I don't take that as a criticism. I'm just doing my job. My job is to be happy on the golf course and perform as well as I possibly can. My job is to be a credit to the brands I represent. My job is to be as good as possible at getting more television time by playing excellent golf, because more television time means better value for my sponsors.

A few months before my Ryder Cup debut at Oakland Hills, I had caused a bit of a stir at the Open at Royal Troon by playing my first round wearing a pair of Union Jack trousers. It was the kind of thing I'd been wanting to do for a long time. I was bored with the clothes I'd been wearing until then. I didn't feel comfortable in them. I didn't feel they were me.

I'm a bit OCD about my clothes. I admit that. In fact, of all my OCD issues, it's the biggest. I iron my own clothes and press my own trousers because I don't want anyone else touching them. No one else presses my trousers. Except my mum. Everyone else leaves tramlines in them. Tramlines really, really, really annoy me. If someone presses my trousers and they have a set of tramlines in them, I will not walk out of the room wearing them. I will re-press them until they are perfect. If my trousers come back from the dry cleaners and the lines don't match, top to bottom, I have got to get the iron out and press them.

My wife, Katie? She washes my clothes, but I have always ironed my own stuff. We have help to make sure my stuff is right. Our housekeeper irons my other golf clothes and she knows how to iron them. But my trousers get pressed at the dry cleaners and, if they are not right, I have to redo them.

When I travel to a tournament, if I unpack my suitcase and some stuff is creased, I will iron it the day I get there and I will hang it in the closet in day order for the entire week: shirt, trousers, shirt, trousers, shirt, trousers, shirt, trousers, so it is all laid out, so it is all ready. Then I am relaxed in my brain for the rest of the week. I know what outfit I am going to wear every day.

I will check the weather forecast and, if it is going to be red hot, I will wear the dark outfit in the morning and the light outfit in the afternoon, so there is some flexibility according to the weather pattern. The weather plays a part as to whether I am going to wear tartans. If it is roasting hot, I will choose a pair of trousers that are slightly cooler to wear than the tartans.

Fashion has always been important in my family. Mum was a manager at a Dorothy Perkins. Before that, she worked in Top Shop. My dad always loved nice clothes, nice shoes, nice everything, but we just couldn't afford it. That was difficult because he always wanted to dress well. When he did have any money in his pocket, he went out and bought himself a new leather jacket or something that was quality.

When I worked on the market stall, I was selling menswear, selling T-shirts, so I was always around clothes. They were right in front of me. I would usually finish packing the stall away by 6 p.m. and then I'd walk to Top Shop in Stevenage New Town to get a lift home with Mum, who would have just finished cashing up.

Then I worked in the pro shop at Chesfield Downs from the age of fifteen, merchandising the stock, always hanging it neatly, in order, making sure it was colour co-ordinated. I definitely knew what looked good and what didn't.

I was never afraid of wearing something different. I didn't do that very often when I was a kid because I couldn't afford it. I would rather go and buy a new pair of trainers than a new shirt or jeans. But I've got a picture of myself at a family wedding when I was ten or eleven and I've got a bright blue cardigan on. A real rascal. It was a little bit out there even then. That cardigan is saying, 'Look at me.' I've always been at it.

Many golfers aren't too bothered what they wear, as long as they're supplied with some nice shirts and trousers and get paid for dressing in them. That was never the way it was for me. Fashion was always important in our family and, when I became interested in golf, I idolised players who had their own identity and whose clothes sense said something about their character.

When I was younger, I always made a point of trying to find out what Payne Stewart was wearing. I absolutely hero-worshipped him. I went to watch the Open at Royal St George's one year and he was wearing this pair of trousers that had been perfectly ironed and which had a little slit at the bottom of each leg so that they sat just right on top of a pair of leather golf shoes with shiny steel toecaps. That seemed like perfection to me. I wanted to model myself on him.

For some time, Stewart had a sponsorship deal with the NFL where he wore the colours of the team nearest to the golf course where a tournament was taking place. He wore the knickerbockers and the socks and the right colour shoes. Whether it was his idea or Reebok's, I don't know, but it was bloody cool. It was clever branding. It worked.

Stewart, who died tragically in a plane accident in 1999, had a great dress sense. He had the confidence to wear those ivy caps and patterned pants, which were a cross between plus fours and knickerbockers, and he carried it off with style. I used to tune in just to see what he was wearing and I was far from being the only one.

It was the same with Jesper Parnevik, too, in his eccentric way. What is he going to be wearing today? Is he going to have the twenty-four-inch cigar hanging out of his mouth on the eighteenth green as he's about to hole his putt? Is he going to have the peak of his hat flipped up? And John Daly. When he first burst on to the scene, I followed him, too. Most people did, because they like the personalities in golf.

You can name the guys that moved the needle: Arnold Palmer, Nicklaus, Player, Seve, Faldo, Woosie, Payne Stewart, John Daly. Seve didn't dress flamboyantly, but when he went somewhere, everybody followed him. He had it in a different way. He carried it. Tiger carries it in a different way, too.

That's why I liked watching them play golf. They were good at golf, they were exciting to watch and eighty per cent of them dressed in a way that was really cool. Seve looked cool. He just looked smart. His dress was conservative but, as wayward as he was, and as bad as some of the weather conditions were that he played in, his shoes were always clean. He looked like he walked on water. He was immaculate, always. I liked that.

I just wanted to look good on the golf course. I wanted to wear a different outfit every single day. I wanted to wear a different pair of shoes every day. I wanted to get to the stage where I felt really comfortable, where I felt special.

When you go and buy a new suit, a new pair of shoes or a new car, it makes you feel really, really good. But if you go and put on an outfit that you have worn a hundred times, you are lying if you say you don't feel shit. I know you're lying. You don't feel as good as when you put something new on. And it's all about the feel-good factor.

As long as you feel good, it doesn't matter what anybody else thinks. If you feel good, then I believe you are going to be in a better frame of mind to be able to perform well. So I try to work out what I need to do to make myself feel good, how I can treat myself to make myself feel good all the time.

There's a reason some players go to a psychologist: it's because they need the confidence to feel good about themselves so they can go out and perform. People may like wearing comfortable things, but if you had an old pair of comfortable trousers and I gave you a brand new pair of

Above left: Anything you can do . . .
No stabilizers at 20 months.

Above right: Having dinner with my
cousins Gary, Emma and brother Danny.

Right: What a rascal outfit.

Below: My nan with Aimee-Leigh, 2002.

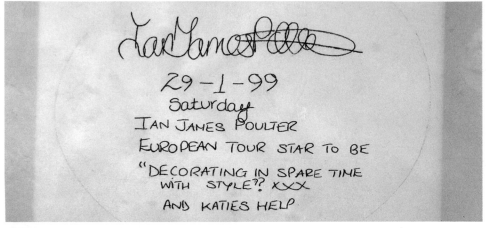

Ian James Poulter

29 – 1 – 99
Saturday
IAN JAMES POULTER
EUROPEAN TOUR STAR TO BE
"DECORATING IN SPARE TIME
WITH STYLE?? XXX
AND KATIES HELP

Above: My inscription behind Katie's mum and dad's wallpaper.

Left: What a heap of rust! £300. My first car. I was 17 years old.

Above: First Ferrari, a 360 Modena.

Right: Mark, Mum, me, Dad, Sue. First Masters 2004.

Do you want to build a snowman, do you want to come and play? At home in England.

Ryder Cup clothes laid out.

Go on, get in . . .

I'm loving this Ryder Cup lark.

Flying at the Ryder Cup, 2004.

Left: My Ryder Cup mascot having a snooze with Daddy on the plane back in 2004.

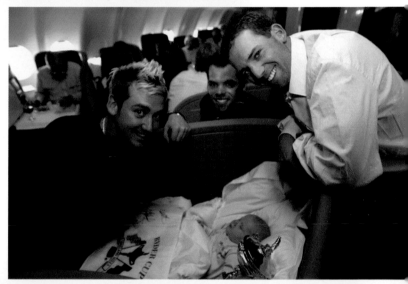

Right: Sergio, did you have to knock the lid off and wake the entire plane?

Below: Aimee dashes over to congratulate Daddy at the Volvo Masters 2004.

Are you sure this isn't a gimme ... Tiger ...

This is how to close out the 2010 Ryder Cup game.

How can you miss my mouth, lads?

How many head starts do you want, boys? Ha ha ha.

There is only one 'Easy Rider'.

Luke says to Aimee, 'It's about bloody time they got married!'

Didn't I get lucky?

Don't we all scrub up nicely . . .

the same trousers, you'd put on the brand new pair. You feel better in something new.

I like the attention clothes bring to me. I understand marketing and branding. The fact that I am good at what I do and I'm identifiable is a good thing for the brands I represent. People can relate to that and people can follow it.

I was very mono when I first started playing on the European Tour in 2000. I had Titleist clubs and was given some shirts from another company which were drab and bland – plain shirts with logo patches. That was one of the reasons I experimented with my hair a bit. I had red streaks put in it at one stage. I spiked it up. I put peroxide in it. I couldn't do anything about my clothes because I was under contract, but no one could tell me what to do with my hair.

The red streaks were just a fad. I suppose they were a nod to Arsenal. I was young. I had a hairdresser who was happy to experiment and so I played around with it. It was nothing new for me. I'd been like that at school. One minute short, one minute a bit longer, centre parting, side parting, longer at the back. I never had a mullet, but that was about the only thing I didn't try.

My mum used to style my hair when I was a kid and put highlights in it now and then. And some of my dad's hairstyles down the years . . . Holy shit. He had a full Afro once; he had a long mullet; he tried pretty much everything. So I suppose experimenting with different haircuts held no terrors for me. They might have held a few terrors for the people who saw them, but not for me.

I switched from Titleist to TaylorMade and Adidas in 2001. There still wasn't much to my outfits because they were all part of the range. But I was getting to the point where I felt like I was a good enough player to be able to express myself with my clothes without getting slaughtered for it.

I began to pester Adidas to make me something more adventurous. The stuff they were giving me was tame; I wanted to be more me. Gradually, I went my own way with the trousers. I was still under contract to Adidas, but they weren't bothered. They didn't have a big trouser collection at that stage, anyway. If I wore more brightly coloured trousers, that got me more attention. That was what mattered to them. I still wore Adidas shirts and the TaylorMade visor, and that was really all they were bothered about. I don't think they were making that much money out of selling trousers. They sold a lot of shirts, a lot of shoes and a lot of equipment.

So I started getting trousers made by a tailor on Savile Row called William Hunt and, sometime around the beginning of 2004, I told him I wanted to wear something cool and patriotic at the Open that summer. He wasn't very enthusiastic about it, but once I convinced him, he got right into it.

The Union Jack trousers were delivered to me at the start of the week of the Open, when I was already up in Scotland. I tried them on in the house that I had rented.

Wow, I thought. These are a little pair of rascals. I wonder if I can pull this off?

Adidas made me a pair of matching shoes with a red, white and blue three-stripe. I had Oakley make a pair of sunglasses which had the Union Jack painted on them. I bought Kangol hats, which I was going to wear back to front, and asked TaylorMade to embroider them.

I planned to wear them for my opening round on Thursday, but, right up until the Wednesday, I was a bit unsure. I gave myself a talking to. I thought, I actually think I can do this. I got all dressed up the night before to check out the outfit in full.

Oof, I thought. I am going to have to play well in this or else I am going to get shot down.

On Thursday morning, I pulled up in the players' car park at Troon, got out of the car and walked towards the archway that leads to the clubhouse. A couple of press photographers started taking pictures. By the time I had walked another hundred yards, there were ten photographers. I made it to the clubhouse. When I came out to head to the driving range, there were twenty photographers. And when I got to the range, they were lined up all down the side.

Oh shit, I thought. What have I done?

That only lasted for a few minutes. I knew it was going to create attention. I knew it was going to be a bit risky. I admit, though, I didn't quite anticipate how much fuss was going to be made. The phone lines lit up at the R&A with people complaining about the trousers. One of the papers rolled some old boy out to say I would never have got through the gates at Troon wearing those trousers if it hadn't been the week of the Open.

People said it was disrespectful to the game of golf. It wasn't disrespectful. It was just a pair of trousers. The next morning, my picture was on the front of almost every national newspaper.

But you know what? I did okay. I shot an even par 71 in my first round. I played fine. And I had fun. I got a few wolf whistles out on the links. There was a lot of laughing and joking, but it was all good-natured. After my round, I told the press that golf needed to be livened up, that it was good for kids to see a player like me wearing something different and that it might make the game attractive to a wider audience.

Of course, there is a kind of pressure that comes with wearing gear like those Union Jack trousers. Some people wouldn't like it, but I think it's a good kind of pressure. It's not like I'm saying, 'Bring it on; I can handle the world.' I'm actually saying, 'I feel comfortable in that and I think I'm going to perform well in it because I feel good.'

It's not taking up any mind space. I am good enough to be able to turn the concentration button on and off. When it's business time, I can turn it on and vice versa. That's a few minutes in a round of golf. Switch it on. Play my shot. Turn it off. Everybody does it. You can't eat your job for twenty-four hours a day. You can't digest it properly. You have got to have a little bit of breathing space in there to get away from it. That's why everybody goes on holiday – to get away from stuff.

Predictably, people said I should be concentrating on my golf, not my clothes. They said I might actually win a Major if I didn't distract myself with all these silly clothes. They said I'd never amount to anything until I focused more on my sport and less on fripperies like Union Jack trousers.

Well, if people are weak enough not to believe in themselves and they translate that weakness into criticism of me, that's their problem. That's a plus for me. Just because I'm confident and I'm able to go out and deliver, that's not my fault. I still get it today. People say I should deliver more, and I agree with them, I should. I have got to continue to work harder to get rid of those little flaws I have in me.

But, Christ, am I not allowed to have fun at the same time? If that means dressing the way I want to dress, I'll do it because it makes me feel good. I'm confident enough to be able to wear whatever takes my fancy. Just because they're not confident enough, just because they're not able to pull that off, it doesn't mean to say I can't.

So don't tell me the Union Jack trousers affected my chances of winning the Open in 2004. Don't tell me they distracted me. Don't tell me they affected my preparation. Because they didn't. I thought about them for five minutes on the eve of the Open while I tried on the outfit and ironed it.

Everyone's comfortable with their own dress sense and that's fine. Just because someone's happy wearing tartans, but you're not, doesn't mean to say it's a bad thing. People don't get it. The people saying I'm causing a distraction for myself by wearing interesting clothes have never stood in my shoes. They have never won a WGC event.

They have never been confident enough to be able to go out and perform at that level. So what they're saying is bollocks.

Because they haven't done it and they don't know anything about it.

CHAPTER 13
Critics

I didn't listen to any of the criticism about my interest in clothes. In fact, I went the other way. I launched my own fashion company. In 2006, I unleashed IJP Design on the world. I employ sixteen people now and our range is made in different factories around the world. And, yes, I am ambitious for the company. Why wouldn't I be?

I want it to succeed. I want it to be a recognisable name in the marketplace. Nike started somewhere, Adidas started somewhere, Fred Perry started somewhere, Lacoste started somewhere. They all started from nothing and grew into something.

I get even more criticism now, because I started my own label. I expected that. If you do anything else apart from golf, if you show any interest in anything apart from hitting a white ball, it is somehow supposed to indicate that you are not truly committed to making yourself the best you can possibly be in your sport.

This frustrates me. A lot. I don't want to be a twenty-four/seven animal that chews golf all day. I can't do it. And yet people throw this stuff at me all the time.

All you're interested in is Twitter.

All you're interested in is fashion.

All you're interested in is selling stuff.

Really? Did people say that about Greg Norman? He was the world's number one golfer and he had his own clothing business and he was an investor in a club-manufacturing business. I don't recall anyone slagging him off. They didn't slag him off because he made an outstanding success of the other things he became involved with.

Then there's the Adam Scott argument. Adam Scott doesn't tweet, so when he goes and wins a Major, everyone says to me, 'There you go – that's what you need to do. He's won a Major because he hasn't got the distraction of Twitter or owning a fashion company.'

Yes, but there's also the small matter of the fact that Adam's unbelievably talented. Adam swings a golf club better than I swing a golf club. From the age of eighteen, or whenever it was that he burst on the scene, Adam was anointed the next Tiger Woods. Everybody fully expected him to go on and win Majors, and now he has.

At eighteen, I was a kid playing in anonymity on a municipal course in Hertfordshire. Nobody – *nobody* – expected me to go out there and win a Major, and I am working my arse off to go and do that. Where I was in the game of golf at the age of twenty-three, did anyone expect me to go on to play in multiple Ryder Cups and spend time in the top ten in the world? No, but I knew I was good enough and I have so much confidence that anything's possible. No one's got a bigger right than me to go and perform on a golf course. That's why I'm doing what I'm doing in the sport today and that's why I can have other business interests if I want to.

I'm passionate about this because people don't get it. People say if I had spent less time doing this or that,

I might have won a Major. Well, there's a wonderful 'if' in there and we'll never know. But I think I have done okay so far and I've got a lot to show for it.

I want to do even better, but I am very happy sitting here in my house in Orlando knowing that I have done – and am doing – everything I possibly can to give myself the best shot of being the best I can be.

I am comfortable with the fact that I have worked hard enough and earned enough money in golf that if I want to go and buy Seve's gold putter and put it on my wall, then I'll do it. I am a massive fan of his and I enjoy surrounding myself with things that make me feel good.

A lot of golfers don't have their trophies on display in their house. That's fine. I do have my trophies on display, to remind me where I have come from and what it is that I have achieved. And by having the stuff around me that I am proud of and which I can talk about when family visits, it makes my family and friends feel good, too.

They come in, they see my trophies, they see the Ryder Cup bags, they see the golf ball that I got a hole-in-one with in Italy and the ball that I got off Monty from the 1993 Ryder Cup. All that stuff is part of my journey, my life, and I'm really proud of it.

When I walk into my cinema room in Orlando, I am proud to have a picture of Muhammad Ali with the 2008 European Ryder Cup team, of which I was a member. I have got a signed glove from Ali, too. I have got one of the special Bank of Scotland five-pound notes with Jack Nicklaus's picture on, which the great man signed for me. These are legends in sport and I enjoy having these things around me.

What gave them the right to be great legends in sport? They worked hard. I believe I am working hard to try to achieve great things, so I want to surround myself with images of them and things they used. I'm not going to start apologising for what I have achieved or hiding the prizes I have won.

That's why I'm happy to show people on Twitter what I've been able to achieve – because I'm proud of it. I hope it will be an inspiration.

I was an assistant in a pro shop when I was nineteen. Everyone knows that. I have worn that one out. But why can't these other kids who follow me on Twitter go ahead and do it, too? Why shouldn't my story, my achievements, my possessions, give them the hope that they can do it?

When I was fourteen, I went to see Nick Faldo open the Jack O'Legs golf course and watched him hitting balls on the driving range. I wanted to do what he did after I saw that because it was unbelievably impressive. I was inspired by that hour that he spent at my golf course.

Faldo pulled up in a lovely car that day. Did everyone have a go at him because he had a nice car? No, because he had worked his arse off to earn the right to spend his money in the way he wanted. And I have earned the right to do it as well. If that inspires some people, that's great.

If people think they can come out of nowhere and play in five Ryder Cups and win fifteen tournaments and be established in the world's top fifty for more than a decade, just like I did, then that has to be a good thing. If they think, 'That could be me one day,' that's what I want.

Hard work pays off. I was not born with a special gene to play golf. I believe anybody can do it. I really do. There is no special reason why I should have done it. I was very sporty from a young age. I loved playing football and athletics at school. It was in me because I was surrounded by sport, because my dad played sport, because my brother wanted to play sport.

I didn't want to sit in the house. It wasn't like we had DVD players. We didn't have luxuries in the house that kept us inside. We wanted to get outside and kick a football around, ride a bike, do something of interest.

Some people accuse me of showing off by posting pictures of my Ferraris, say, on Twitter. I'm not showing off. I'm proud. Why shouldn't I share that? Why shouldn't it be an inspiration for people? If it pisses people off, well, shame on them. They should have a little look in the mirror and understand why it has pissed them off. And the answer is maybe they are not strong-willed enough to better themselves.

Do I flaunt my wealth? No. Just because there's a recession on, should I throw a blanket over everything and not share it with people? No. It's in the public domain how much David Beckham and Wayne Rooney earn, how much Donald Trump is worth. Different people earn different amounts of money and that's what makes the world go round.

Times are hard for a lot of people and I'm not saying that those people don't work hard to earn the money they get. But if me tweeting some pictures of what I'm up to inspires a few people and makes them realise they can do it from nothing and you don't have to be a natural-born genius to do it, then so much the better.

No one's given me anything. No one's given me a Tour card, no one's given me a victory, no one's given me a Ryder Cup win, no one's given me anything I've got today.

Everybody can better themselves. Some people dig themselves out of the 'I'm happy ticking along' mindset and travel to another part of the brain that is going to ask them to be more daring and risky. I didn't go to university and get a master's in business, so how have I got my own business? It's because I have taken a risk and I think I can make it work if I surround myself with the right team of people that are passionate enough and able enough.

I felt it was a big risk when I started the company in 2006. I made a significant level of investment; that was a gamble because I put a lot of things on the line. If people realised what it took to get that off the ground, if people realised what I had risked, they would understand why I want to make sure it works. No one gave me a clothing business on a plate.

It is not as if I am sitting down designing all my own outfits, poring over drawings when I should be practising. I have great people who do that for me. The IJP Design team has an office at Paul Dunkley's building in Leighton Buzzard and the manufacture is placed in different factories around the world that make the various types of garment. That might be Italy for the belts, or material being milled in Scotland and then being sent to Morocco for manufacturing the trousers, or fabric being sent to China to be made into shirts. The business is run from the

UK and it takes up a significant amount of money. It has not been easy.

I haven't taken a penny out of the business and I don't intend to. I wouldn't even say it's successful yet. We are very much in the learning stages and we are still growing within the market to make it work more efficiently. I would like it to grow in a way which will enable me to do a number of other things when my golf game is not as good as it is now.

Whether that's in fashion or in golf or golf-course design, I don't know yet. But there's no reason why this business cannot be a very successful one. It's the route I have chosen. I could have worn another manufacturer's clothes for a certain amount of money per year, but that has limitations. At some stage, when you are not good enough, it runs out. That money dries up. You have earned your money and you have probably spent your money, too.

But if you invest and create a business which can one day multiply by ten, if your business profit is a million bucks – and the multiple on these businesses is generally seven to ten, depending on how the market is and how good the business is – then your million profit is going to earn you ten million sooner or later. Someone's going to give you ten million bucks for your company.

My golf career won't last for ever. God forbid I have an injury or something silly that keeps me out of the game, but I want to do as much as I possibly can as soon as I possibly can to enable me to sustain a level of income for the rest of my life. I have the potential, if it is a successful business, to make more money by taking the risks early. That's how Greg Norman has done it.

Most athletes get paid to wear what they wear and they are happy with that – like Tiger Woods and Nike. Tiger has been paid all his money up front and doesn't have to do anything for it. That's because he's so good.

I'm not going to get paid the money he's been paid. And I'm not prepared to be happy ticking over, being paid a smaller fee and spending that fee. I feel I can make a bigger gain by having my own business, trying to grow a global business, expanding it, seeing where it can take me. The more players that wear it, the more advertising you have.

IJP Design is not at a level yet to start paying lots of people to wear our clothes. We can afford to supply kit to some players because they know it's good quality. It has my name attached to it. It's IJP Design. It doesn't scream out Ian Poulter on the back of a player's collar, though. It's run as a business.

I started IJP Design after I got out of my Adidas contract at the end of 2005 and signed with Cobra and Footjoy. I didn't have any of my own stuff ready immediately, so I wore an Arsenal shirt at the Abu Dhabi Championship towards the end of January 2006. I was asked not to wear it again. I was told football jerseys were not part of golf attire.

There were rumours that spring that I had been warned by Augusta National Golf Club about the standards of dress that were expected of me at the Masters that year. Some people said that the contact had come through a third party, as if there was a great undercover mystery about it. There was no mystery. It was just bollocks. There was no contact. I didn't receive a letter from anybody about anything related to the Masters.

I had some fun that year with my clothes, though. When I played the Johnnie Walker Classic in Perth, Australia, in February, I suggested to the sponsors that I make up outfits in the colours of Johnnie Walker labels – red, black, blue, green and gold. I saw a business opportunity to be able to do something cool with them for the week, and so I did.

I realised quite quickly that we could do something like that with sponsors on a more regular basis. So from then on, it was business, business, business. Why not exploit that? Why not try to find ways to make some extra money? If you have got an idea that works, then crack on. Everybody wants to make more money. I have always thought outside the box to try to make some extra income. It doesn't make me a bad person.

By then, of course, I had followed up my Union Jack trousers at the Open of 2004 with another rather bold design at St Andrews in 2005. This time, I wore a pair of trousers emblazoned with a big print of the Claret Jug, a design that had won a competition run by the BBC called Design Poulter's Pants.

When he saw them, Seve Ballesteros, who was commentating on television, said that that was probably the closest I'd ever get to the Claret Jug. I had that coming, I suppose. I wasn't offended, but Seve was my idol and now he was telling me I would never win the Open. I thought it was a bit unjust. Other people were saying I was all trousers and no golf game. It didn't sting me. It was an inspiration, in a way. I just thought, That's fine; I'll show you different. I haven't quite got it yet, but I have been runner-up and I was close again in 2013. I know I'm capable of it.

It was taking it up a notch, wearing trousers like that at the Home of Golf. It was essentially a photograph of the Claret Jug, so I had to seek permission from the R&A to use the image because it is copyrighted. This time, it was their turn to strike a deal with me. They said they would allow me to wear the trousers on condition that I donated them to the British Golf Museum in St Andrews after the tournament.

So there they hang, a pair of my pants on display at the very heart of the golfing establishment. I always knew the years working on that stall at Stevenage Market were leading somewhere.

CHAPTER 14
Landing on Fractions, Man

Playing in the 2004 Ryder Cup at Oakland Hills signalled a new phase of my life.

A few weeks after I got back from Detroit, I won the biggest tournament of my career so far when I beat Sergio García in a play-off to claim the Volvo Masters at Valderrama. Soon after that, I began to explore the idea of moving to America.

I fulfilled a football ambition of sorts, too. I strode out into the middle of the pitch at Highbury, then the home of Arsenal, and took the applause of a 38,000 capacity crowd. I'd dreamed of being acclaimed by the fans for a spectacular goal or a crunching tackle. It wasn't quite like that, but I wasn't complaining.

I'd been invited by the club to parade the Ryder Cup at half time of the Premier League home-game against Aston Villa on 16 October 2004, and I think I was almost as nervous as I'd been when I was teeing it up at Oakland Hills a few weeks earlier. I couldn't believe I was walking through the Marble Halls, carrying the Ryder Cup and walking into the home dressing-room to show it to heroes of mine like Dennis Bergkamp, Patrick Vieira and Thierry Henry.

I wasn't to know it then, but it was the last game of the

Arsenal Invincibles' forty-nine-match unbeaten run. What a side that was. I got a picture with Bergkamp, Henry, me and the Ryder Cup, which is something I'll always treasure. I was petrified before I went out on to the pitch at half time. You never know what kind of reception you're going to get from football fans, but I got a standing ovation, which made the hairs on the back of my neck stand up on end.

Ten days later, I was teeing off in the Volvo Masters. I had always loved playing Valderrama, with its tight, fiddly fairways, its small greens, difficult winds and the emphasis on distance control. I was full of confidence after my Ryder Cup debut. I was so proud of being a Ryder Cup player and of the prestige it brought and that pride flowed through my game that week in Spain.

I was two strokes off the lead held by Alastair Forsyth going into the final round, but Alastair dropped a couple of shots in the first two holes and it soon became a three-way battle between me, him and Sergio, who was very much the local hero and crowd favourite. Alastair bogeyed the sixteenth to fall back to six under, and I was on seven under, going to the last.

Sergio, who was in the group ahead of us, had missed a seven-foot putt on the eighteenth that would have taken him to eight under. I couldn't get the birdie I needed to win the tournament on the last hole, but I managed a par, which got me into a sudden-death play-off with Sergio. It was the first big play-off I'd ever been in.

We played down the eighteenth and we both missed the fairway. Sergio's ball went into the crowd and a little girl picked it up. Mine went into the trees on the left-hand side. I managed to get my second shot up to the fringes of the green, but Sergio was still struggling. I needed to get up and down to win the tournament and I put my chip to within a couple of feet and holed it.

Aimee and Luke were both there with Katie and, before the trophy presentation, I coaxed Aimee on to the green. She was two by then and she waddled towards me and I lay on my back and lifted her into the air. Her little hands were full of acorns that she had been collecting as she walked around and some of them came spilling out on to the putting surface. She didn't want to let go of the rest, even when we gave her the trophy to hold.

It was a huge win for me. It kept up my record of winning at least one tournament in every year since I joined the European Tour and it gave me big world-ranking points that took me back into the world's top fifty. It gave me a five-year exemption on the European Tour and automatic entry into all four Majors in 2005, plus the World Golf Championship events. It wasn't the same as winning a Major, but it was the closest I had got so far.

Soon after that, I got a phone call from Paul Dunkley. Paul told me that, as a Ryder Cup player, he believed I had an exemption to play on the US PGA Tour in 2005 and was eligible to take up membership. I told him to double check because this was a big deal. He did, and he was right.

I was excited. It was a no-brainer for me. I was playing a few events in the States anyway and this meant I would be able to play some more, so I took up the exemption category and assumed membership of the PGA Tour. The rules changed soon after that, to stop European Ryder Cup players gaining full PGA Tour membership but I was in. Whether it has been through finishing high on the European Order of Merit or winning the Accenture World Matchplay, I have maintained my card for the last eleven years.

I loved the European Tour but there were advantages to playing more in the States. There were more world-ranking points available at tournaments there, the quality of the fields was better and, yes, the prize money was better, too. I understood that, globally, playing more tournaments in the States was going to enable me to be in a different financial position in terms of contracts.

As a European player with global recognition, your sponsorship contracts are going to be worth substantially more if you establish yourself on the PGA Tour. You open yourself up to corporate America, which is obviously going to be much more profitable. I wanted to look at that to better myself, not just financially but by playing against stronger fields. As I contemplated playing more on the PGA Tour, I began to think about buying a house in America, too.

There were a number of attractive things about that. One of them was the prospect of being able to practise all the way through the winter. However good the facilities were at Woburn – and they were first class – there are only so many hours you can stand outside hitting balls in the freezing cold and damp of an English winter.

That's when I started to spend some time in Orlando. I settled on a gated development called Lake Nona that had been built around a golf course just south of the city. I'd stayed there with Justin Rose. It had everything: it was a beautiful development, it was eight minutes from the international airport, it was close to the freeways, it was quiet, it was private and the golf facilities were superb.

In some ways, it didn't feel like real life. All the gardens were beautifully manicured, there were little deer flitting around, the streets were kept meticulously clean and a lot of the residents pottered around the place in golf buggies. It felt like an awful long way from 405 Canterbury Way.

I bought a house on a street called Covent Garden Drive. To begin with, I shared ownership of it with Paul Dunkley while I worked out the details of how long I was going to spend in the States. At that stage, it wasn't really in my mind to move to the States full time. I knew that would have big implications for my family, too.

I did a deal for a house for Justin at the same time because Justin had been spending more time in Florida and was being coached by David Leadbetter. Justin had made the leap to living in Florida full time already. I thought I'd be able to get us a discount by buying two houses at the same time. I got us a great deal.

I could see straight away how much the move might improve my game. I could practise for hours on end in Orlando, all through the winter, because the climate was so lovely. Those first few months of 2005, I really enjoyed being in Orlando and I began to move towards the idea of living in Florida full time rather than just staying temporarily to get some extra practice in.

I knew the tricky bit would be convincing Katie. Katie loved home. We had only recently moved into a barn conversion near Woburn that we had done a lot of work on and which was the big family country home we had always dreamed of. Apart from that, Katie doesn't like to travel because she hates flying.

I tried to work on Katie to spend a bit more time in

Orlando. Practising and playing in the States suited me and I was excited by the challenge of playing more events on the PGA Tour. My family was still in England and my priority was to see them, but travelling back and forth between Orlando and Woburn was really hard work, especially with two young children.

I was spending too much time on an aeroplane, toing and froing between tournaments and not getting any quality time at home. I knew something had to change, so I bought another piece of land on Covent Garden Drive and started to build a new house at Lake Nona. I reasoned that if I could build something nice and make it really homely inside, maybe it would encourage Katie to come out to Orlando more.

At first, I suggested to her that maybe we could spend six months in the States and six months in England. But as soon as she and the kids started having more time in the US, Katie loved it. It was a great lifestyle for the kids. They spent a lot more time outside, messing about in the pool and dashing around in the garden in the sunshine. Also Katie was expecting baby number three. She was due the week of the WGC at Doral, and as I'd missed Luke's birth I didn't want to miss Lilly's.

We have been at Lake Nona ever since, although we live in a house on a different plot now. It has worked really well. It has enabled us to spend more time together as a family and you can't put a price on that. When I play a tournament in the States, I finish some time on Sunday and I am usually at the airport half an hour later. I get home on Sunday evening, in time to put the kids to bed and then see them off to school on Monday morning. I couldn't do that if I had to get the last flight out of an American airport on a Sunday evening and fly home to England. Most of the other guys on the PGA Tour feel the same way. After a tournament, we want to get home. We are in a privileged situation where, most of the time, we can fly privately when we are playing in America, and the main reason for doing that is to maximise your time at home.

I am away for twenty-seven weeks a year, don't forget. I'm away more than I'm at home. I feel like I miss so much, especially at the back end of the year when I am away for a solid month. I come back and my youngest two, Lilly and Joshua, have changed. They might only be small changes, but they bring you up short as a parent sometimes. You think, When did that happen? And, of course, the answer is that it happened while you were playing at a golf tournament on the other side of the world somewhere.

Sure, I see some of it on video when Katie records it for me, but it's not the same as being there and seeing the smile on Joshua's face when I go and lift him up out of his cot. It's worth the money to get home quickly.

You need to get back for your own sanity, sometimes. It's only really when I walk through my front door that I feel like I'm normal. I can be me again. When I'm at a tournament, I'm on duty. I'm at work. There is always somebody who wants something from me. In fact, I kind of assume that if anyone comes up to speak to me at a tournament, they want something from me. Unless it's another player, it's rarely just to chew the fat.

That's difficult because I have a huge problem saying no to things and people. I don't like to do it. But it's bad for my time management. I put my earphones in sometimes when I'm going to the range because I do not want to be distracted and, if someone stops me, I find it hard to ignore them and I end up talking for ten minutes. It's just as it said in my old school reports: easily distracted.

It was around the time of my move to the States that I became friends with a great American icon. I met Dennis Hopper at the Dunhill Links tournament in Scotland in 2004. I didn't know that much about Dennis at the time. I'd heard of *Easy Rider*, of course, but I'm not a great film buff and my dad was more excited than me when I was paired to play with him.

You might think it an unlikely friendship, but Dennis and I really hit it off. Dennis had lived his life to the max, for sure, and people said that, with his lifestyle, it was a miracle he had made it past forty. But by the time I got to know him, he was a softly spoken man, thoughtful and gentle.

I went over to Los Angeles to play the Nissan Open at Riviera Country Club one year and Dennis invited me to stay with him for the week at his house in Venice Beach. I felt a bit nervous about that because I was aware of his reputation as a wild man, but Sonya, the woman who looked after his PR, gave me his address and so, when I arrived, I took a tournament car and drove down there.

I pulled up in his street and I thought I must have been given the wrong address. The street number was 333 and it was hand painted on the outside of this corrugated iron door. The whole street was a little bit dodgy, actually, and I started to have serious doubts I was in the right place. I sat in the car and called Sonya.

'No,' she said, 'if you think you're at the wrong address, you're at the right address.'

So I knocked on the door and went in. The ground floor was the art studio where Dennis had first learned to paint when he was a young man. Then, later in life, he bought the property and converted it into his house. So his studio took up most of the ground floor and Dennis lived upstairs. There was a lot of his artwork hanging in the studio and then, as I walked upstairs, I passed a series of Andy Warhols, one after another. At the end of the line was a portrait that Warhol had done of Dennis.

At one end of one room, there was a bright-pink old-fashioned TV sitting on a stand. I have to confess, I thought it looked awful. Dennis said it was a Banksy. This was 2005. I don't think I had even heard of Banksy then.

I looked more closely at the words on the screen. They said, *In the future, everyone will be anonymous for fifteen minutes.* As horrible as it was, it actually started to grow on me because it was so bizarre. Dennis told me I needed to start buying Banksy pieces as an investment. I didn't take his advice. I wish I had.

I was taken to a kind of wooden outhouse, which looked like it had been there for about eighty years. That was where I was staying. Dennis had another shed which was his den where he chilled out. I went in to see him one day and I could smell the smoke a while before I got to the door. He was chilling out, put it that way.

He was watching television, actually. Dennis Hopper was watching snowboarding in his den. After a little while, he switched over to the golf. I think he discovered golf quite late on in his life. In fact, I think he discovered a lot of things quite late on in his life. I had a great time staying with him in Venice Beach. It was a privilege to become friends with a man who had had such an impact on American culture and I was honoured when he came to my wedding at Woburn a couple of years later.

I would like to say that my embrace of all things American paid immediate dividends in my golf game, but that wouldn't quite be accurate. It took me a little while to adjust to the changes in my schedule and the greater depth of quality of the fields that I was now playing in. I had a couple of decent finishes in the first half of 2005, but I had a run of missed cuts, too, and my year was encapsulated by what happened at the US Open at the Pinehurst No. 2 course in North Carolina in mid-June.

The US Open is difficult enough on a good day. Everyone knows that. The tournament is going to be a tough test, wherever it's played. It's always one of the most testing weeks of the year on one of the toughest golf courses in the States. It's no secret that they really don't like many people being under par. They say they are not aiming for that outcome, but, actually, I think they are.

I had started my first round on the tenth at Pinehurst that year and I had played quite nicely on my front nine. When I got to the eighteenth, which was my ninth hole of the day, I had a three-foot putt for par. I always hit my putts in fairly firm. My putts will always hit the mud or the top of that metal rim and bounce back towards the front of the cup. I never just drop them in. They are always hitting the soil at the back of the cup.

So, on the eighteenth at Pinehurst, I hit this lovely putt into the back of the cup. They were brand new hole-liners and the rims were quite thick and I got the shock of my life when my ball nearly bounced back out. On the next hole, I went through a similar scenario, but this time the ball did bounce out. As you might expect, I threw the teddies out of the pram.

I went bananas. I called the referee and sat on my bag and generally acted like a bit of a knob. This little ball had smiled at me like an imp and gone, 'Reject. Have another go.' I mean, I'd just holed it. I expressed my frustrations to the referee and then expressed them again after my round of golf. I was told to get on with it, basically.

I told reporters after my round that I was trying to choose my words 'very, very, very, very carefully.' It was a big effort, believe me. The organisers said they'd have a look at the holes I'd mentioned, but they just blamed the caddies. They said that, as the caddies were lifting the pin out of the hole, they were lifting the hole-liner out, too. That was nonsense, but I had to get on with it. I made the cut, but the episode didn't do an awful lot for my confidence when I was putting.

It was symptomatic of the struggles I was having as I tried to get used to a new routine and a new life. In 2005, for the first time since joining the European Tour, I failed to win a tournament in a calendar year. I knew the move to America was improving me as a player. It was just taking time to show.

CHAPTER 15
Downtrodden

If something is wrong or something needs addressing, I am always one for offering constructive criticism. In the period after I moved to America, I found myself in a series of run-ins with the golf authorities. I'm not afraid of arguments like that. I'll put my point across and then I'll listen to what others have to say and abide by whatever the powers that be decide.

The fact was that, at Pinehurst, for example, those hole-liners weren't good enough. They were brand new and they were too thick. A couple of the other players made the same point as me, and everything was rectified the following day. It was clear there had been an issue because, the next morning, the liners were lowered further.

Anyway, what had I got to lose by speaking out about an obvious problem? How were Pinehurst going to victimise me? Not give me a good ruling? All I was doing was playing golf. They don't give out invites for US Opens. You have to qualify. I don't think they mind some criticism, as long as it is reasoned, although some may accuse me of being naïve about that.

Look, I probably have been an idiot a number of times and blown my stack when I have overreacted to certain bits and pieces. Some of the people in authority probably wince when I open my mouth and think to themselves, Oh, here he goes again. But for the most part, if I have got something to say, it is intended to be for the benefit of others, not just me.

I had a row with Colin Montgomerie during the Seve Trophy at the Wynyard Golf Club up in the north-east in the autumn of 2005, too, but that was just a matter of me wanting to work on my game on the range, while Monty thought I should have been out supporting the rest of the team on the course.

I admit that what happened at the Nissan Irish Open at Carton House in May 2006 fell into a slightly different category, though. The event was complicated for me by the fact that Arsenal were playing against Barcelona in Paris in the Champions League final on the Wednesday night before the tournament was due to begin.

I was determined not to miss that game. It was the first occasion in my lifetime that Arsenal had made the final and who knows when they will get there again. It hasn't happened since, put it that way. Anyway, I was resolved to make the trip to Paris and I was hoping that the Irish Open organisers might make a few allowances for me. I hoped in vain.

On Wednesday morning I asked the organisers if I could have a late tee-time on Thursday so that I could get a bit of rest after the journey back from Paris. I don't make a habit of asking for favours like that. In fact, I'd never done it before. I just thought that maybe they could take my desire to watch the game into account. It wasn't like I was seeking any sort of advantage.

When the list of tee times was released, I had been given 7.50 a.m. That didn't go down very well. It really pissed me off, actually. I had a word, but the response was not particularly helpful. What did they say? Not a lot. I expressed my opinion. Words were had. I'm not saying I was a marquee player, but I just needed a bit of help from them at the time and they didn't give me any at all.

I'd booked a private plane for the trip to Paris and, after the pro-am had finished, Simon Khan, another Arsenal fan, and I headed for the airport to meet up with my dad and my friend Yvette and her husband. We were in Paris by 5 p.m., in time to get to the Stade de France well before kick-off and soak up some of the atmosphere.

I was full of optimism, but when the Arsenal goalkeeper, Jens Lehmann, was sent off after eighteen minutes, I knew it was going to be an uphill struggle. Sol Campbell put us ahead eight minutes before half time and somehow we hung on and hung on until we were in touching distance of the trophy.

But Barcelona brought Henrik Larsson off the bench after an hour, and he changed the game. Arsenal found it harder and harder to keep Barcelona at bay with ten men and, fourteen minutes from the end, Samuel Eto'o grabbed an equaliser. That was the end for Arsenal. Even if they clung on until full time, it was unrealistic to expect it to stay level until the end of extra time. It never came to that. Five minutes after Eto'o scored, Juliano Belletti got the winner.

It was a massive shame. It would have been a fairy tale to beat Barcelona with ten men and we had come so close. We stayed until the final whistle, of course, and then we began the long journey back to Dublin. We didn't have the adrenaline to keep us going anymore and the thought of that 7.50 a.m. tee-off time started to bear down on me.

There was plane gridlock at the private airport north of Paris that we were flying out of. The planes were stacked up on the tarmac, nose in, nose out. All the corporate hospitality boys were spilling out into their jets and we were well down the list of planes waiting to take off. Then we sat on the tarmac for about an hour before we took off.

I got back to my bed in Ireland about 2.30 a.m., got a couple of hours kip and then headed to the course. I played remarkably well in the circumstances, especially as the weather was so poor that there was a six-hour delay in the middle of my round. I shot 71, which was only two shots off the lead held by Johan Edfors. But the rain started to fall more and more heavily over the weekend and as the weather worsened, so did my mood.

All my frustration with the tee-off time they had given me on the Thursday started to seep out. The weather was beyond horrific and things started to get out of hand when I became involved in an altercation with a marshal on the sixth hole of the final round.

I pulled my tee shot left and saw it bounce twice. When I reached it, my ball was plugged. I'd seen it bounce, so I thought something must have happened to it subsequently. Balls don't bounce and then plug. I asked the marshal if someone had trodden on it. It turned into a very testy exchange.

'No one's trodden on it,' he snapped.

'It's not a problem at all,' I said. 'I just need to know if someone's trodden on it, because it's plugged.'

'No one's been anywhere near it,' he said.

'Well, it bounced twice in the rough, so something must have happened to it,' I told him.

'It didn't bounce at all,' he said.

I wasn't happy. I really thought someone must have trodden on the ball. I'm sure it would have been a mistake, but this guy was being aggressively obstructive. If it had been trodden on I would have been entitled to a drop. I called the referee in. I was explaining the situation to him when my friend, the marshal, stepped in again and piped up about how no one had trodden on the ball.

'Listen, buddy,' I said, 'do me a favour. It's nothing to do with you anymore. I'm talking to the referee.'

I told the referee that you could see the ball had been embedded. Then the marshal butted in again. I was so exasperated by this stage that I told him to fuck off. What I didn't realise was that a camera crew had come up behind me and was about three feet away as I told him to Foxtrot Oscar. So I was turning the air blue, live on TV.

There was a great big footprint next to my ball, but they still didn't rule in my favour so I had to take a penalty drop. I made a load on that hole and that was the start of my fortunes heading seriously downhill. I had been only one shot off the lead after the second round, but I fell apart on the Sunday after the incident with the marshal and shot 85. It was my worst ever day on a golf course. It was my 'I've had enough, get me out of here' moment.

I was fined €5,000 for the incident with the marshal. Or, more accurately, I fined myself €5,000. I realised that, despite all the provocation, I'd behaved inappropriately. I also realised that some sort of sanction was going to be visited on me, so I suggested to the Tour's chief executive, George O'Grady, that we set the fine at that figure. At the time, it was the biggest amount anyone had ever been penalised.

The controversies aside, I was starting to play some decent golf in 2006. I had some good finishes in America, in particular. I came seventh in the Zurich Classic in New Orleans, tied for ninth at the Barclays in New Jersey and finished just outside the top ten at the US Open at Winged Foot in upstate New York.

But there were times when I struggled, too. I missed the cut at the Open at Hoylake. Everyone had a simple explanation for that: it was because I was wearing the Claret Jug on my trousers again. This time, I had gone for a red pair of trousers with a sequin version of the Jug. Seve Ballesteros, who was one of my playing partners, said I looked like a matador.

I was playing more PGA Tour events by then and starting to find my feet, adjusting to playing both tours. I didn't want to move away from Europe, but I wanted to play more tournaments in the US. I wanted to play both, basically. I knew that wouldn't be too popular with the European Tour, but I wasn't the only one and most of the guys who do what I do stay fairly well committed to Europe because it has always been their home tour.

Europe has forty events a year. I play the Majors and WGCs, which now adds up to eight. And I play five other events. All in all, I play maybe fourteen or fifteen events on the European Tour. Eight of them double count on both orders of merits. Three of the Majors are in America and three of the WGCs are in America, but there are a lot of smaller events in Europe that I have played down the years.

There are advantages to the PGA Tour. Each event in America is very similar in terms of prize fund. It only fluctuates a tiny bit between the smallest event and the largest. But in Europe, you can go from eight million dollars in prize money to one million dollars. That's one of the reasons why guys have moved over to the States.

As 2006 wore on, it became apparent I was going to struggle to make it as an automatic pick for the European team for the 2006 Ryder Cup at the K Club. My world ranking was in the fifties and falling and, at the last qualifying event, the BMW International Open in Munich, I missed the cut by three shots. My back-nine charge there to make the team two years earlier was a distant memory.

I didn't hold out much hope of a captain's pick, either. Ian Woosnam was the skipper and he had several outstanding candidates to choose from, notably Darren Clarke and Lee Westwood. Darren had had a traumatic time in the run-up to the competition when he lost his wife, Heather, to cancer. Picking him was an emotional decision, but it was also the right decision.

Woosnam went for Lee as his other pick and I had no quarrel with that, either. Westwood is a great player and he had a good record at the K Club. Thomas Bjørn felt he should have been chosen instead of Westwood and launched a furious tirade at Woosnam, calling him 'pathetic'. I just tried to get on with my golf.

It was really painful to miss out. After playing in 2004, after experiencing the intense emotion of the event and all the highs it brought, I had hoped I would never miss one for the rest of my career. That is how infectious they are. Like I said, they mean everything. I got a call from Woosnam to say I hadn't made it, which showed that I must at least have been close. I didn't have any complaints.

I dealt with it the way I deal with all setbacks. I shut the disappointment away and I try not to dwell on it too long. I block it. I try to blank it out of my memory. The golf journalist Lawrence Donegan, who is a journalist I admire, once wrote that I was unique in my ability to hide what I really think. That was a clever observation.

I don't share a lot with people, if that's what he was trying to get at. I don't open up to many people at all. The inner circle I have is very, very small. I can count my mates on a number of fingers, but out of all of them, the amount of people I would really open up to would be less than one handful.

It's different to chatting with your pals on the tour. I might talk about my game loosely with them. Sometimes you give advice and sometimes you take it. Steve Stricker gave Tiger Woods some putting tips a couple of years back. I spent time practising in a bunker with Rosie at the World Cup once and I noticed he wasn't playing his bunker shots like he used to. We were in there for an hour together, trying out different things. But those kinds of conversations with fellow players don't go far down the line. It's not going to go more than a few players deep.

I did watch a bit of the competition at the K Club, but when you are that disappointed about missing something, you are not going to sit down and pore over it from dawn until dusk.

I kept an eye on the scores and, of course, I was pleased that Europe gained the upper hand and eased towards a fantastic victory. It was such a memorable win and such a momentous, emotional occasion for Darren, who played superbly throughout and then finally broke down at the end of his singles match, that it was impossible not to get caught up in it in the end.

In 2002, I had fallen apart when I missed out on selection for the Ryder Cup. This time, I reacted differently. A week before the Ryder Cup began, I played some of the best tournament golf I've ever played at the Banco Madrid Valle Romano Open in Spain, and won the tournament by five shots.

I wanted to show people what I could do. I wanted to prove a point, I suppose. I didn't even drop a shot until the sixty-seventh hole. I was livid about that bogey, but I pulled a tee shot on the par three, chipped on and missed the putt. It would have been a dream to play a clean tournament without making a single bogey. It was galling to have got so close.

Still, it was great to get another tournament win under my belt after a fallow year in 2005. I kept my form going, too. I won in Madrid, waited for the Ryder Cup to be played out and then went and played well at the WGC American Express Championship at the Grove in Hertfordshire. I shot 64 in the first round, which still wasn't good enough to take the lead. That was because Tiger Woods shot 63. I finished second in the tournament. Tiger won it by eight shots. Just as much as ever, he was the man to aim for.

CHAPTER 16
Mooching

This will disappoint some people, but I do not believe there is any needle between me and Tiger Woods in any way, shape or form. Golf.com named me in a list of 'Tiger Woods' enemies' a couple of years ago. Well, I'm sorry, but I just don't see it. I certainly don't consider him an enemy.

I created some of the media chatter myself, inadvertently, when I gave the 'Just Tiger and Me' interview to *Golf World* magazine at the start of 2008. That gave people material for a thousand jokes and provided them with a licence to speculate, too.

Tiger's former coach, Hank Haney, did the rest when he wrote a kind of kiss-and-tell book called *The Big Miss* about his time with Woods. He revealed, in the midst of it, his rather excitable and melodramatic version of an innocuous episode that occurred when my path crossed with Tiger's at Oakmont in the spring of 2007.

I'm not saying I'm mates with Tiger. I don't have his telephone number, nor do I spend time with him socially. Nor does he have my telephone number. But I do have the utmost respect for him. What he has been able to do in the game of golf is simply unbelievable. He has meant a lot for golf, and a lot of golfers that were coming up at the time used him as a role model.

I was in the pro shop at Leighton Buzzard when he became the youngest player ever to win the Masters in 1997. Tiger is eleven days older than me and here he was winning his first Major at the age of twenty-one, blowing the rest of the field away, smashing records left, right and centre. And I was working in a pro shop, selling Mars Bars and giving one-pound group-lessons to kids.

My perception of him has not really changed from that day. What he has achieved in golf inspires awe. It should provoke admiration, too. I am competing against him week in, week out and I have massive respect for him. That is really all that matters.

I don't want to go and have a drink with the guy because we have got nothing to talk about.

'Let's talk about our Major victories. Oh, you've got fourteen and I haven't got any.'

That's the end of that conversation, then.

Tiger is not the type of guy who is going to share any of the wonderful secrets of those fourteen Majors with me, because I am a competitor. So there is not a lot to talk about. That is not a bad thing. I don't know the real Tiger Woods. I know the golfer Tiger Woods, but I don't know Tiger Woods the non-golfer. I don't think many people do.

He was taught by his dad at an early age to be very disciplined on the golf course with his practice routines. He was taught to be selfish and ruthless, and that turned him into the golfer he is today. I think his dad was fairly tough on him, but tough in a good way. Earl Woods was a

Vietnam veteran and he was military in the way he went about his son's mental training, his practice. He tried to distract him. He made noises on his downswing, stuff like that. He was thorough.

I know all about the legend of Woods. If you want to get better, you study people who are better than you. You find out about them. I studied Tiger. I know his mental training started very early. He was a loner as a kid. He was able to challenge himself every time he was out there practising. It stood him in good stead for later in his life. It shows in all of his performances. That is why he has been able to test himself against the best and become comfortably the best in our sport.

It is said he had a chaotic private life. I don't know about that. It's none of my business. What I do know is that he has delivered on a level no one else will get close to. He does the same things. His swing has changed, but when you see those moments of brilliance, it is the same fist-pump, the same emotion. It's exactly the same.

All I know is that Tiger Woods the golfer is someone that everyone respects because of what he has done in the sport and the kind of domination he has achieved. It's the same as people idolising Michael Jordan. Tiger is phenomenal. He is one of the greatest sportsmen there has ever been. He is up there with Muhammad Ali and all the greats. I don't think many people would argue with that.

When Haney published *The Big Miss* in 2012, he was benefiting from his relationship with Tiger. I only featured briefly, but the tone of what Haney wrote about me fed the fiction that there is some deep antipathy between Tiger and me.

Haney said that, a couple of weeks before the US Open at Oakmont, in Pennsylvania, in June 2007, I had bumped into Tiger during a practice round at the course, asked for a lift back to Orlando on his private plane and then effectively turned up uninvited at the Fixed Base Operations part of the airfield where the private flights fly from.

Among other things, Haney wrote that, while he was sitting talking to me on the plane journey to Florida, he had received a text from Woods, who was sitting a few seats away, that read: *Can you believe how this dick mooched a ride on my plane?*

It is true that I was playing a practice round at Oakmont and so was Tiger. I had flown in privately, but I had booked a Southwest Airlines flight back to Orlando from Pittsburgh about 9 p.m. that evening. I had picked up the tab for my flight to Oakmont, but I knew that it would be quite a big financial hit to fly back privately, too, so I'd decided to take a scheduled flight instead.

Tiger and I were on completely separate rounds. We crossed over and I saw him on the ninth green. He lived in Isleworth, near Orlando, at the time. I asked him if he was flying back that evening and he said he was.

'Look,' I said, 'I'm on a Southwest Airlines flight at 9 p.m. but it looks like we're going to be finished way earlier than that. Have you got any room on your plane? Because I'd love to hop on, if you'd let me?'

'Yeah,' he said. 'No problem. We're taking off at 6 p.m. I'll see you at the FBO at 5.30 p.m.'

'Perfect,' I said. 'See you there.'

To get on a private aircraft, you have to be on the flight manifest. I can't physically put myself on someone's aircraft without their express permission. I have to be signed up for it. The only way that could have happened was for Tiger to call his agent or one of his assistants and say, 'Can you put Ian on the manifest?'

So I didn't exactly just waltz into the terminal, arrive at the steps of Tiger's aircraft and say, 'How about a lift?' It would actually be illegal, for a start. You are not allowed to board an aircraft if you are not on the manifest. It is against FAA regulations. I can't just invite myself.

Okay, I asked him for a lift, the same as if you were getting a ride in someone's car.

'Is there any chance of a lift back?'

'Yeah, no problem.'

It was fairly straightforward.

So I pitched up at the FBO, Tiger's plane was there and I got on board. Tiger was sitting at the front of the plane and Hank was with him. I sat at the back because I wanted to be respectful that Tiger was with Hank and he was giving me a lift. I knew that was really, really kind of him and I didn't want to disturb their conversation in any way.

I was doing my thing and they were up at the front talking and doing theirs. Whether Tiger sent a message to Hank saying, 'Look at this person mooching a lift', I have got no idea. Maybe he didn't really want to give me a lift – I don't know. But Haney never came to sit at the back of the plane to talk to me. I never exchanged a word with him.

It wasn't a particularly long flight. A couple of hours. It passed pretty quickly and uneventfully. When we landed in Orlando, I thanked Tiger for the lift and got off the plane. That was it.

I didn't react to the story when *The Big Miss* was published. I felt awkward about it, but there was no point countering it. It was disappointing to read. It's a shame that Haney felt the need to write the book in the first place. If you have a relationship with someone like the one he had with Tiger, I think it is wrong to divulge private conversations.

What Haney did felt like a kind of betrayal and it's a shame that people feel the need to cross those boundaries. People do funny things when there's money involved, I guess.

To me, the whole story about the plane was a big, fat nothing. As golfers, we travel a lot and certain people have their own planes. I've asked Ernie Els for a lift several times. I choose my moments. If he's travelling with his family, I wouldn't think about intruding. If I know he's on his own and he's going in my direction, I might ask him the question.

I don't think that's disrespectful. If someone has fifteen spare seats and you know them a bit and you're going in the same direction, what's the issue? There isn't one. Sometimes Ernie's said yes, sometimes he's said no. Tiger could have said no. If he had business to do, if he didn't want me on the plane, he would have said as much. I don't think he's the kind of guy who gets bounced into stuff he doesn't want to do.

I didn't speak to Tiger about it when Haney's book was published. I didn't see the need. He knows the truth, so why do I need to say anything to him? And I don't really care whether he wrote the text to Haney or not. That's up to him. Whether Tiger has respect for me or not, I don't know, either. I know I have respect for him.

I don't know if it matters to me whether Tiger respects me or not. It wouldn't particularly affect me if he said yes or no. I think there might be some level of respect there. Every professional has a degree of respect for their counterparts. I have a respect for everyone I compete against.

Whether Tiger respects the events I have won or not, whether he knows what I have been able to achieve from where I came from . . . again, I don't know. I am pretty proud of what I have been able to achieve. Whether anybody else respects that is out of my control. As long as I feel I have done my bit and played my part and given it one hundred per cent, that's all I'm in control of. Controlling someone else's thoughts is not something I'm going to dwell on. But I think Tiger respects his peers, yes.

Tiger Woods is still such a big figure in the sport that the narrative of golf for the next few years will be dominated by his attempt to match and go beyond Jack Nicklaus's record of eighteen wins in Major championships. When Tiger was out of the game for five months at the end of 2009 and the beginning of 2010, people began to think that record had fallen out of reach.

He has not won a Major since the 2008 US Open, so will he get to eighteen? Well, until the spring of 2014, I would have said he was going to get damn close. I still think it's possible he'll do it, but the odds got longer when he had back surgery before the 2014 Masters and was forced to miss the tournament for the first time in his career.

He still wasn't right by the time he played the Open at Hoylake, and it showed – particularly in his final round.

He has time, but it gets more and more difficult the older you get and the more injuries you pick up. But Ernie Els won the Open at forty-three. Nicklaus won the Masters when he was forty-six. Tiger is only thirty-eight. And Tiger's mentally strong and he's great down the stretch. If he can steer clear of any more injuries, he could have twenty chances in the next five years and he only needs to take a quarter of them to get past the record. For someone like him, even with his recent problems, that's within reach.

He will get to fifteen and sixteen. He's probably going to get to seventeen. Then the pressure will really kick in – big, big pressure to get eighteen and nineteen. He will be so, so close, but he will be a lot older and he will be feeling the heat. He'll be in his early forties and moving into the mid-forties with the young guns snapping at his heels. The ones that are already showing face now will be the ones ticking the boxes.

But Tiger is still capable of embarrassing a field in a round of golf. He still shows signs of absolute brilliance. Think about the year that Henrik Stenson had in 2013, for instance, and Tiger still won the PGA Tour Player of the Year Award. He won five of the sixteen tournaments he played on the tour and finished in the top ten in three others.

He didn't win a Major, but his game is right there. He is someone who has totally dominated our game in the past. At one point, the gap between him and Phil Mickelson, who was second in the world rankings, was as wide as the gap between Mickelson and the player ranked 1,200. When you have achieved that kind of dominance, you know it is only a matter of time until you start winning Majors again.

He is still the player that the other players aspire to be. He is the player we all want to join at the top of the tree. And that, of course, is how I came to get myself in trouble when I gave my interview to *Golf World* magazine.

CHAPTER 17
Just Me and Tiger

I look at the world rankings every week. Every single week. Most of the time, it's the same people up there: Tiger, Mickelson, Adam Scott, Henrik Stenson, Rory. When I'm studying the list, I think about what it would be like to have my name up there next to Tiger's. I still do it. I visualise it. I think about what I've got to do to get there.

When I gave an interview to *Golf World* magazine sometime around the end of 2007, that was one of the things I talked about. There was plenty of other stuff, too. It was a long interview and we covered a lot of ground. I tried to be open. I always try to be open. I don't see the point in fending a journalist off with clichés and platitudes. That's never been my style.

It was a lively interview and I did a lively photo shoot to go with it, for the cover. I posed naked with only a pink-and-black Cobra golf bag to spare my blushes. The headline was: 'Poulter Laid Bare – Why There's a Lot More to Me Than Fancy Pants'. Some themes never change, I guess.

I thought that the cover might cause a bit of a stir. But I was wrong. No one really seemed to notice the cover that much – they were all concentrating on something I'd said. Extracts from the interview were released while I was in

Dubai at the end of January 2008, preparing for the Dubai Desert Classic. I finished a practice round, came off the course and found a lot of excited journalists waiting for me.

Everybody had latched on to part of an answer I had given in response to a question about my self-belief and how much potential I believed I had to improve. At that time, Tiger was way, way out in front in the world rankings and was dominating the sport completely, both on the course and commercially. He sells tickets. He moves the needle. There are not many people in sport who can move the needle like Tiger can.

But I am ambitious and I am confident. I have come from a long way back and I have prospered despite an unconventional start in the sport. I have overcome a lot of obstacles and got further than anyone ever thought I would. I aim high now and I was aiming high then, when I sat down and started chatting with the guy from the magazine about the world rankings, me and Tiger.

'The trouble is,' I told the interviewer from *Golf World*, 'I don't rate anyone else. Don't get me wrong, I respect everyone who is a professional, but the problem is I know I haven't played to my full potential yet. And when that happens, it will just be me and Tiger.'

It didn't look great. I accept that. It was part of a longer answer, the gist of which I have just mentioned. So I felt it had been taken out of context a bit, or at least not properly explained. Pretty soon, it felt like the whole thing was running out of control. I was accused of being arrogant, disrespectful to my fellow golfers and delusional about my own abilities.

Apart from that, the interview was a great success.

I tried to explain. I would have been the first to admit if I had meant it in an arrogant way. I haven't got anything to hide. I am open with everybody. What I meant was that my dream was to get to number one in the world, and if you can't get to number one, you want to be number two. So that was my dream of how the world rankings would read. Just me and Tiger.

As I was explaining that to the *Golf World* interviewer, I was visualising the world rankings in that way. And my point was that, when I reach my potential, it's going to be Tiger and me, and I'm visualising the world rankings as I'm saying it. Things can read differently when they have to be summarised, and I guess I didn't explain it properly. I didn't spend enough time explaining what I was trying to say.

I agonised over what I should have said. I meant that if I clicked on to the computer and looked at the world rankings, it would read Tiger, then me. Everything I do in my mind is a visual. I was envisaging reading the world rankings. I was trying to say that, if I couldn't get to world number one, then I could get to two. No one thought they could take the top spot from Tiger at that point. He could have taken two years off and still come back as number one.

What I'd said in the interview became a big issue because it involved Tiger. Tiger sells newspapers. Tiger makes news. Everybody latched on to it. Everybody had fun with it. Even Tiger. Later that week, he was asked about the gap between him and the world's second best player, Phil Mickelson.

'I thought Poulter was number two,' he said.

Which was funny. Some of the other guys took to calling me Number Two for a while. There was talk of playing a big joke where they all walked off the practice range in unison and left me alone with Tiger, just the two of us hitting balls. Fortunately, they never went through with that particular jape.

Not too much gets to me but, I have to confess, I hated the fuss about the Tiger interview. I felt it was causing me a real problem. It was the first time I felt I had been really stung by a media interview. I didn't mean it in the way that it came across. I guess that was naivety on my part, but still, it hurt. It made me really, really sore.

I was mortified and I was really angry. I thought, Stuff all these people; I'm not going to talk to them anymore; I'm going to let them have what they want to hear and not what I really think. I am confident in my own ability, but I felt I had been misrepresented. I had been made to look like an idiot.

I got the piss taken out of me by the other players. For a long time. I got ripped about it in the papers day after day and week after week. The comment kept coming up. I couldn't get rid of it. It definitely affected me on the golf course for a while. I was getting angry. You get a lot of time to think about things on the course.

I knew I would have to speak to journalists at the end of my round and they were probably going to ask me a question about 'just me and Tiger'. And this was for weeks and months after the interview appeared. It was tough. I didn't play well for a little while. I don't know if I was embarrassed. I was pissed off, certainly.

I was a good enough player that what I had said couldn't be viewed as disrespectful to too many golfers. I wasn't ranked a hundred and something in the world. Having the other boys taking the piss wasn't nice because I felt it was unjust. What I'd said didn't warrant six months or a year of continual repetition of that one quote.

Every time I did something well, it was all about 'here's Tiger and Ian'. Every time I did something badly, it was turned into a joke about how I thought I was Tiger's equal. I couldn't get rid of it. I couldn't get out of the way of it. All the commentators kept mentioning it. It was driving me nuts.

The other lads would be saying stuff like, 'I suppose we're all shit now,' and then fall about laughing. They had every right to take the piss. We take the piss out of each other all the time. Every time there's a little chink in the armour, they're going to have a go. I would have done the same if the roles had been reversed.

I dish it out now and again, so I had to take it. Over and over and over again. I would have been kidding myself if I'd told myself it wasn't going to get me down, because the other boys were relentless with it. They got every ounce of value that they could out of it.

It was the usual suspects who were tearing into me: Westwood, Clarke, Rosie. All the guys you would expect, the ones who knew they could do it because they were my mates. In the end, it kind of normalised the whole thing and eventually I started to laugh about it, too.

That happens on the tour when you've got mates together. You try and make fun of adversity. When I failed to qualify for the Masters in 2006, they sent me a 'Missing

You' card in the post from Augusta. 'Missing you very much,' the wording said inside. 'Wish you were here.' Same guys: Westwood, Clarke, Rosie. They actually got Tiger to sign it as well.

I should have kept that card, but I ripped it up and threw it in the bin. Not long after that, one of them failed to make it to the Masters (not Tiger, obviously) and I thought, Right, you bastards, it's your turn now. I had grand plans for a card of my own, but I never got round to sending it.

Ultimately, I suppose, the 'just me and Tiger' interview was a lesson learned. Be a bit more careful. Don't leave room for misinterpretation. Be alive to the fact that anything with Tiger's name in it has the potential to make big news. Be a bit more cute.

But I didn't change dramatically. I didn't want to. My relationship with the press has always been good. I can say what I want. I can have a jab at them and they can have a jab at me. So if my guard's down, I'm going to get one back. I think journalists prefer that to a closed shop, anyway. You don't want someone saying, 'It is what it is,' and stonewalling you all the time. You don't want some human PR machine. You want the guy to give you an honest answer.

There are no hard feelings on my part now. You have to have media coverage. If you're not getting media space, something is wrong. If you are being asked questions, it's for a reason. You are obviously doing something well or you have done something wrong. If nobody comes to ask you a question, you need to have a look in the mirror and see why and find out the reasons. I would rather keep being honest and giving people my opinion. Whether they like it or not is up to them.

CHAPTER 18

Rough with the Smooth

Despite the fuss about the *Golf World* interview, which was still an issue going into the Masters, I played well at Augusta in 2008. It was Ryder Cup year, Nick Faldo, one of my golfing heroes, was the captain of the European team, and I was desperate to get myself into a position where I didn't miss out again, like I had at the K Club.

I shot 70 in the first round at the Masters, my lowest score to date, and I got the first hole-in-one at the tournament for three years. I hit a lovely eight-iron into the sixteenth green and it rolled back down the slope and into the cup. I shot 69 in the second round and was in a tie for third going into the weekend, three shots behind the eventual winner, Trevor Immelman.

I fell away a bit over Saturday and Sunday and finished in a tie for twenty-fifth, but I was encouraged by my performance overall. I had some uneven results over the rest of the spring, but I went into the US Open at Torrey Pines outside San Diego that June with some optimism. It turned out the optimism was misplaced.

The rough that week was absolutely brutal. It was one of the toughest set-ups I have ever seen and it wasn't helped by the fact that I struggled with my game. I shot 78 in the first round, so I knew I was going to be in a battle to make the cut on the Friday. It is a battle, too. It beats you up. Every single tee-shot is like taking a jab in the face. By the time you get to the seventy-second hole, it has worn you out.

In the second round, I had a nightmare on the twelfth hole. I was level-par up to that point, but I pushed my tee-shot right and it found the rough. I took a wedge, but only managed to get the ball out a few feet. I felt incredibly frustrated. I had been carrying a slight wrist injury and I could feel that I was aggravating it by trying to chop my way around the course.

At the US Open, we play on the toughest golf courses and they set it up so that it's very difficult. At the bottom of the order, you have got guys who are twenty-five over par. It gets ugly. There is no other word for it. You have got some of the best players in the world shooting fifteen or sixteen over par. It's not enjoyable for anybody to play in that, nor is it enjoyable for some of the spectators. Some people like it, some people don't. It's just the way it is and it is something you have to deal with because it's not going to change.

I like it tough, but you have to start with the mindset that par for the week might be 75 a day. If you start with the mindset that it's a twenty-over week, then you'll have a good week. If you start with the mindset that you're going to shoot four under, then it's going to be a long week. What are your expectations? You have to manage your expectations because it is easy to be pushed over the edge too early. I have done it several times.

Things got worse for me on the twelfth. My next shot landed short of the green. My pitch wasn't great and I three-putted. That meant a triple bogey. Then I double-bogeyed the fourteenth. By the fifteenth, I was really struggling with my wrist and with the course. I missed a six-foot par-putt and then tried to backhand the tap-in and missed again from six inches.

I was now in a lot of pain from my wrist and I wasn't going to put myself in a position to play the remaining three holes and risk injuring myself any more than I needed to. I was fourteen-over-par for the tournament by then. I had to get off the golf course. If I hit it in the rough again and damaged my wrist further, it could have taken me out for the rest of the season.

You can't play with that kind of injury. It's dangerous. You have got to be careful. You push it a bit too much and you are done for a month or six weeks and it takes you out of the Ryder Cup and all sorts of stuff. It was particularly brutal that week at Torrey Pines and, on the fifteenth green, I turned to my playing partners, Luke Donald and Paul Casey, wished them luck and walked back to the clubhouse. Luke would also be forced to retire later in the weekend.

I knew I'd get some criticism for that and, up to a point, I understood where people were coming from. It's not over until it's over: that's the mantra I've always abided by and I hated walking off early. But if you're in a position where you might injure yourself badly, you need to get yourself out of there.

I need to keep myself fit. All golfers do. It's our livelihood. I can't afford to be injured. So I need to play well or else I am out of pocket. I don't see a footballer having to pay his expenses each week. Golfers have to cover all those costs. Some footballers might not even be playing; they might be sitting on a bench. They still get paid if they're injured. We don't.

Pulling out of the US Open prompted a few people to jump back on the bandwagon of suggesting that I would benefit from seeing a sports psychologist. It crops up every now and again, that one. I know a lot of sportsmen do it. I've read about Sir Chris Hoy, Victoria Pendleton, Craig Bellamy and how they've all benefited from seeing the psychologist Steve Peters, who accompanied the England football team to the World Cup in Brazil.

Well, I'm sorry, but it's not for me. People say I'll regret not going to consult someone. But I'll never regret it if I don't do it. I'm stubborn like that.

My thought process is different to some other people. I don't really have a sports psychologist, but I would say that Paul Dunkley often fulfils that role for me. I speak to him about everything. In 2007, at the Belfry, for instance, I was tired and I was struggling mentally. I played a pro-am on the Wednesday and shot a big number. I was hitting it all over the place. I was really pissed off. I didn't want to play golf. I just wanted to be at home. I don't know why, but I wasn't feeling it.

I called Paul and told him I was going home and was going to withdraw. We chatted for two hours on the phone. Paul talked to me in the same way a psychologist would, trying to dissect why I wasn't ready or prepared, why I was feeling so down. I rationalised everything by talking to him and, by the time I got off the telephone, I felt fine.

So, on the Wednesday night, I had my head up my arse and didn't want to play golf, and then, in the first round, I went out and shot 67. I finished second that week to

Lee Westwood. It confirmed that Paul Dunkley is the person for me to speak to. He has known me from day one, from me working in the shop. He has got the knack of rationalising things and explaining them in a way that helps me.

He helps me throw everything out of my brain that is bothering me. It might happen twice a year that I am pissed off and then I pitch up saying things on Twitter that I probably shouldn't. Paul and I have a discussion and put everything back in the boxes where they need to be, have a mental spring clean and off we go again.

I have never felt the need, as complex as my brain is (and I would say that it is fairly complex), to divulge everything that is going on in there to somebody. I haven't got the time. It is not a two-second fix. It takes hours to fix. And Paul and I go through those hours of fixing it every now and then.

I see it as a sign of weakness, having to open up and spill your beans and show all your cards. So I like to keep that circle of people I talk to very, very small. Paul is successful enough that I respect everything he has done and everything he says. We have known each other for nineteen years, which is a hell of a long time.

I guess I was just lucky that my path crossed with Paul's when it did.

As the years went by, and I started winning tournaments, I began to receive enquiries from many management firms and agencies. I never fancied any of them. Although it wasn't Paul's primary source of business, he managed me throughout that entire time. Every now and again, we would work with an agency on a deal or appearance, but

I never felt the need to make a formal arrangement with an agency. Paul looked after my business.

Around the end of 2008, Katie and I decided that it would be better for my career, and our family life, to relocate full-time to the US. I was playing more in the States, which meant seeing my family less and less. It was just too hard, and I missed my wife and kids too much. Moving to Florida seemed like a great step for many reasons. This of course meant that Paul and I would be in different time zones and a long way away from each other. We thought it may make sense to have a US-based agent join the team. We just had no idea who that person would be. As luck would have it, that's when R.J. Nemer at ICON Sports appeared in the picture. I first accidentally met R.J. in the clubhouse during the US Open at Torrey Pines in 2008, and we struck up a conversation. We hit it off very quickly, and I think our first chat actually dealt more with fashion than golf. I phoned up Paul and asked him to meet up with R.J. They got on equally well. In fact, he and Paul are now business partners, and having the two of them in my corner is absolutely perfect. Over the past seven years now, R.J. has become invaluable to me. R.J. is a lawyer by trade, and he impressed me straight away. He understood me and what I wanted to build. He also has a background in fashion and marketing which fits my interests very well. We are close mates, and our families have gone on holiday together too. One year in the Bahamas, we sat by the pool and did a few deals over burgers while our kids swam together. It was a fantastic work day for us!

Since I joined up with R.J., he has made the whole team

around me even stronger. R.J. negotiates and deals with all my sponsors, endorsements, media requests, including this book deal. He also sorts out all my taxes and banking and anything else that comes up in my off-course life. As many people know, I have a love of Ferarris, and my collection has grown nicely. They are not only pieces of art to me, they are real investments. I feel safe having my money in collectible cars, and I like being able to see my investments everyday. It took a long while to convince R.J. that cars were the right way for me to invest. Like most people, R.J. views cars as something that quickly lose value. I finally got R.J. educated on cars now, and he oversees that collection too. R.J. would probably tell you that he is the head of Ian Poulter, Inc., and that's a very good description. Recently, we began hosting a radio show together on Sirius XM in the States, and the listeners seem to enjoy hearing us discuss and banter over bits and pieces.

Most of the top golfers have people with them during tournaments or other business events. For example, if you've got a corporate function you've got to go to, it helps to have someone with you who can keep you to a schedule and make sure that, if you're supposed to be there for an hour, you're out after an hour. You need someone who says, 'We need to move on now.'

Paul Dunkley's son, James, worked for ICON for about a year, and travelled with me during that time and he was brilliant, as well as being a good mate. ICON Sports have got quite a few people who work for them, and I usually have one of their guys, Chad Poling, with me all the time now. Chad played college golf, and really understands the game. He helps to analyse my stats, and puts together most of my practice routine.

So I didn't feel the need to run to a sports psychologist after what happened at Torrey Pines. I regrouped, and a month later I pitched up at the Open at Royal Birkdale. I played some steady golf in the first two rounds and, even though I started the final round six shots behind the leader, Greg Norman, I thought I had a real chance.

Norman has always been one of my idols, but he fell back on Sunday and I started to motor. I was running higher and higher up the leaderboard and, when I birdied the sixteenth, I started to think it might be my day. Padraig Harrington was a couple of shots clear, but he was a few holes behind me on the course and the wind was really starting to get up. I thought if I could perhaps pick up another shot, I'd be hard to beat.

As I went up the last, there was a brutal wind pounding off the left and my approach ballooned in the wind so it came up twenty yards short of the green. I hit a chip to within about eighteen feet, so I needed to hole it for par. Terry, my caddy, hadn't read a putt for me all day, but after he had given me my ball and wandered off, I called him over. He looked surprised.

'Yeah?' he said.

'Did you ever imagine when you were a kid and you were messing about on a putting green,' I said, 'that you would have a putt to win the Open?'

'Yeah,' he said.

'Well, I've got it,' I said. 'Now sod off.'

So he walked away and I stood over the ball and holed it.

It got me to within two shots of Harrington and made

me the leader in the clubhouse. I thought I had a massive chance. To post a number like that with it being as windy as it was put me in with a real shot. I went over to the practice ground for some peace and quiet and to get my head together in case I needed to go out for a play-off. I watched Harrington's final few holes on a television in the Porta-kabin where they do all the ball washing.

In the end, failing to pick up shots on the par fives cost me because, in the last few holes, Harrington went berserk. He birdied the thirteenth and the fifteenth to move to five over, which was two ahead of me. I still had a decent chance, but then, on the par-five seventeenth, his second shot bounced over a bunker instead of bouncing into it. Those are the breaks. He rolled in his eagle putt from six feet and it was all over. He finished four shots ahead of me. He had played a superb final round.

If I had lost by a shot, I would have been full of regrets because I had three-putted the seventeenth and I would have felt like I had thrown it away. But I had played a great final round myself and, the way Padraig finished, there was no way I could have bridged that gap.

As it was, I got a lovely silver salver for second and the confidence boost that came with recording my highest ever finish in a Major. In many ways, I was delighted. I felt that my season was about to take off and I dared to hope that qualifying for the European Ryder Cup team to take on the Americans at Valhalla that autumn would now be straightforward.

CHAPTER 19
Monty being Monty

I was wrong about qualifying for the 2008 Ryder Cup. It wasn't straightforward at all. In fact, it was anything but. It actually got very messy. By the time we got to the middle of August and the final qualifying events for Valhalla came around, I was tantalisingly close to automatic selection. I was also caught on the horns of a dilemma that brought me into a public conflict with Colin Montgomerie.

At the heart of the dilemma was a clash in my schedules on the PGA Tour and the European Tour. I had missed the cut in the opening event of the PGA Tour's FedEx Cup play-offs – the Barclays tournament in New York – so to try to secure a place in the final two tournaments, the BMW Championship and the Tour Championship, I had to play at the Deutsche Bank Championship in Boston in the last week in August.

It was also the only chance I had to get up to the fifteen events I needed to maintain my membership of the PGA Tour. I didn't want to give that up. I lived in America for most of the time now and it would cause huge disruption to my life, as well as my career, to surrender membership of the tour.

And, of course, there was the small matter of the fact that the FedEx Cup was potentially very, very lucrative. It was a volatile competition and I felt that I had a chance of winning it. It wasn't peanuts we were playing for, here. It was the richest prize in golf. The FedEx Cup was worth at least ten million dollars to the winner.

The problem was that I had not quite got over the line in terms of qualifying automatically for Sir Nick Faldo's European team at Valhalla. If I played at the Johnnie Walker Championship at Gleneagles instead of the Deutsche Bank Championship in Boston (the two events were being staged at the same time), it was possible I could grab the last of the points I needed to make the team.

My choice came down to this: did I play in Boston and gamble on Faldo giving me one of his two wild-card picks, or did I fly across the Atlantic and try to do enough at Gleneagles to force my way into the team by right? I went through agonies of indecision about it. I was in turmoil. I didn't know what to do and I phoned Faldo about it.

'Nick,' I said, 'I am going to make a decision and it is solely based on me as a player and nothing else. I am going to do exactly what Nick Faldo would have done in this situation, back in the day. Nick Faldo would have done what was right for him. So I'm not going to do what is right for everybody else, just to please everybody else. I'm going to do what I need to do for myself and whatever the repercussions are of that, I will take them on the chin.'

'I respect that and that's fine,' Faldo said. 'I'm not going to lie; I'd like you to play Gleneagles. But if you are telling me you are not going to come back, you are not going to come back. I'm not going to tell you to do something. You have to make your own decision.'

'I'm happy you have said that,' I said, 'because I am going to make the decision for Ian Poulter and nobody else.'

'Okay,' he said. 'I hear you.'

I felt I owed it to him to say that because I didn't want the furore to continue to rage without me having communicated my thoughts to him. So I stayed in the US and decided to play the Deutsche Bank. I believed, if I was selected for the team, I would be in a better shape to play my best golf without flying across the Pond to play at Gleneagles and then flying back for the Ryder Cup at Valhalla, which was near Louisville, Kentucky.

There was no guarantee I was going to do well enough at Gleneagles to force my way into an automatic qualification place, so why should I jeopardise my FedEx Cup rankings? If I went back to Gleneagles, I missed out on the Deutsche Bank, dropped down the rankings and lost the chance to compete for ten million dollars.

I thought I had had a decent year. I'd finished runner-up at the Open and I'd played well at the Masters. I thought I'd done enough to get one of the wild cards. If I were a betting man, I would have said I had a really good chance of getting a pick.

I knew I wasn't making things easy for Faldo. If I'd pitched up at Gleneagles, it would have been easy. Even if I didn't play well, people would have said I'd shown willing, that I'd made a big commitment by flying over to Scotland. Faldo wouldn't have got any flak for giving me a wild card in that situation, but if he picked me now, he would. I was still in turmoil after I'd made my decision. I kept thinking, Shit, what's going to happen?

It got worse when Monty stuck his oar in. Soon enough,

my decision not to play Gleneagles became public and I said openly that I had let Faldo know that I would be playing the Deutsche Bank instead. That sent Monty into a proper tizzy. He had played in every Ryder Cup since he made his debut at Kiawah Island in 1991, but now he was one of my rivals for a captain's pick.

Monty reacted badly to the fact that I'd rung Faldo to let him know of my decision about not playing Gleneagles. He said I was the only one of the European players to have a 'hotline' to Faldo and he suggested that the reason I wasn't playing in Scotland was that I had already been tipped off that I was going to get one of the wild cards.

That started a war of words between us in the media.

'He has got enough work to do this week to try to make the side himself,' I told a press conference in Boston when I heard Monty's accusation about the hotline. 'He should just be getting his head down and trying to play good golf.'

Monty had a go, straight back from Gleneagles.

'It's nice to be told what to do by one so young and one so inexperienced,' he said.

The idea that I had already been given the nod is bullshit. That is flat-out bullshit. That is one hundred per cent flat-out bullshit. Even now, some people still persist with that garbage. Well, they can say what they want, write what they want, but I am happy to take a lie detector test to prove them all wrong.

It's bollocks. I would quite happily say if Faldo had given me the nod. I will say it again: there was no nod given.

Monty and I had history. He was the captain of the Great Britain and Ireland team at the Seve Trophy at Wynyard Hall in 2005 and, on the first morning of that competition, we had a big argument. I hadn't played well in the morning and Nick Dougherty and I had lost our fourball to Thomas Bjørn and Henrik Stenson.

We had been the first match out and, as soon as our defeat was confirmed, I just wanted to get straight on to the practice range, which was fairly close to the eighteenth green, and try to fix some of the faults that had just cost me and the team that morning.

I was annoyed about how badly I had played and I wanted to get my head down and do some work so that I could play better the following day. So, after a couple of the other matches had finished, I went over to the range and started hitting some balls.

The last match of the day was a tight contest between Padraig Harrington and Paul McGinley, and Jean-François Remésy and Thomas Levet. Monty and some of the other Great Britain and Ireland players were waiting by the eighteenth green as the game reached its conclusion. The match went the wrong way and Remesy and Levet sealed it on the last.

Monty's reaction was to come stomping up to the range and start having a go at me. He said I should have been by the eighteenth with him and the rest of the team, supporting Harrington and McGinley. He got himself in a real lather. He was having a right pop. I was bemused. It wasn't like I was sitting there having a beer, or something.

'Fuck off,' I said. 'I'm working. I know you're captain, but I'm actually working for your benefit here. I want to hit some balls to better myself, to better the team score, so I can come out and play better tomorrow. And you're having a pop at me.

'Go and have a pop at one of the others by the green who lost this morning and who didn't fancy going to hit some balls. Don't have a pop at me. I'm doing my thing. For you, I'm doing my thing. And you're having a dig at me.'

We both went at it in a fairly forthright manner. That can happen with Monty and it can happen with me. He was throwing his toys out of his pram, which he does sometimes. But that doesn't mean he and I are sworn enemies. Actually, I think that, most of the time, I've got a great relationship with him.

Look, Monty's Monty. I have got massive respect for him. He's an unbelievably good golfer, a Ryder Cup captain. Everything he has done in the game, I have got respect for it. But, like I say, Monty's Monty. And I'm me.

It is no secret that sometimes he's miserable and sometimes he's stroppy. He'll say that himself. He won't mind me saying it. Well, he might, but that's fine. I don't care. He's been stroppy and moody. He's Monty. That's what makes him a fun character. Everybody knows – one minute he's great, the next minute he's a bit moody.

I've not had proper run-ins with him. I don't count what happened at the Seve Trophy as a proper run-in. It was just silly because he was having a pop at me when I was working. If I had been sitting doing naff all, then he would have been entitled to have a go. But, in that instance, I felt I was well within my rights to tell him to Foxtrot Oscar.

We had had another little spat a few months before the controversy about my 'hotline' to Faldo blew up, too. We were in the same group at the European Open at the London Golf Club in Kent in July, and we were on a par four. There was a water hazard at a 290-yard run out. Unbelievably to me, Monty pulled a driver out of the bag and hit the driver through the fairway into the water. He proceeded to make five or six, or whatever.

Then he was whingeing and moaning all the way down the next hole. He's hit driver on a par four. It was just stupid. I mean, it was a lovely drive. It was just that it went straight in the water. He was frustrated, so he vented at a cameraman an for nothing in particular. I made a gesture then to signify, 'Here we go, Monty's going off on one, yapping and moaning,' and the cameras picked it up and Monty didn't like it.

That was Monty's hot-and-cold for you. That's what you get with him sometimes. When he said the stuff about me having a 'hotline' to Faldo, it was because he was worried he wasn't going to get picked. And it just ended up with us having a few games of tennis back and forth in the papers.

He's on one side of the Pond. I'm on the other. I didn't go back to Gleneagles to play when he thought I should be there. But Monty's got such a tight connection with Gleneagles that he believes everybody should be back there playing because it benefits the tournament. But it would have been better if he had caught his breath and remembered that everyone has their own schedules for a reason.

I didn't hold any of that against him and I don't think he harbours any grudges against me. Monty's open; I'm open. He's honest; I'm honest. He has a private-club background and I don't, but for what he's done in golf, for being an eight-time Order of Merit winner and winning a boatload of tournaments and having a great Ryder Cup record, I have got massive respect for him.

He can be frustrating, but I'm sure I can be frustrating too. He knows me well enough to tell me to sod off if the mood takes him and I can tell him to sod off if he's getting on my nerves. You would only be able to do that if you know someone pretty well. With us, the friction disappears as quickly as it flares up.

There were some stories after the team had been announced that Monty and I had had a stand-up row in Zuma, the Japanese restaurant in Knightsbridge that's my favourite place to eat in London. There was even some suggestion that we had to be pulled apart because the argument was getting physical. That was absolute nonsense.

I was with Katie, Monty was with his wife and we wished each other all the best. It was very civil. The idea that there was a row was a fantasy.

By then, we had learned our fates, as far as getting into Faldo's side for Valhalla was concerned. Monty didn't make it. And when I arrived in Boston to play the Deutsche Bank, I still had no idea whether I was going to make it, either. My mind was all over the place that week. After all that, I missed the cut in Boston and all that was left was to wait for Faldo's decision. I was staying at the Omni Hotel in downtown Providence, Rhode Island, and I had wandered over to the adjoining shopping mall with Katie and my mum, who had been out watching me that week. I was going stir crazy waiting for the decision, so I just wanted to get out of the room.

I saw an Indian stall at the food court and I thought, Fuck it, I'll have a curry. I'd had one mouthful of my curry and my mobile started to ring. It was Faldo. I got up and started pacing around.

'Ian,' he said.

'Nick,' I said.

'How are you?' he asked.

'I'll tell you in a minute,' I said.

Faldo, like a lot of other people, used to make fun of me for looking like Rodney, the character from *Only Fools and Horses*. Rodney was my nickname at school, actually. And now, Faldo started doing his best Del Boy impersonation.

'Ian,' he said. 'Get your coat. You're coming to the Ryder Cup.'

I turned to my mum and gave her the thumbs-up. She started crying.

CHAPTER 20

Valhalla, Faldo and Søren Stenson

I know that some people are hoping I will fail at Valhalla. Nick Faldo has made a lot of enemies during his time as a player. He is no fan of the press. He made that abundantly clear when he thanked reporters from 'the heart of my bottom' after he won the Open at Muirfield in 1992. I am one of his wild card picks. If I fail, it is another stick to beat him with.

Faldo has not gone for the popular choices with his captain's picks. The popular choices would have been Monty and Darren Clarke, who has had a late run of form and won twice on the European Tour in 2008. Faldo ignores them both. He goes for Paul Casey, who has also passed up the chance to play at Gleneagles, and me. It is a big call.

Most of the criticism centres on my selection, not Casey's. Many say that Faldo has made a mistake selecting me ahead of Darren and the Swede, Carl Pettersson, who has also had a good season. Darren has won two tournaments since mid-April, including the KLM Open in Holland just eight days before the team announcement.

Faldo had said several months earlier that he would make his captain's picks on the basis of form, which means Darren should have had a strong case. That is one reason his omission raises eyebrows. Another is that his Ryder Cup partnership with Lee Westwood has been particularly successful.

Clarke and Westwood have beaten the world number one and number two in three of the recent Ryder Cups – Woods and Duval in the fourballs at Brookline in 1999, Woods and Mickelson in the foursomes at Oakland Hills in 2004 and Woods and Furyk in the fourballs in 2006. 'To discard such a potent partnership seems to be brave at the very least,' the *Times* golf correspondent John Hopkins writes.

Faldo is subjected to a reasonable amount of hostile questioning about my inclusion when he faces the media at the Gleneagles press conference to announce the team. It is pointed out to him, among other things, that I have recorded only one round of 68 or better on either side of the Atlantic all year. Faldo counters this by talking up my attitude and my performance in that year's Open.

I am fully aware some people see my selection as a controversial pick because Monty and Darren have been left out. They think they can scent Faldo's blood in the water already. I am going out there with the spotlight on me and I know there is plenty of potential for Faldo to get slaughtered because of me. I am determined that isn't going to happen.

I was a Faldo fan, back then. I still am. He is someone I have always followed closely. He opened Chesfield Downs in 1991 and I still have the golf ball he signed that day in my trophy cabinet. He won six Majors, which says all you need to know. He lived in Florida when I first moved out to Orlando and I got to know him really well down the years.

He has won more Majors than any other European golfer, don't forget, and it is right and fitting that he should be asked to captain our Ryder Cup team. He has become a celebrity in America because of his television work and it makes sense for his captaincy to coincide with a Ryder Cup on US soil. He is a good choice. I firmly believe that.

In many ways, his captaincy is the opposite of Bernhard Langer's in 2004. Everything is quite casual and relaxed. Langer had us in team meetings at 7 a.m. on the dot. Everything was regimented. Faldo is more about trusting us to do our own thing.

I'll tell you how casual he is about the whole thing – he is still writing his opening-ceremony speech in the team room in the minutes before we go out on to the stage. Unfortunately, it shows. It isn't an overly good speech. This is a ceremony that is going out to millions and his address goes down like a lead balloon.

Nick makes a few mistakes. He gets Søren Hansen and Henrik Stenson mixed up and introduces Søren as 'Søren Stenson'. That isn't a good start. Then, when he turns to Padraig Harrington, he says he has 'hit more golf balls than they have planted potatoes in Ireland'. That makes a few more people wince. Then he moves on to Graeme McDowell and says, 'Where do you come from again? Ireland or Northern Ireland?'

We are getting uncomfortably close to Hal Sutton territory but, again, it just shows you what the pressure of the Ryder Cup can do, even to people like Nick, who are used to the public eye. Nick gets quite emotional about it all. Even before the competition starts, he says it has been one of the best weeks of his life. In terms of the press coverage, that opening ceremony sets a tone and the media take every chance they can to settle a few scores with Nick.

Actually, the fun and games started the previous day when we were practising. A photographer had trained a long lens on a piece of paper Nick was holding while he was chatting to Stenson. It had sets of initials on it and it looked as though it was a list of pairings that the captain was considering.

Nick is asked about it at his press conference on Wednesday afternoon and denies it has anything to do with the pairings. 'It just had the lunch list,' he says. 'It had sandwich requests for the guys. Just making sure who wants tuna, who wants the beef, who wants the ham. That's all it was.' The press have a ball with that. 'Nick Fal-Doh,' somebody calls him in one of the papers.

It feels as if the press have been biding their time with Faldo and now they are enjoying giving him both barrels. He gets it in the neck over every detail. He has asked DJ Spoony to come in and play some music in the team room to lighten the mood a bit, and that is criticised as well. People are saying, 'What's a DJ doing in there?' even though it is totally irrelevant.

The atmosphere is actually all right within the team. We are fine. There isn't the same sense of meticulous preparation there had been under Langer, but that's okay. Faldo is different to Langer. He does things a different way. Spoony's presence is Nick's way of trying to provide a distraction. If we win at Valhalla, he'll be hailed a genius for it.

It's a tense week. There's so much pressure from every angle that you really don't get a lot of time in the team room to yourself. At every Ryder Cup, there's a night where the captains try to let the players chill out and have a bit of fun together before the competition starts, to break it up with something, and Spoony is Faldo's way of trying to do that. Nicko McBrain from Iron Maiden comes in to show us how to play the drums, which was a nice way of relaxing. You can't eat, sleep and talk Ryder Cup 24/7 that week because you are going to get to Saturday and you will be exhausted. It is too much sometimes.

At Medinah, four years later, José María Olazábal, who is a vice-captain at Valhalla, sets up a kind of *Strictly Come Dancing* night on the eve of the tournament. That is a good laugh, just like it is a good laugh having Spoony around. But if we had lost at Medinah, Olly would have been ridiculed for the dancing thing. It would have been held up as an example of where he got it wrong. The way you're viewed as a Ryder Cup captain depends entirely on the result.

The fact is, at Valhalla, we come up against an American team packed with hungry, young rookies and desperate to reverse the trend of recent results that strongly favoured Europe. Tiger Woods is missing because of injury and they are the underdogs. They thrive on that. They have a ballsy, stubborn, meticulously prepared captain in Paul Azinger and they are determined to wipe out the memories of the humiliations at Oakland Hills and the K Club. They come out hard, right from the start.

They have six rookies altogether and those rookies show no fear. They are inspired by the partisan support and they milk it. I'm not sure anyone's ever been more fired up than Boo Weekley is at Valhalla in 2008. Boo is a southern lad from Florida and he gets all he can from his good ol' boy reputation. Once at Valhalla, he hits his tee shot and, swept away by the cheers of the crowd, sticks his club between his legs and sets off down the fairway, riding it as if it were a horse. That kind of thing stokes up the crowd big time. I don't mind that. It is part of the deal. We have made it work for us in Europe in the past. They are doing the same.

I go out with Justin Rose in the third match of the morning foursomes on the first day. We start well against Stewart Cink and Chad Campbell. In fact, we start brilliantly. We birdie the third, fifth and seventh holes and we are 3 up and flying. Then they start to fight back.

We are still 1 up going to the thirteenth, but I hit a poor approach shot and it bounces off a rock wall near the front of the green and comes to rest in the water hazard. It is a stupid shot. It is a wedge and I should hit it stiff, but I mess it up. If I could play a shot again from any of my matches at Valhalla, it would be that one.

We had control of the match and now we are losing it. They bring the match all square at the thirteenth and then I hit my tee shot at the fourteenth into the deep rough behind the green. That is another hole gone and they are in the lead for the first time.

We get a hole back at the fifteenth and we are all square going up the eighteenth. Justin and I both make mistakes and, when I miss a par putt from five feet, I concede the hole and the match. They have won, 1 up. It is hugely disappointing. I feel I have let Justin and the team down, particularly with that shot that ended up in the water at the thirteenth.

I get incredibly determined from that point on. I want

to make amends. I want to prove I am worth my place in the team after all the hot air that has been wasted about my selection. We are 3-1 down after the morning session and I want to do my bit to turn things around. That afternoon, Justin and I go out together in the fourballs and duff up Steve Stricker and Ben Curtis. We win that, 4&2, but by the end of the day Europe trail the US 5½–2½.

I feel as though Justin and I are on a roll then. Faldo senses it, too. He puts us out first in the Saturday morning foursomes and we are drawn against Cink and Campbell again. There are no screw-ups from me this time. We batter them 4&3 and, by the end of the session, we claw the score back to 7-5 in favour of the USA.

That day marks the start of me becoming a Ryder Cup pain in the arse.

The way I started to perform over those first three sessions in Valhalla makes me feel like one of the leaders of the team. I feel like I am utterly inspired by the spirit of the event. I feel more driven and pumped up than I have ever felt before.

Faldo sends me out again in the afternoon. That means I am the only member of our team who is going to play in all five sessions. I feel proud of that and I respond to it. I need to be at my best, as well. I go out with Graeme McDowell against Kenny Perry, the local hero, and Jim Furyk, and it is one of the best, most highly charged Ryder Cup matches I will ever play.

Those Kentucky fans are hard to play in front of, that afternoon. They are a brutal set of fans. They have got every right to be loud for their team. I am not getting anything I am not able to soak up, but they are giving it everything they can in support of Perry, and the atmosphere is so loud that it gets to both teams.

I am up for it and I am showing it. They are too. It even gets to the point, on the tee at the par-three fourteenth, where one of the American team takes it into his head to give me a shoulder barge. I am taken aback by what Anthony Kim does, I have to say. He crosses a line.

It happens when we have all teed off. GMac and I set off towards the green and Kim, who has been going nuts all weekend, strides straight at me. He said later he wanted to go and encourage Perry. I see him coming, but I don't move out of the way and nor does he. What's he doing coming on to the tee box? I'm playing, so I certainly ain't moving. And he just barges straight into me.

Are there words exchanged? Yes, there are two words exchanged, both spoken by me: 'fuck' and 'off'. I think he is a bit overexcited by it all. And that is it. It happens. He is a fiery character. I'm fiery in the Ryder Cup. He tried to claim later it was a mistake and he hadn't seen me coming. I don't know about that. I think, at the time, it is intended and it only fires me up to finish that match off. I use it to my advantage.

I get even more pumped up for the last few holes of that match. It suits me in match play. Sure, you can show emotion in stroke play, but you are only ever going to show it when you are in a position to win. You are not going to show that emotion when you are lying twenty-fourth or tenth. The only chance you have got to show that emotion is down the stretch when you are in contention to win and you start hitting big shots and big putts and you can finish it off.

But every shot you hit in a Ryder Cup is the equivalent of finishing the job off for a tournament win. I play five matches that week at Valhalla and each one feels like the equivalent of playing a final round to win five tournaments. If that doesn't get your brain switched on and able to show some feeling then you are not wired right.

In one week, I have the opportunity to try to win five massive, massive matches. It's the equivalent of five massive tournament wins and the reality is that I might not get the opportunity to do that in stroke play in a calendar year, let alone in one week.

There is more pressure to win at the Ryder Cup than there is to win a tournament – even a Major. You see people fist-pumping who don't normally fist-pump. At Medinah in 2012, even Jason Dufner was fist-pumping. It's incredible. You see people firing the crowd up that don't normally act like that. It just doesn't happen any other week.

The game against Furyk and Perry is immense. GMac and I get to the turn 2up, but then Furyk starts to play like a demon. He birdies five of the last nine holes and GMac and I are clinging on. It is an absolute ding-dong. When GMac doesn't make birdies, I do. When I don't make birdies, GMac does. We dovetail brilliantly.

By the time we get to the fourteenth tee, we are only 1up and they are putting us under all sorts of pressure. But somehow, if I am struggling, GMac steps up and vice versa. So, when I make a mistake on the sixteenth, GMac drains a fifteen-foot par-putt to keep us ahead. Furyk never lets up. I think we have won it on the seventeenth, but he holes a ten-footer to keep them in the match going to the eighteenth.

On the eighteenth green, Furyk has an eagle putt that will win the hole and halve the match. He misses it right, but only just. We need a birdie to halve the hole and win the match. GMac goes first and misses to the right. That leaves me with a nasty six-footer. I make it. Winning that match goes down as one of my best memories of all time.

The two teams are all square in that afternoon session. Europe has gained two points and so has the USA, which means that they have a two-point lead going into the final day's singles. We still feel we have a good chance, but the momentum is with them. They are still on an emotional high and, even though we are battling them every step of the way, there have been a few issues in the team.

On the Friday afternoon, for instance, Faldo goes to the tenth tee to speak to Westwood, who is at a crucial stage of a foursomes match. Faldo tells Lee that he is going to rest him the next morning. Bear in mind that Lee has never been dropped for a single session at a Ryder Cup before, and that he is in the middle of a tight match with Søren Hansen against Boo Weekley and J. B. Holmes, and you'll appreciate that it is a strange move.

I think Faldo is trying to be helpful. Lee is suffering with blisters on his feet and my guess is that Nick is trying to say to him, 'Just give everything for the rest of this match and then you can rest up in the morning,' but actually it is the biggest kick in the nuts Faldo can give him.

Lee, me, all of us – we would play with one arm hanging

off in the Ryder Cup. No one wants to take a rest because they have blisters. Lee is admirably loyal to Nick in all the post-match press conferences, but he admits in an interview a year or so later that the timing of Faldo's intervention was not particularly helpful.

Who knows how much it affects Westwood, but he and Hansen are 1up going to the tenth, then Faldo speaks to him, they lose that hole and never regain the lead. The match is halved, but it is obvious that Lee is struggling a bit with what has happened. Anybody would.

You give blood, sweat and tears that week and you don't even think about it. So for Faldo to tell him that news on the golf course was a mistake. It would completely suck every piece of energy out of any player. And now one of our best players is feeling dejected. That can't be good. You potentially switch someone off. It's very easy for that person then to get down when things aren't going our way.

Some of the players on the European team at Valhalla say subsequently they feel a bit isolated on the course. Azinger has three vice-captains: Ray Floyd, Dave Stockton and Olin Browne. Faldo just has Olazábal, which leaves things a bit thin with four matches going on at a time. It doesn't bother me, but others feel it is odd that Faldo doesn't have more back-up.

One of the criticisms regularly aimed at Faldo during that Ryder Cup and its aftermath is that he is not a good man-manager. I probably agree with that. He's his own man. That's how he was able to be so focused and so single-minded in all his years playing golf. Does that make you a good team person? Perhaps, as a player. But probably not as the captain.

CHAPTER 21
Trouble in the Team Room

On Saturday night at Valhalla, José María Olazábal stands up in the team room and makes a great speech, an unbelievable speech. It has several people in tears. He tries to make us understand his view of what it is we are playing for at the Ryder Cup, who it is that we are playing for and what it should mean to us as we put that shirt on.

Maybe he doesn't come across as a great orator in his public persona, but he is an inspirational speaker. He speaks about the Ryder Cup in a way that I have never heard anybody speak about the Ryder Cup before. He is able to convey what it means to him and how much he wishes he could help the side by putting that shirt on and getting out there himself.

But, of course, he can't get out there, and he talks about how much it upsets him that he can't play in the team anymore. He talks about how vital and alive it made him feel to play Ryder Cup and that now something has been taken away from him. He says we have to treasure it while we can because it is the most precious thing in golf.

He talks about how much it had meant to him and Seve, and how it breaks his heart that his best playing days are behind him and that he can't be one of us anymore. It cripples him, he says. At Medinah, four years later, he

The Ferrari collection growing nicely . . .

Mr Wenger, can't I just play for a few minutes? I promise I will score.

Why can't Superman wear sandals and socks?

OK, team, let's win the Masters.

Always taking the piss, will Terry ever stop chuffing?

Luke's birthday trophy, the Volvo World Matchplay.

WGC Accenture matchplay, 2010.

WGC HSBC Champions – I quite like Wedgwood Pots.

Heart rate 180 and pumping. Rosie, let's do this.

Now boys, time to start the 'Miracle at Medinah'.

They just keep dropping...

Terry, you better be right, I hope it cuts . . .

Olly. You got what you wanted.
To take this home.

No words required.

Left: 'Dad, are you sure we can eat Cheerios out of the Ryder Cup trophy?' 'Of course . . .'

Below left: Me, Pat and Katie. As if this 'QUIET' sign makes any difference at the Ryder Cup!

Below: Dreamflight is the trip of a lifetime for such special kids.

Dad, let's go for a spin in the red one . . .

Above: Nice day trip to Universal Studios with the family.

Left and Below: Katie's surprise 40th birthday pictures. I had them taken and hung while we were out for the day.

Better late than never.

would go on to make that speech in the closing ceremony about how all men die but not all men live. That is the message he is trying to get across to us at Valhalla: make sure you go out there and feel what this means. Make sure you go out there and live it.

We go into the final day two points down, but sure that we can overhaul them. That is when Faldo makes the move that earns him the most criticism of all. He backloads the singles line-up. He gambles on the fact that the match is going to go down to the wire and puts some of his strongest players out at the end of the line-up. The last four players are GMac, me, Westwood and Harrington.

The truth is, that line-up isn't all down to Faldo. What happens is that we all sit round a big table to discuss who wants to go out when. At one stage, I am going second. Harrington says I need to go later on in the order, in case it comes down to the last few groups. I am fine with that. I don't care where in the order I go.

'I'll bring you a point from wherever I am,' I say.

In the end, I go out tenth. Would it have made a difference if I'd gone out second instead of tenth? No, because we get well and truly walloped. Does it make a difference if we are front-loaded and leave the rear up to some of the rookies? I don't know because I can't predict being slapped that hard.

The US get off to a storming start when Kim blitzes Sergio García five and four in the opening match. In fact, the US win five of the opening eight matches and halve another. And so, when the last of those, Jim Furyk, beats Miguel Ángel Jiménez two and one, it takes the US to fourteen and a half points. It means they win the Ryder Cup for the first time since 1999.

The opening match sets the tone. There is one hole early on when both Sergio and Kim hit their tee shots stiff. They're both gimmes, but Sergio is a tiny bit further away and Kim refuses to concede the putt. Sergio taps in and then picks up Kim's marker. It's obvious straight away there is a lot of tension in that match. I think then, This ain't going to be good. Anthony is right up for it.

The matches that make the difference are Kenny Perry beating Henrik Stenson, Boo Weekley beating Ollie Wilson, J. B. Holmes beating Søren Hansen, and Furyk beating Jiménez. So matches five to eight all go red. And matches nine to twelve become irrelevant. It takes it past the point where we can do anything about it. By the time my match with Steve Stricker reaches the fourteenth, the Ryder Cup is effectively over. So you are playing the last few holes with nothing in your body. It's horrible.

We have firepower late on in the order, but it is too late. It is all done and dusted. It is totally deflating. Being left out on the golf course at that Ryder Cup is the worst feeling I have ever had in a competition. It's over. You have got the adrenaline in your body to play, to keep fighting and fighting because you think you have got a chance, but then you realise it's been taken away from you.

A roar echoes around the course because each scoreboard is changed at slightly different times. The roar goes from green to green – the roar that says the US has taken back the Ryder Cup. And you can hear those roars as they come at you in a long series.

It's horrible. One minute, you're right in the thick of it, surrounded by a great buzz. The next minute, it's like someone has put you on a golf hole five hundred miles out in the middle of the ocean. It's awful. You go from surging adrenaline to emptiness.

I am stuck out on the course. GMac, Westwood, Harrington and I are all stranded, our matches an irrelevance. I beat Stricker three and two, for what it is worth, but the eventual margin of victory is sixteen and a half to eleven and a half for the US. It is a crushing defeat and Faldo, more than any of the players, gets it in the neck.

I feel for Faldo. History says he is a losing European Ryder Cup captain in an era when Europe has been relatively dominant. That will hurt his pride because he is a winner. But will it bother him long term? No. It's Nick Faldo you're talking about. I think he would have liked it to be a win, but he's not going to lose any sleep over it.

He's ruthless and that's the reason he was so good. It doesn't alter his playing record. It doesn't change the fact he won six Majors. He is still the most successful European golfer ever. It is just disappointing that, in the record books, it says USA regained the Ryder Cup in the year Nick was Europe's captain.

It is a brutal feeling to be part of a losing side, but I am able to dredge up some personal satisfaction from the way I played. I hadn't been the weak link that many said I would be. In fact, I am the only player on the European team to play in all five sessions and I am the top scorer on either side, with four points. That doesn't make me happy, because we just had our backsides kicked, but I would be lying if I said it doesn't sugar the pill.

I am proud that I did my job because there was a lot of heat there for me in the build-up. To win four out of five matches is personally rewarding. To be able to go out there and deliver and validate my pick at least makes me feel I have done my bit. I haven't let anybody down and I am not going to get slaughtered, which is a small measure of consolation.

There is a postscript, too. Normally the winners pay a visit to the other side's team room to socialise a bit after the hostilities are over and show there are no hard feelings and that we're all pals again. You have a beer or two and smooth things over. This time, it doesn't quite work out like that.

This time, we go up to the US team room and things get a little bit out of hand. Everyone has had quite a lot to drink and Lee Westwood and I start messing around with some of the pictures the US boys have pinned up on the walls. They are motivational photographs of the players in the US team and Lee and I draw a few things on them.

We are down in the dumps after the loss, but we're trying to lift our spirits and have a joke. We want to take our mind off things, I suppose, and we assume that they are so carried away by their victory that they will not be in the mood to take offence at us larking around. We are just letting our hair down, nothing more. We have lost a match. We are trying to drown our sorrows.

Some people are drinking and chatting. Some of the boys are playing table tennis. It is a loud, boisterous atmosphere and we think we'll have a bit of fun. There is a picture of Boo Weekley pinned up on the wall and I write, *Who Ate All The Pies?* on it. Westwood writes something similarly frivolous on a picture of Stricker. We are just having a bit of a laugh. But the American boys don't like it. They don't like it at all.

There is no malice involved, but they think it is disrespectful. A couple of the American players get upset and Boo gets annoyed. They are a bit pissed off and, when you sit back and think about it, probably rightly so. We shouldn't be drawing on their pictures. Some of their players start shouting, 'You can't do this.' There is a melee. It starts to look a bit dicey.

There is a lot of finger pointing and a bit of barging. People are being held back. Some people are trying to calm the situation. Others have lost it. Look, if you get twenty-four emotional lads in a room together at 2 a.m. after a really intense, high-pressure week when they've been in each other's faces and desperately trying to win, there's always going to be something going on.

I don't want to be on the wrong end of it if Boo launches one. He can handle himself, I reckon. But it never gets to the stage where there are fisticuffs. We defuse the situation and back off a bit. We decide we ought to go back to our team room.

'Come on, guys,' I say, 'we're sorry. We'll leave. If we're offending anyone, we'll get out of here.'

We have another couple of drinks in there and then go downstairs to our own team room. Justin Leonard and a couple of the other US players come down to have a few drinks with us to show there are no hard feelings and, a little bit later, Boo comes down, too. So it isn't like it's a lasting thing. We have a laugh and a bit of a sing-song and try to forget about the fact that the Ryder Cup belongs to America for the next two years.

CHAPTER 22
Addicted to Twitter

I came second at the Players' Championship at TPC Saw-grass in May 2009. Henrik Stenson shot a final round of 66 and beat me by four shots. People call that tournament the fifth major, so it was another good result for me – my biggest result so far in America and another sign that my move to the States was paying off. I mentioned it a few times on Twitter.

I'd joined Twitter a month or so earlier. I loved it from the start and now I'm addicted to it. I'm way addicted to it. I use it as both a news source and a source of information, I tweet what's going on in my life and career, and it's a business thing, too. Of course it is. I've got more than 1.7 million followers. How many newspapers worldwide have got 1.7 million readers? Not that many.

I like following accounts like Piers Morgan, Peter Jones, Lord Sugar, Lee Westwood, Ferrari, Spoony, my mate and car dealer Tom Hartley, and a number of my fellow golfers. Every morning I wake up and I have a little look and scroll down my Twitter feed. It's like me catching up on news. It's like reading the newspaper. I skim through. I'll open some links to news stories. It's perfect for me. It suits my attention span.

I tweet business stuff and the more numbers you reach,

the more it helps to build your brand. People who have television shows that have the biggest ratings, well, there's a reason why they're paid the most money.

I get abuse on Twitter, sure. Plenty of it. Doesn't everybody? Westwood gets some serious grief on it. He had a full meltdown last year. I don't blame him for that, but Twitter and several beers are not a good combo. You don't have enough time to process the information and the potential consequences before you press *send*.

I do it sober and I still sometimes think, What am I doing? Why have I just bitten on that? But it's so hard when these people are constantly at you. They wouldn't say the things they tweet to my face because they know how disrespectful and stupid it is, and if you're not prepared to say it to somebody's face, why are you going to write it on Twitter?

So I block people all the time. It's a no-brainer. It's not in your nature to allow people to abuse you. It's a cheap form of bullying. Especially if it's coming from someone who isn't qualified to criticise you in any way, let alone shower you with foul insults.

If Jack Nicklaus was having a pop at me and it was justified, I'd have to sit back and take note of that because I'd respect his comments, but I don't have to take it from some nobody who doesn't know me and comes and abuses me out of the blue.

I think of my Twitter feed as being a bit like reality TV. I'm not trying to create my own show, but people want to know what I'm doing. People want to get an inside look at a sportsman's life. And if I'm going to be on Twitter, I don't want to be bland and just tout all my gear and indulge in a series of platitudes. I want to put my opinions out there and try to give people an impression of what my life is like.

People get offended sometimes, as if they think I'm just using Twitter as a platform to boast. All I'm doing is trying to give an honest look at what my life's like. I know it's not normal. It's not my idea of normal, anyway. I know I have a privileged life now. I have to pinch myself sometimes to make sure I'm really leading this life. But I try to make it a real view of the way it is, the way I am.

I get butchered on Twitter sometimes for that. But why should I feel guilty about jumping on a plane to go and watch the Monaco Grand Prix just after I have missed the cut at a tournament, like I did after the BMW PGA Championship at Wentworth in 2013? I got absolutely hammered for it. Am I supposed to go and watch my counterparts play for money? Am I supposed to feel sorry for myself that I have missed the cut? Am I supposed to dwell on the fact that I am not earning any money that week and that I have actually lost money on the week because I have paid my caddy and my hotel bills and my flights from the US to the UK and I have got to fly myself back? I am out of pocket that week. So if I'm out of pocket and I want to be out of pocket a bit more in order to go and watch an F1 race that has always been on my bucket list of things to do, why should that annoy people?

I got stick for that and it blew my mind. It's obviously jealous people who resent me because I can do it. Some people take offence and I think those people are very sad.

So are the ones who bang on all the time on Twitter about my interest in fashion.

'All you are is a clothes horse; you're shit at golf,' they say.

Well, I'm looking at my trophy cabinet and I think I'll be okay. I think I'll cope. I think I'll sleep at night. People take this as an arrogant thing to say, but I'm happy. I'm really happy with what I've been able to achieve, so I don't give a shit if that's what they think, really.

People on Twitter can say I'm shit at golf, but that just makes them look stupid. Look at what I have been able to achieve. The top twenty all-time money list on the European Tour goes like this: Els, Westwood, Montgomerie, Harrington, Jiménez, McIlroy, Goosen, Poulter, García, Clarke, Bjørn, McDowell, Stenson, Kaymer, Donald, Casey, Rose, Karlsson, Cabrera, Singh. I have done pretty well. I'm eighth in Europe, all time. Enough said.

Of course, I pinch myself sometimes. My life seems absolutely stupid now and again. Flying to the Bahamas for a day to check out an apartment: how does that seem right, coming from a small house on a Stevenage estate, earning £120 a week in a pro shop? How is that a normal progression? It's not normal.

I'm not trying to separate myself from everyone else. The opposite, actually. I'm as normal as everyone else. I don't look at people differently because they are in a different pay bracket. I am unbelievably fortunate to be in the position I am in, and that's why none of this makes sense.

I never have to play golf again, as far as being comfortable financially for the rest of my life is concerned. I could just do corporate gigs and that would be enough. I could shut up today. I could lock that front door and say, 'Bollocks to everyone,' and never have to work again and be really comfortable and the kids would be comfortable.

I wouldn't be happy, though, because I know I am capable of more. I would go stir crazy. I could say, 'Bollocks to it all,' but that's not in me. I can't sit still for two minutes. I can't handle the phone not ringing. I can't handle not doing something. I want to be involved in everything I touch. Therefore, I have always got the want – the want to get better at being a businessman and making better decisions – and what comes with that is rewarding.

I don't feel guilty for enjoying what I have earned, nor will I ever. I am prepared to work really hard and I am going to enjoy everything I get from it. I am not frivolously throwing money away. Yes, I am a big spender, but I think I have done a good job spending money and building stuff around me that makes me feel secure.

I have a garage full of Ferraris and that is a luxury. But the cars are an investment, too. I have houses, which are an investment. I am able to surround myself with what I have been able to achieve. I could put every penny into a trust fund and not see any of it and let it tick over, but I want to enjoy it and I want my kids to enjoy it.

I'd rather do that than give it to someone else to have a play with – some big shot investor, some stocks-and-shares guru, some dodge pot. As we've seen in the past, sometimes that's been great and sometimes it hasn't been great. I'd rather be in control of my money than entrust it to someone else. If it goes wrong, it's down to nobody else apart from me.

I did Business Studies in my PGA exam but, apart from that, I have never studied business. None of it, not one bit of it, not once. I have never read a book on it. I can add up, I can do my multiplication and I know what two and two makes. If you can do that and you understand how the business world works, it is not rocket science to know where to put money or what to do with it and how it's going to benefit you.

If two and two make four, but you can put it somewhere and it makes six, then it's going to be a good thing. I want my money to work for me as much as possible. I enjoy the challenge of trying to make it work for me by doing it myself. I get to enjoy it that way, as well. That's my personality. I have an issue. I like to be in control.

That's why I take time off during the year at some stage, because I have got so much going on in my head that I have a meltdown when I can't process everything. As good as I am at processing, people have no idea how much there is rushing around in my mind. If they spent every day with me, from 7 a.m. to midnight, when I shut my mind down, for a week, that might help.

My life is not just hitting a golf ball at the driving range and going to play golf. It is no secret that there is the clothing business, but I am separated from that in some respects. I don't have to give it an hour a day, or anything like that. It's minimal. I have got people to run that for me. But it's still busy. The phone's non-stop. There's still stuff that I've got to make a decision on because it's my stuff.

I'm still addicted to Twitter. It's a million miles a minute, which suits me. Sure, now and again I get drawn into conversations with people who are intent on abusing me. But I'm okay with that. I'm a relatively robust character. I can take it.

CHAPTER 23
Amen to All That

At the end of 2009, Tiger Woods announced he was taking an indefinite break from the game of golf. He had been involved in a minor car accident outside his house in Isleworth, near Orlando, and the incident unleashed a storm of revelations about his personal life. He needed some time away and no one knew when he was coming back.

I've never commented on Tiger's personal life and I'm not going to start now. I was only concerned about it in golfing terms. At first, I didn't even think about who might take over from Tiger as the world number one. I just thought about the enormous gap his absence would leave in the sport.

If the world's best player takes any time out of his sport, then it is going to be difficult for that sport to deal with it. There aren't many players who move the needle like Tiger Woods, but one player who can is Rory McIlroy. He did it at the US Open in 2011. He won by eight shots with a record low score. He was the youngest US Open champion for eighty-eight years. He blew the rest of the field away, much like Tiger had done at Pebble Beach. A year later, Rory did it again, winning the US PGA by eight shots. And, in the summer of 2014, he dominated the field at Hoylake to add the Open to his growing list of Majors.

I like Rory. He had to grow up quickly as a golfer after he had the meltdown at the Masters in 2011. And he did grow up quickly. He is only twenty-five and he has already won three Majors. It's a lot to deal with – a lot of attention, a lot of pressure, a lot of expectation. Players like Graeme McDowell were a bit older and better equipped to deal with it all when they broke through.

I laughed, though, at the people who said Rory would find it hard to recover from his final round collapse at Augusta in 2011. If you take a four-stroke lead into the last day at the Masters, that is going to give you encouragement in the long term no matter what happens on the final day. Sure, you've had a bad Sunday, but it's not going to affect you indefinitely. It should actually make you stronger because it shows what you are capable of.

Rory has so much natural talent that he is capable of lapping a field. You can't learn that. You can't just find that talent. And his natural ability will make it easier for him to cut out any mistakes he makes under pressure.

People ask me sometimes if I envy Rory's talent. I don't envy anybody's talent. I respect their talent. The reality is that I wasn't capable of doing what Rory did at the ages he was doing it. I just wasn't. I wasn't able to spend the time he spent hitting balls at the age he was doing it. He was practising his golf and practising and practising when I was playing football and working on a market stall.

It's not just the practice. I'm not saying that. I don't have the talent that he has. I have never swung it like Rory McIlroy. When you look at guys like him, who swing the club that naturally and are that talented, you don't envy them. There's nothing you can do about it. Your DNA is your DNA.

If you look at how Tiger Woods swung it as a three-year-old, you would recognise his swing as an adult. You hold a lot of that DNA through all your years of playing. You just try and fine-tune it. That's why some guys are natural and some guys aren't. Padraig Harrington is not a natural. He wasn't the straightest hitter as a kid. He was erratic and he changed his swing a million times.

There are a number of players who have done exactly the same. There are guys who have to work really, really hard at maintaining what they have and getting better, and there are guys who don't have to work hard at all. Rory doesn't have to work very hard because it is so natural for him to swing a golf club.

For me, it's a bit of both. I think I swing it pretty well, but I have had to work really hard to get to that point. It's not entirely natural. I still have the same tendencies I had when I was an assistant at Chesfield Downs. I have always taken my swing slightly outside the line on the way back. I have always laid off at the top and, because it has been laid off, I can get myself in a position where it is not pulled down on the perfect line. It took me years to make the changes I needed to.

My timing always needs to be right for me to be absolutely flushing it. I have quite a bit of leg movement. These are all minor flaws I am constantly trying to improve. I am hyper mobile, so it is easy for me to let the club run on, as opposed to holding it short in the backswing. I play my best golf when I have got it shorter than parallel, as opposed to past parallel.

There are all these little things that have been the same since I first started playing, but I manage them better today than I did back then. That's the same as everybody. Every-body will have essentially the same traits they did when they were younger. There are not many guys that will swing a golf club early in their teens and change their style so much as to be unrecognisable by the time they reach their thirties.

It was coincidence, but I played some of the best golf of my career while Tiger was taking his break from the game. I had a six-week break myself in September and October 2009, and then came back and won the Singapore Open at the start of November. That was a huge boost because it was one of the first tournaments that counted towards Ryder Cup qualification for the following autumn at Celtic Manor in South Wales.

A few months after that, in February 2010, I won the biggest event of my career so far, the WGC Accenture Match Play Championship in Tucson, Arizona. That was a massive victory for me: my first tournament win in the US, and it pushed me up to a new high of fifth in the world rankings.

Winning in Tucson was the next best thing to winning a Major. I beat Justin Leonard, Adam Scott, Jeev Milkha Singh, Thongchai Jaidee and Sergio García on the way to the final, shooting twenty-seven birdies. I was playing beautifully and, in the thirty-six-hole final, I beat Paul Casey four and two. It was a great boost. It counted on the Order of Merit on both the European and US tours, which made it even bigger and strengthened my position for Ryder Cup selection.

Tiger returned for the Masters a couple of months later, but my good form continued. In fact, I was the joint leader of the Masters with Lee Westwood going into the third round. I had a great chance to press forward and try to win the tournament, but I started my round on Saturday in the worst possible way.

The big mistake came on the first. I hit it way left, which rattled me a little bit because, when I had been warming up on the driving range, I had never hit it so well. It was flawless. Then I got on the first tee and hit it fifty yards left on to the ninth hole.

I wasn't sure why I hit it that far left, and I got on the next hole and hit it left again. I made two great pars on the first two holes after those poor tee shots. I started to settle down and recover, but then I made bogeys on five and six. I clawed those back with birdies on seven and eight, and then bogeyed eleven and double-bogeyed twelve.

Let me tell you a bit about the twelfth at Augusta. It's the par three that's the centrepiece of the Amen Corner complex. The twelfth is one of the most beautiful and most devilishly difficult tests of golf in the world. It is one of the top ten hardest par threes on the planet and when you factor in the pressure that is always on you at Augusta, it makes it even more difficult.

You are talking about a par three that is 145 yards. The flag at eleven is only sixty foot away from you when you are standing on the twelfth tee. You can see that flag blowing straight in your face and yet you stand on that twelfth tee box and you know it's straight down wind. If it's 145 and it's into the wind, it's like playing 160. So sixty feet to your left, it's playing 160 yards. But on the tee box, it's playing downwind and it's like playing 130 yards.

So you are trying to deal with a mental adjustment of

thirty yards and reminding yourself that the green is only eight yards deep. That's like preparing to take a penalty in a football match and looking at a goal that is only three feet by three feet. If you are eight yards short, you are in the water. It is one of the most volatile holes in the sport. It feels like you are trying to land your ball on a table-tennis table. It is ridiculously tough. Look at the guys over the years that have made double or triple there. It has ruined scorecards, mine included.

I rallied at the end of the round and finished with a 74. It was a good 74 and I still thought I was in with a chance, going into Sunday. But Mickelson shot 67, 67 in his final two rounds and ran away with it. I think the Masters probably represents my best chance of winning a Major and another opportunity had slipped away.

It's difficult to get the balance right with friends and family at Augusta, too. It is hard to rent a house and have twelve people stay in it and not get excited when you are leading the Masters at the halfway stage. It's hard to be in the house and turn the telly off when your friends and family are flicking it on, wanting to watch the coverage, and they are buzzing because you are leading the Masters.

It's hard because you just want to do your thing and shut yourself away. You want to be a hermit for the week and it is draining to have the television droning in the background with wall-to-wall coverage of the tournament. It's not that I want to get back to the house and go straight to bed, but you have to separate your brain from the golf for a while so it's not 24/7.

You can't deal with the pressure, the excitement and the

level of expectation over four days for twenty-four hours a day. You have got to have some break in there to get your mind off what you're doing. Everybody in that house wants you to win, but sometimes it's hard to get them to understand what you're trying to deal with mentally. Maybe it's something I'll change.

By that summer, though, people were finally starting to talk about me as a talented golfer, rather than someone who was all trousers and no bollocks. The win in Tucson had put me up to number five in the world, my highest ever ranking.

I was happy and confident and, when summer turned to autumn and the Ryder Cup approached, I knew that this time I wouldn't have to worry about whether I was going to get a wild card in order to secure my place on the European team. I was in the team on merit and ready to tear lumps out of the Americans again.

CHAPTER 24
Celtic Manor

How will I get on with Colin Montgomerie? That's what everyone seems to want to know. Am I nervous that he's the European Ryder Cup captain at Celtic Manor? Will I be able to play for him? Will our 'feud' get in the way? All that sort of stuff. It is a good job I qualified automatically, people say, because, after the fuss Monty had made about my wild card in 2008, there is no way he would have picked me out for one when, as captain, they are in his gift.

Well, I am certainly glad I'm not in a fight for a wild card. That much is true. But that's mainly because the competition is so intense and the quality of the players fighting it out so high. Luke Donald, Padraig Harrington, Paul Casey and Justin Rose have all failed to qualify automatically for the team and I wouldn't want to be the captain who leaves two of them out. In the end, Monty has to tell Justin and Paul that they will not be making the trip to South Wales.

I am not nervous about Monty being captain at all. Honestly. Even if we have had our differences in the past, I respect him as a golfer and I think he respects me back. That pitter-patter game of tennis in the papers is all a bit bollocks. He blows hot, I blow hot. He blows cold, I blow cold. That's what makes us feisty individuals.

As far as Celtic Manor is concerned, Monty is my captain and I am going to go out there and make sure I deliver for him. I am not afraid I'm not going to be able to perform at my best. When I am pulling a Ryder Cup shirt on, it makes no difference to me who is captain. Be it Monty or Olazábal or Faldo or Langer, I'll give the same. No difference at all.

Actually, I think Monty is a good captain at Celtic Manor. He is Monty, and Monty likes talking. Monty gets himself in his team room and loves to talk. There are not many guys who have played as many Ryder Cups as he has, so he has got every right to hold forth up there and talk about everything that needs to happen in the Ryder Cup. And that is what he does.

For the most part, the art of being successful as a Ryder Cup captain is making sure you can make twelve guys feel at home and comfortable. Okay, there are a number of players in there you probably don't have to worry about, but you have got a percentage of them that you do. It is that feel-good factor: how can I make sure that A, B, C and D are looked after in a way where they feel like they can deliver? How can I get them to play their best?

I don't really need any of that. I just need to make sure my Duracell batteries are put in that week and then let me go. I'm off and running and that's it. Everybody's different. Twelve individuals are in a team, there is no 'I' in team, and you need to look after whatever they need that week.

Some players like an hour's massage. Some players like ten minutes. Some players like a glass of wine. Jiménez – he'll have a glass of wine. Doesn't matter if it's the Ryder Cup, doesn't matter if it's the Welsh Open; Jiménez will have a glass of wine. That's his thing. Other players won't even sniff anything – drink-wise, I mean, obviously. Maybe someone's fallen asleep in his room when he should be in a team meeting. There's usually one. It gives everyone a laugh. It's fun and that's what makes it fun, because you don't have twelve robots. Everybody's personality that week makes it so enjoyable.

Does a player want still water or sparkling water in his room? Loads of little things like that. The captain has to look after the details. What's going to make that person do what he needs to do? It's getting all your ducks in a row so you don't even have to think that something is bugging one of your players.

The wives being well looked after? I've got to be honest, that's the least of the captain's worries at the Ryder Cup. There is stuff that they need to do and the women look after themselves. I don't mean to be insensitive but the last thing on a player's mind that week is making sure his wife is hunky dory.

Of course, they need to be involved. You want to share it with them, but they take care of themselves. We've got enough stuff on our minds. We don't have time to think about them. We're too busy. Sure, the Ryder Cup involves some ceremonial duties, but it's important to remember that, first of all, it's about trying to win the most famous golf competition in the world.

There are always a few last-minute hitches. At Valhalla, all the team outfits were held up in customs. Or you'll put your suit on and it doesn't fit. You've been measured for it and you would expect it to fit, but sometimes it just doesn't. So there's a seamstress at the end of the corridor and

she's fitting twelve suits on the eve of the opening ceremony. You've got to make sure all your shoes fit, that the
outfits are right and that your name's spelled right on your
bag. Søren Hansen's name was spelled wrong at Valhalla.

There is one thing that dominates the build-up to the
2010 Ryder Cup for the players, though. On the Tuesday
evening, three days before the competition starts, we all
gather in the team room around a telephone. Monty
switches it on to speaker so we can all listen and, from the
other end of the line, we hear the lovely, lilting, deep voice
of Severiano Ballesteros.

Seve is ill. He is very ill. He collapsed at Madrid airport
in October 2008 and tests had revealed that he was suffering from a malignant brain tumour. He has had four
operations and several courses of chemotherapy and,
although he isn't well enough to travel to Wales, he is able
to speak to us from his home in Pedreña, near Santander.

We don't know what is coming and it is very uplifting
for the team to hear his voice. Men like Monty and José
María Olazábal are great orators in their own way, and passionate men, but there is no one better than Seve to talk to
you about the Ryder Cup.

He is obviously in poor health, but he talks about the
Ryder Cup and what it means to Europe and her players.
This is the man, after all, who has done so much to make
the Ryder Cup what it is today, whose charisma has helped
to popularise it and reinvent it. He talks about the pride
and the passion and the drive you need to bring the trophy
back and put it where it belongs.

He talks for five or ten minutes. Everyone listens, spell-
bound. No one says a word. He is talking and so we listen.

We realise how poorly he is and so, of course, it is emotional. It is hard to hear someone suffering like that. When he speaks, we understand how much he wants to be there with us, because that is his life.

As he speaks, I think back to the images I have seen of him at Valderrama in 1997 when he was Europe's Ryder Cup captain. I listen to him and I sense he wants to live all of it with us, he wants to be with us, to know what it is like at Celtic Manor, to feel the spirit of the Ryder Cup one more time. You can't teach that or buy that. That's either in you or it isn't. It's in Olly and it's in Seve and it's in a number of players, including me.

The conversation with Seve adds to everything we learn that week. It makes it even bigger than it would otherwise be. The pressure builds even more, but in the right way, because you sense what it means to everybody and what it means to people who have played it, lived it, done it.

You know then what you have to do. The sense of drive builds within you even more. We don't need to speak to Seve to want to go out and win the Ryder Cup that weekend, but I think that ten-minute talk gives us all something extra.

How many opportunities will you have to sit and listen to Seve Ballesteros and then go out on a golf course and try to honour the way he performed over the years? I feel even more than ever as I leave the room that I am in a privileged position.

I am very confident going into the competition and, as a team, we are bullish about winning the trophy back. I had won the Wales Open at Celtic Manor in 2003, when I had red streaks in my hair to celebrate Arsenal winning the

FA Cup a couple of weeks earlier, and even though they have changed a few holes since then, I know I'll feel comfortable around the course.

I have won in Tucson, I've led the Masters and now I am about to play in another Ryder Cup. I couldn't be any happier. I am so eager, that I am the first player on either of the two teams to arrive at Celtic Manor. In fact, I am there before the captains and a lot of the officials.

I get there on Sunday morning, wander over to the range and start hitting balls by myself. There is no one else around and I just do my thing. It is absolutely fantastic to be there early, to soak up some of the atmosphere, to get ready. I am eager to play. I am bang up for it. I have had two weeks off. I am bursting to get out there.

Unfortunately, the weather is not quite in the same mood. It is absolutely awful. I am paired with Ross Fisher against Tiger Woods and Steve Stricker in the third match of the morning fourballs, and somehow play starts on time, but by 10 a.m. it has been suspended because of the pouring rain.

The course, and particularly the spectator areas, soon turn into a quagmire. A couple of times, I am standing over my ball and I look to my right or my left and see some poor guy sliding thirty or forty yards down a hill on his backside, powerless to do anything to stop.

There are reports of fans breaking their legs as they slide and fall down some of the steep banks in the slippery conditions. At one stage during the long suspension, I look out of the clubhouse windows and see that a river of water is flowing down the eighteenth fairway.

This is going to sound daft, but it is tiring just sitting

there with nothing to do. You have got all that nervous energy to spend and nothing to do with it. We know there is a rain delay, but we don't know when we are going back out. We have to manage that. Everyone is going stir crazy.

You are cooped up in a hotel. You can't go anywhere, can't hit golf balls because the range is under water and there's only a certain amount of food you can eat and fluid you can put in your body. Everybody's trying to get as much rest as possible because you know that, when you eventually do go out to play, you are going to be on it.

Monty has asked us not to tweet. Or he has said that, if we feel we have to tweet, at least be careful and don't do something that allows the tweet to become an issue. I respect that, but I have to tweet. I'm addicted. And during the rain delay, there is quite a lot of harmless fun to be had recording what the lads are up to. I post a couple of pictures of Padraig having a kip in the locker room which Sky, who are desperately trying to fill time, discuss for about an hour.

Ross and I had been 1up when play was suspended in the morning, but when the rain finally eases and the surface water drains away, we go back out in the early evening and Woods and Stricker turn the tables on us. They win the eighth and ninth holes to go 1up. We level things on the tenth before the heavens open again and play is suspended once more.

When we go back out on Saturday morning, things turn bad. Neither Ross nor I play well enough. I make two birdies during the entire round and Ross is similar. That's not good enough in fourballs, when you have got two chances on every single hole.

And it's certainly not good enough when one of the players you are up against is Tiger Woods. He and Stricker go back into the lead on the twelfth and keep us at arm's length relatively easily. We go up the eighteenth, still in with a chance of halving the match, but Woods and Stricker win the hole to finish 2up. No one likes losing, and this is horrible.

It hasn't gelled with me and Ross. I don't know why. I have played World Cup with him before. I have played a lot of golf with him. It isn't like we are strangers, but for some reason, it doesn't work. I don't know if it is him or me. It isn't a clash of personalities or anything like that. The spark isn't there. The click isn't there.

I mention it to the vice-captains. If something doesn't work, you don't want to repeat it. I say, 'I'm going to make a suggestion to you that that didn't work.' I say it might be that they need to put Ross with somebody else or me with somebody else to get the best out of us. I am just giving my opinion because I want to win.

I want to make sure that everybody else is capable of winning and, if I have an insight into how that might happen, I'm not just going to sit on my hands and keep my mouth shut. That wouldn't help anybody. It's about the team winning. It's about us getting to 14½ points to get that trophy back.

So in the next session, which was foursomes, Ross is paired with Harrington and plays some amazing golf. Maybe he feels more comfortable with Padraig. Harrington is really helping him read his putts and Ross is able to draw on Harrington's talents in a different way than he is able to pull on me. It works better for him and, when I go out with Luke Donald, it works better for me, too.

Because of the bad weather, the organisers sit down after the first day's play and decide to alter the format. What should have been three sessions of four matches is changed to two sessions of six matches, meaning that every player from both teams is involved in both those sessions. The intention is to try to finish the competition on schedule on Sunday. That doesn't happen.

Europe are a point behind when the rain-interrupted foursomes finally finish. The fact that Ross and I lose makes me even more pumped up to put that right during the rest of the weekend. It is the same dynamic that had worked for me at Valhalla. For the rest of the 2010 Ryder Cup, I feel like there is no way on this earth that any man or any combination of men is going to beat me.

When I'm in that mode, I am the type of player that will definitely piss opponents off. They want to stuff me as much as I want to stuff them. I don't see that as a problem. I see that as a compliment. I don't care who I play; I want to go out there and beat them. I want to get my match done as early as possible because I want to get back out on the golf course and go again so I can stuff someone else.

And I fully expect whoever I am playing to go out there and want to do the same to me. I have got absolutely no problem with that at all. If I am going to fist-pump on the first hole, I'm going to fist-pump. Nobody should take offence at that. It's not personal. I'm just going to show my passion and what it means to me to play Ryder Cup for Europe.

You might say it's screaming and hollering. It's not. Look, there is so much noise at the Ryder Cup, you can probably hardly hear me against the roars. Listen, bring it on. Let's go play golf. It's the Ryder Cup. Let's go and do it. If that pisses you off, so be it. If you can't show any passion in the Ryder Cup, something's wrong with you.

So I go out and play with Donald in the foursomes against Bubba Watson and Jeff Overton. At that point in his Ryder Cup career, Donald has never lost a foursomes. He'd played five and won five. I love playing with him, and his caddie, John, says that the way I am on the golf course fires Luke up as well.

You play foursomes with Luke and you know you're going to be on the fairway and you know you're going to be in a good position because he's going to back you up. He's a great player to play golf with, especially in that format. He is really, really solid. He can be quite quiet. I can't be quite quiet. Not in the Ryder Cup, anyway. And the difference is good. It makes us a really, really good pair.

It is a brilliant match from start to finish. We go 1up on the first when Luke sinks a great putt, but it swings back and forth until we win the eighteenth to seal victory, two up. We win our match and Fisher and Harrington beat Mickelson and Dustin Johnson. Those are Europe's only victories in the six matches, though. At the end of the second session, the USA hold a 6-4 lead. It is looking a bit messy.

CHAPTER 25
The Postman

On the Saturday at Celtic Manor, when things are going wrong and every match seems to be turning against us, there is a lot of agonising about why it is happening, why none of this is turning out how we have planned it and what we can do to turn things around.

I suggest changing the scoreboards. Not changing the scores – that would have been nice – but changing the actual scoreboards themselves. It sounds daft, I know, but for the first time, at that Ryder Cup, the scoreboards are digital rather than manually operated. And it takes something away.

The screens go black as you are approaching the green and they flick the coverage off so it won't disturb the players. But that means that the crowds and the players are robbed of the drama that is happening around the course.

On Friday, before the rains came, we had got off to a flying start and the boards were blue. Except you couldn't see they were blue because they kept being switched off. Stop the coverage, sure, but keep showing the scores on the left-hand side of the screen. It was killing the atmosphere because the spectators couldn't see the shifts in momentum.

That's part of the buzz. It's a big part of the Ryder Cup

experience. You hear the roar, the roar, the roar, the roar. If that board is blue, I want to see it. The momentum shifts are massively important. There aren't enough visuals at Celtic Manor. We need to feed off that stuff. So some of the tecchie guys work through the night to change the graphics and I think it helps. I think it helps massively.

Psychological things are important. We are down after the second session, but we start the third session, which is a mixture of foursomes and fourballs, really well. We can't finish the third session before the end of Saturday, but we want to make sure we do everything possible to keep the momentum of our recovery going when we restart on Sunday.

We have been wearing black and white with a touch of red for the start of that third session and we decide as a team that, even though there is supposed to be a new out-fit for each day, we will wear the same clothes to finish that session.

It is superstition, I suppose. Whatever is working, is working. So let's not change that feeling. Let's keep those boards blue. Let's go and get that bit done and see what happens. Everybody agrees we will wear the same outfits, and it all works. The boards stay blue that day. It is almost a clean sweep. We turn things around completely.

I play in the last match of the third session and, by the time I get to the first tee, those scoreboards I have been banging on about are bathed in beautiful blue. I am playing with Martin Kaymer in a fourball against Phil Mickelson and Rickie Fowler, and we jump on the coat-tails of our teammates straight away. We are 1up after the first, 2up after the second and 3up after the fifth. The whole team suddenly feels unstoppable. We are riding a huge wave of momentum. Everybody forgets the weather. The spectators are going mad.

It is another terrific game. Phil and Rickie come right back at us and level the match by the thirteenth, but then we pull away and win, 2up. I draw a lot of satisfaction from that win with Kaymer. I have played with three different partners at Celtic Manor and won with two of them. I take some pride in the fact that I am compatible. Just get me out on the golf course and let me play. Sure, it didn't work with Ross and me, but Ross gets out with someone else and wins. If you've got someone in the team who can only play with one player, it's a bit awkward.

By the end of the third session, the competition is totally transformed. Europe wins five of the six matches and halves the other. We go into the singles, which are now to be played on Monday for the first time in Ryder Cup history, leading 9½-6½.

Monday is a beautiful day. It shows the best of Wales: crisp, blue sky, the sunshine and the Vale of Usk. And what a day of golf it is, too. What a day to be involved in the Ryder Cup. What a day to be a sportsman somewhere near the centre of the best kind of drama that sport can bring.

I wind things up a bit before I even start my round. I am going out fifth in the order and have been drawn against Matt Kuchar. Kuchar is the form guy on the American team. He has been on a hot streak on the PGA Tour and he hasn't lost a match at Celtic Manor. I am supposed to be the underdog, but I don't see it that way.

Sometime before we are due to go out on Monday

morning, I do a television interview at the range with Tim Barter from Sky. When Tim asks me what I think my chances are against Kuchar, I tell him what I have already told my captain. 'I will deliver my point,' I say.

Tiger is watching, apparently, and goes rushing straight down to the locker room to tell Kuchar. He is incensed by what I said, I'm told. My teammates seem rather amused by it all. They start calling me the Postman after that – because I always deliver.

A lot of people claim what I said was disrespectful. I'm sure Tiger was telling Kuchar it was disrespectful. I don't blame him. I would have done the same. He was just trying to fire his guy up. That's what the Ryder Cup is all about: passion. Whatever you feel you have to do to believe, you just have to do it.

I didn't mean any disrespect to Kuchar, although I suppose it's hard not to sound disrespectful when you say you're definitely going to beat someone. But I said it for a reason. I'm not sure I could have wanted to win any more, but saying it puts even more pressure on myself to win. I will be hammered if I don't win after that comment. I also want to show my team how confident I am. I feel very good at the time. It comes off. It's fine.

I didn't say it an obnoxious way, but the Americans take offence. It gets under their skin. That's fine, too. I tend to do that in Ryder Cup week. But, as far as I am concerned, I was asked a question and I answered it. It's the Ryder Cup. You've got to have the mindset that you're going to win. I don't want any other mindset, put it that way.

Yes, the Americans probably want to punch me in the face. I rile them up. I guess it's because I'm one of the most vocal in the team. I have got form in Ryder Cup, which is very, very good, so you know they want to shut you up. They don't like the fist-pump and they don't like the fact that you are getting your crowd fired up.

I'm not sure if they get intimidated by me. I doubt it. These guys are seasoned professionals at the top of their game. But they are certainly told to shut me up, that I do know. That's fine. I am one of the loudest people in the European team. I am someone that tries to get everyone fired up. It's crazy what the Ryder Cup does to me.

Nobody likes being beaten and I have dished out some punishment at the Ryder Cup. I have come up against a number of players and I have played fifteen, won twelve and lost three. I have put a lot of points on the board. There have been a lot of fist-pumps in there.

But what I do is no different to Bubba Watson and Keegan Bradley firing their crowd up. That is what they will do for the first two days at Medinah in 2012. In fact, Bubba will go considerably further than I have ever been before. And you can't be any more vocal than Phil Mickelson or any more pumped up than Keegan. At Medinah, Keegan's caddie, Steven 'Pepsi' Hale, will get so pumped he will start whirling one of the flags around his head after the US win a hole.

I know the Americans want to take me down. Steve Stricker says that at a press conference before Valhalla. He says he wants to shut me up. That's fine. It is no secret they want to beat you. That's fine, too. I want to beat them, as well. And it's fun. That stand-off is fun. It's part of the magic of playing the Ryder Cup.

I beat Kuchar 5&4, by the way. I am 3up after ten, four up after eleven and five up after fourteen. Game over.

I play great. I play unbelievable. I make birdie after birdie after birdie. I am six under par after fourteen holes. I am flying. Look, I have got respect for Kuchar. He is someone who has played phenomenally in the last few years. But that doesn't count for anything on an occasion like that. Ryder Cup is one-on-one and I want to put a point on the board and take you down. That day, I do my job. I deliver my point like I said I would.

There is no room for any sympathy for Kuchar. None at all. You should never feel guilty about beating anybody. I take my hat off and shake his hand to show my respect for him. The respect level is no different whether I have beaten him heavily or it is all square. I wanted to win that match, so there is no point feeling sympathy. After I win, I look up at the scoreboard. I know things have been going slightly awry, but now I realise it is all in the balance. The US has mounted a brilliant comeback. Mine is the third match to finish. The first two have been won by America. So now the score is ten and a half to eight and a half in Europe's favour.

The problem is that Jeff Overton, Tiger, Mickelson and Zach Johnson are all ahead in their games, and the others are too close to call. It is going to be tight. I have to do a few television interviews and then I decide to head out and watch Edoardo Molinari's match against Rickie Fowler.

By this point, Rory has halved his match with Stewart Cink and Luke Donald has beaten Jim Furyk so we are twelve-nine up. Miguel Ángel Jiménez beats Bubba. That's

13-9. GMac is neck-and-neck with Hunter Mahan in the last match, but if Molinari beats Fowler, GMac will only have to halve his match for us to win the trophy back.

And Molinari seems certain to win. He was 4up after twelve and, even though Rickie has clawed a hole back at the thirteenth, Edoardo is still 3up with three to play when I catch up with the match. I walk down the sixteenth with them. I think I'll see Edoardo close out the match. Rickie wins the hole.

On the seventeenth, Edoardo misses a putt for a birdie. Rickie drains his. Rickie wins the hole. Edoardo is 1up with one to play. By now, Mickelson has beaten Peter Hanson, which leaves the competition score at 13-12 to Europe. Molinari and Fowler go to the eighteenth. Fowler has a fifteen-foot putt to stop Molinari winning the match. He drains it. He wins the hole. He halves the match.

That makes it $13\frac{1}{2}$-$12\frac{1}{2}$ to Europe. Soon after that, Zach Johnson completes a comfortable victory over Harrington. The scores are tied at thirteen and a half. It is all down to the last match out on the course: GMac against Hunter Mahan.

I haven't gone down to the eighteenth green with Rickie and Molinari. I can sense the way it is going. I stay back on the fairway and, as soon as Fowler's putt disappears into the cup, I turn around and head back to watch GMac. I am nervous but I am still confident. There is a reason Monty has put GMac out in the last game. He is the reigning US Open champion. He is in brilliant form. He is the man to get the job done.

I manage to get back to them when they are halfway up

sixteen. GMac had been 3up. Now, he is just 1up. If Mahan halves the match, the USA retain the Ryder Cup. It is all on GMac. Simple as that.

He has a long putt for birdie at sixteen. He judges it beautifully. It rolls all around the cup as the crowd holds its breath and then there is a monumental roar as it drops in. He is 2up with two to play.

They move to the par-three seventeenth. I head towards the green. I have never witnessed scenes like this at a golfing event. The marshals have been overwhelmed by the crowds. There are fewer of them than there should be, presumably because the competition has spilled over into an extra day. All semblance of order has disappeared. It's chaos, and chaos and golf don't normally go together.

There are 35,000 fans around that seventeenth green. There are no ropes anymore. It is close to madness, a wonderful kind of madness. GMac tees off first. His ball comes to rest on the fringe at the right edge of the green. Mahan mishits his tee shot and comes up short of the green. Both men march up to the green to gauge their next shots. The crowd has moved forward by then. They are practically on the green now.

Mahan goes first. He fluffs his chip shot. It only goes a few feet. He looks at it with horror in his eyes. The crowd goes wild. My heart is pounding and pounding in my chest. GMac has two putts to halve the hole. Two putts to win the Ryder Cup for Europe. He leaves his first putt four feet short. Mahan misses his putt and concedes the hole and the match.

Bedlam. Bedlam. Bedlam.

I am on the green straight away – along with 35,000 other people. It is utter chaos. I manage to get to GMac and cup his face in my hands and just scream with joy. There is an overwhelming feeling of elation. I haven't experienced winning a Ryder Cup at home before. It is beautiful. The crowd is singing and cheering. Champagne is spraying. It feels like it is raining champagne. It's nuts.

I get quite scared at one point. It actually gets really dangerous. There is a friend of mine, Ken Parker, in the crowd with his son, who is about eight years old at the time. I see them as everyone rushes on the green as Mahan concedes the hole. It feels like a stampede. I am panicking because Ken and his son are right behind me. It is so chaotic that, if his son goes down, he is going to get trampled. Fortunately, that didn't happen.

Some people, including Rory and some other players and a few journalists, manage to get off the green by forming a kind of long conga line, but the situation still seems close to getting out of hand.

Eventually, it eases and I walk up a steep grass bank to a point where some buggies are waiting in a line. I hop on one and we drive back down the hill towards the clubhouse. The fans are marching, too, marching down the Welsh hillside like a tired but victorious army. They have just witnessed something very special. A sporting epic has been fought out at Celtic Manor.

It is still chaos. Great chaos. The right chaos. The celebrations are phenomenal. I am flinging shoes off the clubhouse balcony. I am hosed with a jeroboam of champagne by Thomas Bjørn and we are all spraying champagne over the fans below. There are sing-songs in the team room followed by the press conference. Then we get ourselves together for the closing ceremony.

There is a big picture of Olazábal and Seve in our team room, the one with Olly using Seve's shoulders for leverage as he jumps up to try to see something in the distance. It is a famous picture. A lovely picture. It has meant even more to us since Seve spoke to us on the eve of the competition.

Billy Foster and a couple of the other caddies take it down and put it on the steps of the stage. As we go to take our seats, the American players and the European players have to walk right past it. You can't miss it. It is perched right there, up front and centre. Just where it should be.

CHAPTER 26
Distractions

In 2011, I moved house. Well, I tried to move house. I had bought another plot of land in the same gated community, this time in one of the prime spots right by Lake Nona, and my new place, the dream home for me and my family, was being built from scratch. Things didn't go smoothly.

At the beginning of 2012, when I was knocked out of the World Match Play Championship in Tucson in the first round by Bae Sang-moon, Nick Faldo gave an interview to the *Daily Mail* where he said he was worried I had too much going on away from the golf course. It wasn't the first time that criticism had been levelled at me and usually I railed against it. This time, for once, I found it hard to argue.

Look, I'm OCD. I've already mentioned that. My walk-in closet has to be just so, all nicely laid out, perfectly neat. The creases in my trousers have to be right. I'm hands-on. I'm a control freak. So, if I build a house, if I invest more money in a project than I've ever invested in anything before, there is no way in this world that I am just going to sit back and let other people take charge.

There are some people out there who would have just paid the money, gone away for a year, trusted everyone else to do the job, turned up when the house was ready and moved in. Some people might be happy to do that, but I'm not. It's not me.

This is a big house and the building work dragged on a year longer than it should have done because the builder didn't manage the job properly. I was naïve, too, which isn't something I'm proud of. I learned a lot of lessons. I signed some contracts without putting penalty clauses in for breaches of delivery dates. I won't be doing that again.

The whole thing was a painful process. The idiot that was building my staircase was nine months late delivering and fitting it. The front door was several months late. The flooring was delayed. The tiles from Italy were delayed. It was one thing after another. It was just laughable, in the end, that something could get that far out of control.

I was getting seriously pissed off. I wanted to be in my new house. It got to the spring of 2012 and we still weren't in and it was a year behind schedule by then. My fourth child, Joshua, was born in January 2012 and, because we were still in our old house, we didn't have a bedroom for him.

I know that probably sounds spoiled and, yes, we made do. But having a baby and trying to move house at the same time is stressful. Katie was stressed. I was stressed. She was heavily pregnant and we didn't have a bedroom for the baby. Parents like to decorate a nursery for their new baby. We couldn't do it. We were supposed to have moved in five months before he was born. It made me tense.

Why should I accept all these delays from so many people who are unable to pull this thing together to the point where my newborn baby doesn't have a bedroom?

That's just ridiculous. People are crying out to do good work and to be paid good money. I didn't go to the cheapest staircase maker. I was putting premium products in and I expected to get premium service, and that's not what I got.

So, yes, the house was definitely a distraction. Especially when the new house, the half-built house, the house that people didn't seem able to build, was 800 yards from the driving range and the phone went whenever something had happened. I was hitting balls thinking, What have they done now?

It's annoying when you can see the way it's going.

'You'll be in by the end of November,' someone says.

November comes and goes.

'You'll be in by the end of December,' someone says.

December comes and goes.

'You'll be in by the end of January,' someone says.

You look at the house at each juncture and listen to their promises and think, No way. I'm not a builder and I can work that one out. That was a pain in the arse.

I was hands-on. Totally hands-on. I chose everything: granites, cabinets, doors, handles, screens, sofas, materials, power sockets, door brackets, every frame for every picture and the design of the house itself. I hand-selected all of them myself with the help of our interior designer, Angie Kline. I was way too involved. Way, way, way too involved.

My obsession with detail is everywhere in my personal life and in my career. There are a million ways it manifests itself. If I walk past the table in the dining room at home and one of the chairs has been left at a slightly crooked angle, I have to straighten it. I like all the labels on the tins and packets in our cupboards to be facing the right way, too. I don't have time to do that all the time, but we have a nanny/helper and, luckily, she's detail-orientated too, so she does it for me.

When I'm out on the course, I have to have a full bag of tee pegs. It stresses me if there aren't enough. But I will only carry three tee pegs in my right-hand pocket when I'm playing. I don't know why, because I usually don't like the number three.

I can't use a number three golf ball, for instance. That's a legacy of my friendship with Lee Scarbrow. When I worked with him at Leighton Buzzard, he used to tell me to make sure I took all the number threes out of a pack of a dozen balls if he was going to use it. That was his stupid superstition that fed its way into me.

I asked him once why he refused to play with a ball with the number three printed on it and he said it was because he would three-putt with it. That was it, then. I was infected with that superstition, too. So I had to sift all the number three balls out of every box of Titleist I ever used.

When Terry Mundy started caddying for me, it used to drive him mad. In the end, he hit on a solution. He asked me if I'd got any objection to balls with five, six, seven or eight printed on them. I said I hadn't, so we switched to the higher numbers. Problem solved.

Then there's the coin that I used to mark my ball with. I used to use a regular ten-pence piece, but when I marked my ball, I always made sure that the Queen's head was facing upwards to the sky. Not just that; her head could not be at an angle to the hole. It had to be aligned so that her head was facing the hole. That was a trait I couldn't get rid of. I used to spend ages twisting it and moving it on the green so it was at exactly the right angle.

I thought I'd kicked it when I commissioned a special ball-marker with my kids' names on it. But I made a critical error. I added the IJP Design logo to the coin and pretty soon I found myself up to my old tricks again. Instead of the Queen's head, I became obsessed about making sure the logo was lined up correctly when I marked my ball.

My golf shoes have to be clean all the way through my round. If I've been in the bunker, I make sure all the sand is off them when I get to the next tee. I like cleaning my golf shoes myself. But that's nothing new. When I was a kid, I turned the act of cleaning my football boots into an art form. I'd clean them of dirt, stuff newspaper inside them to make them dry evenly and then polish them up the next day. I always had perfect football boots. I took great pride in all my possessions back then, and I still do today.

I have to have all my clubs in order in my golf bag, too. All the irons have to be in number order. I arrange them so they're all neatly aligned, but then, when Terry picks the bag up and walks off down the fairway with them, they get all jumbled up again, so I have to sort them out on the next tee.

I arrange things for other people, too. When I go into the scorer's hut, there's always a row of pencils on the table where other players have signed their cards and then just discarded their pencil. There are often ten or twelve pencils lying there. I can't leave them like that. I have to line them all up neatly and make sure the erasers on the end are all the right way up and that the sponsor's name on the pencil is facing outwards so you can see it. Some of the other lads know I've got a thing about it and they'll swish them across the table when they come in, just to wind me up.

When GMac, Justin Rose and I fly back to Orlando in a private jet, I've perfected a way of packing our clubs into the luggage area. I like to pack the back of the plane efficiently. I can't stand it when people leave their suitcase or their clubs on a seat in the plane. I often have to unpack the back of the plane and then pack it up again more neatly. It has got to the point now where GMac and Justin dump their bags on the tarmac when they arrive because they know I like to pack for them.

What I worked out was that, if you take the woods out of the golf bags, you can pack the bags standing up and then load the suitcases around them to keep them upright.

What else? Well, I iron the snooker table at home before I play to make sure the baize is absolutely perfect. And when I park my car in the garage, the wing mirrors have to be lined up exactly the same as the other cars beside it. Some of them are on lifts at the moment, but I want to get to a point where I can have them all spaced out neatly on the same level. I'd like them lit nicely, too. Having those cars – that's my art.

When I go into the pro shop at Woburn, I like to straighten the shirts and arrange them in size order, just like I did at Chesfield Downs in the old days. In fact, any shop that I go in, if I ever take an item of clothing off a shelf and then decide I don't want it, I have to make sure that I fold it up neatly and put it back exactly where it came from. You see some people just put stuff back loosely and unfolded. I can't do that.

I do take an awful lot of time over my yardage book, too, particularly if it's a Major. I normally get there on the Monday before the event and I draw in my green lines (the paths I think putts will take) during my practice rounds. I'll draw them on grid lines, like a little sketch. But then things get way more complicated. I have a routine I like to go through where I mark out a space in yellow highlighter pen in the top right-hand corner of each of those boxes so Terry can write in where the pin is on each day, on each hole.

I measure those pages practically to the millimetre. I measure from the top of the page and the lines have to be parallel. Look, graphic design was the only thing I was good at when I was at school. I have to use it somewhere. Terry adopts a long-suffering attitude to all this. He'll come up to me at the start of the week to get my yardage book and he'll open it and look at the detail. If it's the full Monty, the yellow highlighter pen and everything, he'll look at me and say, 'It's a Major this week then, is it?'

My OCD tendencies don't make life easy for Terry. I like him to have a particular kind of Sharpie so that he can draw the line on my ball nice and thin. If I bogey a hole, we change the ball immediately, and I try to give that ball to a kid in the crowd. I have seven brand new gloves at the start of each week. If there's a Wednesday pro-am, I use one of the new gloves until, perhaps, the last five shots of the day and then I fold it up and put it away and get another new glove out to wear it in a bit for the next day. I always take two drivers to an event. I had one stolen in China four years ago and I didn't have a back-up. They caught it on CCTV. I'd left it outside the locker room in the clubhouse and some bloke came up and got it out of the bag and took a few practice swings with it. Then he just sauntered off with it. So I'm not getting caught out like that again.

Sometimes, I take a duplicate set of wedges, in case the greens are very firm and I need extra spin. I have a three-wood in my bag, a three-iron hybrid and a four-iron hybrid. I have a windproof top and a waterproof suit. I take six pairs of shoes to every tournament, which are, of course, colour co-ordinated with the outfits I will wear on each day. I have to take an inhaler for my asthma, too.

I have sun cream, a ball-line marker, twelve balls and a penknife. I always take a penknife. You never know when you might need a penknife. A thread might come loose on your shirt or you might need to cut a lace. Or you might have to sharpen your pencil when you are filling out your scorecard. Terry likes to fill the bag with new pencils, but that drives me mad. So I take the penknife.

That's what my OCD is like, so it's not really much of a surprise to anyone close to me that I got over-involved when we were building the new house. And yes, okay, the people who said I was doing too much at that time were right. But I'm the type of character that likes to be busy in my brain. I always have been and always will be. Time management is something I am terrible at, but I'm trying to get better. I've got Chad here now to try and help me with that. And Terry keeps me on track, too.

Faldo also said I spent too much time playing with my mobile. Okay, guilty. I do want to get to a stage where I can turn the phone off for several hours and do what I need to do. I don't turn my phone off on the range when I'm at Lake Nona, in case Katie calls.

When I'm on the range with Chad, then my phone will go on silent. If it's buzzing, he can look at it. Most guys don't turn their phones off unless it's tournament day or tournament practice. Everybody's phone rings while they are on the range. It's not just me, but, yes, I am probably too reliant on it.

Again, though, it's partly just my personality. I can't help it. People ask me how I unwind and the answer is, I don't know if I ever unwind. We don't really go on that many family holidays. Our holiday, mainly, is having a six-week stay in the UK during the summer, although, obviously, I'm playing golf for some of that time. I go to Orlando Magic games as much as I can, but that's another way of spending more time with Katie and the kids.

We finally moved into the new house in May 2012 and things improved massively then. It was a huge relief, but it also felt like a great achievement. More than anything else, I suppose, that house is the embodiment of how much success I have had in my career and what I have been able to provide for my family.

I am a patriotic Englishman. I will always love my country. But Florida is home now. The standard of living I have been able to create here for my family is very nice. To be able to get the kids playing outside all the time is great.

When the sun shines, there is no better place in the world than England. There is no humidity in the English summer, very few mozzies but the odd horsefly that might bite, and it is perfect. But when it gets to October and it starts to get a bit miserable, then give me Orlando every time.

Katie and I had got married back in England at the end of September 2007. I'd only kept her waiting for eleven years. People had begun to tease us, and particularly her, about whether we were trying to set a world record for the longest ever engagement, but I wanted it to be a big day. I wanted it to be the perfect day for her and I wanted to be able to put some proper money behind it.

I didn't want a small wedding. I had worked and worked to get my Tour card. I had earned a big chunk of cash in the first year, but then we bought a house and the cash went. I was happy being engaged, anyway, and I was happy we had Aimee and Luke when we did. It wasn't that getting married was ever put on the back burner, but it wasn't a desperate necessity either.

My brother got married and then divorced. My dad and his brothers were all married and then divorced. I'm not saying Katie and I ever would, but I just didn't want it to go wrong. I wanted it to be a meaningful day. Not that a tiny do wouldn't have been meaningful, but I have always had a want for bigger and better things.

I am one of those people who says, 'Go big or go home.' You know, do it or don't do it. And it was one of those 'do it' days. If you are going to tie the knot, then tie it properly.

We hired the putting green at Woburn Abbey and, because I have got a great relationship with the Duke of Bedford and Woburn, where I'm the touring professional, they allowed me to put an enormous marquee on the putting green lawn, which looked out towards the house.

We had the reception in the Sculpture Gallery with just over 200 guests. Then we had 400 or more people in the evening. It was big bash. I had my old schoolteachers there – the ones I got on well with, anyway – my old schoolmates, some ex-sponsors. Beverley Knight sang in the evening, which was awesome, and Spoony rolled the decks. We had sushi, a hog roast, Indian, Asian. I wanted a bit of everything.

It was emotional. We had waited a long time. It was Katie's day. I wanted to make sure it was great and it was. I was very nervous about making a speech, but I got through it. I wasn't born to make public speeches. I might look different on TV, but it's nice to have a little barrier there. That barrier isn't there when you're standing with a microphone in front of all your closest friends. I am still the same guy I was when I was working in a pro shop, and I have kept all my old friends.

When we finally moved into the new house, it felt like everything was complete. Katie and the kids love it in Orlando, and I do, too. But, ultimately, the choice of where we live is about golf. October through March is the best time to be in Orlando, and October and January are the months when I get chunks of time off from the playing schedule. So those are the two opportunities I have to work really hard to get my game in shape. And I can't do that in England because of the weather.

I intend for us to be here for a long time. That's why I have invested my money in making sure I am comfortable in my house and have also bought a holiday home in the Bahamas. My money's invested Stateside. Aimee has got an American accent. Luke hasn't. If Aimee was to talk to you on the telephone, you would have no idea she had ever set foot in England. But she can switch on her English accent, too.

Of course, I miss my wider family and I miss the friends

I have back in England, who I only get to see for a few weeks of the year. I miss the TV. I miss my Sky Sports remote control and I desperately miss bacon. A nice, juicy piece of bacon. You can't beat a good bacon butty.

Even though we've got PG Tips and stuff here, there's something different about an English cup of tea, too. I don't know if the kettle boils the water a fraction hotter. I don't know if it's because the semi-skimmed milk in the UK is different to the two per-cent milk here. It just tastes different. Is the water different? I don't know what it is, but an English cup of tea is better than an American cup of tea.

And I miss a curry. I crave curry. All the years Katie and I were struggling for money, that was our treat: a Chinese or a curry. We went to Asda and ate in most of the time, so our weekly treat would be a curry or a Chinese on a Friday or Saturday night. For thirteen years, that was our routine.

You can get a decent Chinese in Orlando, but you can't get the Indian. That's tough. My doctor, who is Malaysian, cooks an absolutely phenomenal curry and we have got all of the ingredients and his recipe, so now we cook it ourselves.

The Chinese food is good. The sweet and sour chicken balls are not quite the same as the sweet and sour chicken balls back home, but there are some sacrifices you just have to make.

Still, there are compensations. I can nip round to Publix, our local supermarket, and buy a lovely piece of fillet steak and be back in ten minutes to stick it on the BBQ. Everything is easier about living here. There is a bank outside the gates and a post office, and there is so much space that parking is easier. GMac owns a great pub-restaurant round the corner called Nona Blue and sometimes we have get-togethers down there with some of the other golfers who live in the area.

It wasn't like building the house and the delays had wiped out my golf career, by the way. I had got on a roll at the Ryder Cup. And I stayed on it pretty much until the end of 2010. I played the Hong Kong Open in the middle of November and, in the second round, I shot sixty, my best ever score as a professional. I won the tournament by one stroke from Simon Dyson and then jumped straight into contention for the Dubai World Championship the following week.

I led by two shots from Ross Fisher going into the final day, but Robert Karlsson, who had been three shots back, caught me near the end and forced the tournament into a play-off. I thought I had won it on the first sudden-death hole when I hit a sand wedge to three feet, but Karlsson almost matched it with a sand wedge that he got to within four feet.

On the second extra hole, things unravelled for me. I had a pitch to the green but I left it slightly short. Karlsson had a similar shot and hit it stiff again. Effectively, I had a thirty-foot birdie putt to force the play-off into a third hole. But as I bent down to mark my ball with my platinum ball-marker, which has got my kids' names engraved on it, I picked the ball up and then dropped it. It landed on the marker and flipped it forward by a centimetre.

I wasn't sure what the rule was, so I called over the referee, Andy McAfee. He told me it meant an immediate one-stroke penalty. It felt tough. I didn't know that rule. I took my putt and missed. Karlsson now had two putts from four feet to win the tournament. He didn't miss. Karlsson probably would have won anyway, and at least my misfortune gave some of my Ryder Cup buddies cause for amusement.

'Poults may not have won the Dubai World Championship,' Rory McIlroy wrote on Twitter, 'but he could be in with a shout for the tiddlywinks world championship.'

The next year didn't start quite as well, but in May 2011, with the house hassle in full swing, I changed all that when I played the Volvo World Match Play Championship at Casares in Andalucía, Spain. Things had been a little lean and I was not exactly brimming with optimism. In fact, when I found myself behind in an early match against Lee Westwood, I asked Terry, my caddie, if he knew what time the next flight back to England was.

But I halved that match with Francesco Molinari, and another one with Paul Lawrie, and squeezed through to the last sixteen. Then I had a ding-dong match against Westwood. Lee was in tremendous form. He had shot six or seven under, every round. After five matches, he was something crazy like thirty under par. He would have been leading any tournament – by a lot. He shot six under against me and I shot seven under. It was just one of those matches where I couldn't do anything wrong and I beat him at the final hole.

That put me through to a quarter-final against Francesco Molinari. I was two holes down against him, too, but I birdied the last three to win the match. My short game was in great shape that week.

The short game has always been one of my strengths, really. Why? Well, learning my trade on the par-three course at Chesfield Downs didn't hurt. My brother and I used to go over there and play four rounds around the par-three course, chipping and putting, chipping and putting, over and over and over again. It's ingrained in me. I have always been comfortable around the green, in terms of using my imagination and how I work the golf club through impact.

The part of my game that needs the work now is from 50 to 120. It's not the short game, but it's distance control. I need to put that extra effort in there because my stats aren't that good.

I'm happy hitting flop shots and chip shots and getting out of thick rough and playing bunker shots. That's the fun part. That's the imaginative side of golf. It's having that imagination to work out how to play around the greens. I always watched how Seve hit his chip shots and bunker shots. It was fascinating. He was the master.

There was no one better in the game of golf than him with the club he used. He never had any more loft than fifty-six degrees. He could do with a fifty-six-degree wedge things that people couldn't do with a sixty-degree wedge. That's how good Seve was.

That week in Andalucía, I never gave up. I was 3 down to Nicolas Colsaerts in the semi-final at one point and still had one shot to make up coming down the last. Colsaerts is a monster hitter and he smashed a 340-yard drive down the middle on the par-five eighteenth, which meant he would be going into the green with a six iron.

I knew I couldn't reach, so he was right in the driving seat. I laid up to my good number and got up and down for a birdie. He hit a poor approach shot and couldn't make birdie, so we went to an extra hole. The same thing happened again. He hit a massive drive and then put his approach shot in the greenside bunker. I laid up and then hit a great shot to five feet and holed the putt. I was in the final.

That was what it was like every game. I was down, I was down, I was down. I played Luke Donald in the final. If he won, he would overtake Westwood and claim the world-number-one spot and I struggled to stay on level terms with him. He went into the lead three times and three times I pegged him back.

After the turn, I eased ahead for the first time and when we reached the seventeenth, I was 2up. My approach there left me with a ten-foot putt for victory and I sank it. My son, Luke, was seven that day, 22nd May, and I had told him on the phone before the round started that I would bring him home a trophy. So now I rang him again and told him the trophy was on its way. He loved that. It made up a little bit for me not being there to celebrate his birthday with him.

The rest of the year was uneven. I missed the cut at the US Open at Congressional in Maryland and also at the Open at Royal St George's. Then Justin Rose and I finished second at the Omega Mission Hills World Cup in China and, in my final event of the year, I won the JBWere Masters in Melbourne with four rounds in the sixties. That victory moved me back into the top twenty in the world.

Joshua was born at the beginning of 2012 and then there was that loss to Bae Sang-moon in Tucson. But I finished seventh at the Masters in April, ninth in the Open at

Royal Lytham & St Annes, and third at the US PGA at Kiawah Island. If the European Ryder Cup captain, José María Olazábal, needed any reassurance about my form, those results provided it for him.

I just missed out on an automatic spot for the team for the 2012 competition at Medinah Country Club just outside Chicago, but I had finished eleventh on the Ryder Cup points list, I had a good pedigree in the competition and I was confident I would be chosen as one of Olly's wild cards.

My struggle to make the team on merit was partly a product of playing both tours. If you just play one, you have got a better chance because you are committing all to one side. By playing both, it's unlikely you will be high in the European rankings unless you play fantastically well in the WGCs and the Majors, which count on both.

I took the call from Olly the Monday before the Barclays tournament at Liberty National in Jersey City. I knew the phone was going to ring at some point because there was a press conference scheduled for the next day and I guessed that, whatever his decision was, good or bad, Olly would let me know.

I was in the apartment that I was renting for the week, which had a fantastic view of the Statue of Liberty, when the phone rang. Olly told me that Colsaerts and I were his picks. I was as excited as ever. I didn't know it then, but Medinah was to be the stage for the defining performance of my career so far.

CHAPTER 27
Bubba Golf

When Seve Ballesteros dies in May 2011, many of Europe's greatest golfers travel to his home village of Pedreña in northern Spain for his funeral. Three of Europe's most recent Ryder Cup captains are there: Colin Montgomerie, Nick Faldo and Sam Torrance. And so is the man who will lead us at Medinah, José María Olazábal.

Olly had been one of Seve's closest friends. Seve had been his mentor and hero when he was breaking through, and they had formed a magical partnership in the Ryder Cup. They played together fifteen times over the years and lost only twice. When Seve dies, Olly is overcome with grief. 'He has lost an older brother, almost,' Monty says at the time.

So it is inevitable and it is right that Seve should be remembered and honoured by the European Ryder Cup team at Medinah. He had inspired us in life at Celtic Manor and now he inspires us in death as we travel to the USA to try to win the competition that he had done so much to revitalise and popularise.

None of us know that an image of Seve is going to be on our golf bags and on the arms of our jumpers, until we arrive in the States. We know his name will be mentioned a ton of times, obviously, but adding the silhouette of

Seve punching the air after beating Tom Watson to win the Open at St Andrews in 1984 is a lovely touch.

'Seve always said that was the sweetest moment in his career, winning at St Andrews, making that putt to beat Tom Watson,' Olly says. 'It's tough for me; it's the first time Seve is not going to be with us at the Ryder Cup. He has meant a lot to me and to the team, and I wanted to have something that was present to each and every player.

'We came up with the idea that it would be nice to have Seve's silhouette, and so every time somebody gets to grab a club or something from the bag, they can see the silhouette. I thought it was important for us to have Seve's memory and presence during this week.'

The bags look old-school. The embroidery with Seve on the front pocket is awesome. When I get to my room and see my outfits laid out for each day of the Ryder Cup week and see the Sunday one in navy and white, which are Seve's colours, it is spine-tingling. It feels like it is going to be a belter of a week.

I am keen to get the balance right. I am aware that a lot of people in the media in particular are saying, 'Seve, Seve, Seve, Seve,' but we want it to be Olly's week, as well. It gets to the point where planes hired by a betting company are circling the course and writing *Do it for Seve* in smoke in the sky. I worry that Olly is being overshadowed a bit, that his captaincy is being lost in the understandable outpouring of sentiment about Seve.

Seve had been captain. He had had his famous captaincy at Valderrama. It is part of his legend. But that means there is an extra pressure on Olazábal to be a winning captain as well. He wants to enjoy what it will mean for him and Seve both to be winning captains. It is natural he wants them to be bracketed together. Because of that, if we lose, I think it will hurt him more than we could ever imagine.

After all my striving and all my excitement about playing in another Ryder Cup, I nearly blow it right at the last moment. On the night before the competition begins, after we go to the opening ceremony and sign all the stuff we are required to sign, I get involved in a game of table tennis with Sergio García and Peter Hanson and his wife, Susanna.

Sergio asks me to help him out because Swedes are pretty useful at table tennis, so I say, 'Go on, I'll have a quick game.' We have a little knock-up, the competitive instinct kicks in, the ball comes flying over the net and I lunge for a backhand. I catch my foot on a sofa, twist my left ankle and yell out in pain.

What have you done? I think. What on earth have you done?

Sergio looks really concerned. He comes over and tries to help me up. I tell him I am fine, but I am panicking inside. I get some ice to put on it and then I go straight to see the physio.

He gives me some anti-inflammatories and tells me we'll have to wait to see how the ankle reacts. I am in a reasonable amount of pain. I can't really put much weight on it. I wake up the next morning wondering whether it will have swelled up like a balloon, whether I'll even be able to walk on it.

I think about what it will be like telling the press what has happened. Or telling my captain.

'Sorry, Olly, I can't play; I tripped over playing table tennis.'

I wake up. I move the sheets aside and stare at my ankle. It hasn't swelled up hugely, but when I put my foot on the floor, it's sore. I start chewing Advil to get rid of the pain. I am thinking, How is this going to feel when I get to the range? It is sore when I walk on it, so how is it going to feel when I am hitting balls? How is it going to feel if I try to play thirty-six holes?

Shit, I think. This better not be an issue.

In the end, I am okay. I feel some discomfort before I go out to play in each session, but the second my adrenaline kicks in, I don't feel any pain. It doesn't matter where the ache is. It all goes away. Anything is possible with adrenaline. Boxers fight with broken hands and all that kind of thing. Nobody ever finds out about my ankle, but that was a scary twelve hours waiting to see how it would be. I did't get a lot of sleep.

The rest of the build-up is fun. Olly organises a kind of *Strictly Come Dancing* night one evening to bring a bit of light relief to the preparations. They get a couple of dancers in from the American version of the show, *Dancing with the Stars*, who do a bit of a display. Then some of the players have a go.

Some guys don't want anything to do with it, while others have a right laugh with it. I don't dance with anyone. I don't want to get involved. I have a tracksuit and hoodie on. I am just happy to be in the team room, slobbing. You go to your room after your day of practice and official functions and have a shower and put on anything you want. You don't do your hair. You just go down and relax.

Some people are dancing so, in the end, I get down and do the old-fashioned worm across the floor. Miguel Ángel Jiménez is one of the vice-captains and he is loving it. He is up for a drink every night, polishing the Rioja off at pace. He is up there, jigging himself. Martin Kaymer is up there having a bit. It is funny to watch. It is a little icebreaker.

Olly has put together a great video compilation, too. Everyone gathers round, Olly says a few words and then plays this emotional video to get us all even more pumped up. It shows the great shots we have hit in tournaments, the wins that we have had, shots in previous Ryder Cups. There is a team talk on Thursday night. It is short and to the point. He goes through the pairings and tells us to get out there and get after it.

We know the atmosphere is going to be hostile. Medinah is only about thirty miles west of Chicago, one of America's most passionate sports-supporting cities. And even though Olly and the US captain, Davis Love III, are two of the most dignified men in golf and remain diplomatic in the build-up, some of the players speak frankly about what the tournament means to them. One of those players is me.

At my press conference a couple of days before the competition begins, I say that, even though the players on both teams are normally all friends, there is a divide between us at Ryder Cup. 'There's something about the Ryder Cup that kind of intrigues me,' I say. 'How can you be great mates with somebody but, boy, you want to kill them in Ryder Cup?'

Some people, predictably, try to inflate the meaning of that comment. It is a turn of phrase. Of course I don't actually want to kill anyone on the American team. I just want to beat them on the golf course. Everybody knows what I mean, really. A couple of hours later, Brandt Snedeker talks about the European team at his press conference and says he wants 'to beat their brains in'. That's the kind of rhetoric that comes with the Ryder Cup. It's something and nothing.

I am paired with Justin Rose on Friday morning. Olly sends us out in the last of the four foursomes matches and we are drawn against Tiger Woods and Steve Stricker. What a start. I have only lost three Ryder Cup matches and two of them have involved Woods. I have never beaten him in the competition, so I want to make amends for that. It is a massive challenge.

The morning goes okay for Europe, but there are some worrying signs. One is the dynamic partnership between Phil Mickelson and Keegan Bradley, who crush Sergio and Luke Donald. Mickelson has sometimes not been at his best in previous Ryder Cups, but he looks like he is really enjoying playing with Keegan.

Tiger and Stricker do not play very well that morning, though, and Justin and I take advantage of it. From the fourth hole onwards, we are in the lead and they never get back on level terms. Tiger is a little wayward and Stricker is not one hundred per cent on his game. That makes it easier for us and we close it out on the seventeenth to win two and one.

Maybe some people have been expecting that there will be a hostile atmosphere between Tiger and me after the so-called revelations in Hank Haney's book. I've already told you what I think about those 'revelations'. There is certainly no hostility on my part, other than that I desperately want to beat him and put a point on the board for my team.

It isn't frosty, but it isn't friendly, either. I'm not going to start sharing a conversation with him. I'm with Justin and that's my conversation. The exchanges with Woods and Stricker are restricted to, 'Good shot,' 'Good drive,' 'Nice putt,' 'Nice chip,' and a shake of hands afterwards. That is as you would expect.

It is a big result for me personally to be part of a pair that has beaten Tiger Woods. It is brilliant to beat him, to be honest. Whether he plays well or badly, it is always good to beat him because it doesn't happen often in any form of the game. He has had the upper hand on me in the Ryder Cup and it is definitely a big scalp and a good point on the board to tie up the morning session at two-two before the team goes into the afternoon fourballs.

The mood out on the course isn't pretty. I wouldn't expect it to be. We're in Chicago, the home team has got the upper hand and the supporters are loud. There are a lot of nasty things said. You have got guys there drinking from seven in the morning until six o'clock at night, so unfortunately a few Bud Lights are going to get to them.

A few of them make unpleasant remarks about Seve. They cross the line. In fact, they go way, way over the line. There are times when the American caddies have to step in and say, 'Look, guys, enough. That's not what we're here for; we're here to play golf.' I don't want to make a big song and dance of what is said because it is just a couple of sad people who can't handle their drink.

For the most part, it is just a wonderful, nerve-tingling, properly hostile atmosphere. It keeps the needle pushing in a way that makes it particularly rewarding if you can turn things around.

I know I am not going to play in the afternoon. I have been told the previous day I am going to be rested for a session. Olly wants me fresh for Saturday. I am fine with that. I am not expecting to play five matches. I just focus on being ready when he needs me.

So after Justin and I win our match, I ask Darren Clarke, one of Olly's vice-captains, whether he wants me to go back to the hotel to try to get some sleep or stay at the course to support the other guys.

I want to be at the course, but I could do with a rest. Darren says that's fine. So I go back to the locker room, get a duvet and a couple of pillows and lie on the sofa in our team room with the telly on and manage to get an hour's sleep.

How you get your heart rate back down to be able to sleep after a morning when you've played Tiger Woods in the Ryder Cup, I don't know, but I doze for a little while. I can't rest for long, though. I want to get back out on the course.

Things aren't looking good. The Americans are on a roll. They are doing to us what we have done to them in so many recent Ryder Cups. They are feeding off the support of the crowd, which is going absolutely wild, and riding on the adrenaline. I've never seen an American team that pumped up and that together. They are playing as if they feel they are invincible.

The bottom line is that they have a really strong team. I would expect them to play well. Mickelson and Bradley are more than pumped. I have never seen Mickelson fist-pump as much. I don't know what Keegan is on, but he is going berserk. His caddie is whirling the flag around his head when Keegan holes a putt on fifteen. They have all that early momentum and they are absolutely lapping it up.

They are letting us have it. It is full on. They have got every right to do it, but it is unnerving. I haven't experienced too much like that before. Even Valhalla didn't feel as intense as Medinah. For Mickelson to be as pumped as that takes me aback. He is loving Keegan as a partner, he is loving adding points to the board and Keegan is loving playing with him. Even Jason Dufner is fist-pumping.

They are taking things up a gear from anything I have ever seen. Bubba Watson is playing with Webb Simpson and, on the first tee, he encourages the massive crowd in the stands there to keep on cheering and screaming while he hits his shot. This is proper rabble-rousing stuff. Not that I am against it. Actually, I admire it. They are taking the game to us.

I don't know if their opponents, Paul Lawrie and Peter Hanson, are unnerved by what Bubba does, but Watson and Simpson sweep them away. They beat them five and four. Mickelson and Bradley beat Rory and GMac, and Dustin Johnson and Matt Kuchar beat Justin and Kaymer.

We are fortunate that, in the last match of the day, Colsaerts produces a round of golf that is near miraculous. Playing with Lee Westwood, Colsaerts holes pretty much every putt he has in the match against Woods and Stricker. The US team is absolutely rampant and Colsaerts is like a bloke forcing back the tide. He makes eight birdies and an eagle in one of the most remarkable rounds a rookie has ever played at the Ryder Cup.

The match goes all the way down to the wire. Lee and Colsaerts prevail 1up, but the team score makes very uncomfortable reading at the end of that first day. The USA are 5-3 up and they have momentum on their side. Lots of it. At our team meeting that evening, Olly doesn't pull any punches.

Olly can be a mild-mannered guy. That's the side you see most of the time. But he isn't mild mannered in that meeting. He goes for us. We all get a bollocking. Olly explodes, and rightly so. His face and his mood have changed dramatically between Thursday and Friday night. We go into the team room and everyone is dead quiet, and then Olly lets rip.

I have never heard him speak in that way before. He is pissed off and he lets us have it. He says our performance, collectively, is not good enough from a Ryder Cup team of this stature. He says we need to sort it out. It is the Ryder Cup, not a monthly medal. He says we are better than this. We have to ride out their momentum and turn it round.

We are all quiet. Very, very quiet. There is not a lot you can say. After the way we have played, no one really has the right to make any objections. A couple of people respond, but not in an argumentative way. Your captain's giving you a bollocking and, when he's got the hairdryer out, you have to sit there and take it. We are being beaten fair and square. The truth is, it isn't even that close. And it is about to get worse.

CHAPTER 28
Where the Miracle Begins

That Friday evening, someone calls me over and says, 'You've got to see what Bubba did on the first tee.' I haven't seen the footage at that point. I sit down and watch the highlights and see Bubba whooping them up.

Olly sticks me and Justin out at the top of the line-up for the morning foursomes on Saturday. When the matches are revealed on Friday night, we are drawn against Bubba Watson and Webb Simpson.

The moment I see that, I know what I have to do.

I'm sitting with Justin.

'I'm going to give Bubba some of his own medicine tomorrow,' I say.

Justin looks at me, a little bit quizzical, a little bit worried. 'What do you mean?' he says.

'Wait and see,' I tell him.

It's a no-brainer, as far as I'm concerned. I'm going to let Bubba have it like he is letting us have it. If he wants to do that on the first tee, that's fine, but two can play that game. I feel it's important. Bubba needs to experience it from the other side. I can handle it, so let's see if he can.

I get to the first tee on Saturday morning. Team Europe is leading off and I choose to take the odd numbers, which means I'm teeing off first. There are about 15,000 fans around that tee, all going nuts. I stand on the tee, looking around, trying to take it all in. We are announced to the crowd. The crowd starts cheering and chanting and screaming, and then the US fans try to drown out the European supporters.

'USA! USA! USA!'

I peg it up and stand back off my ball and go through my routine. Then I start egging them on, exactly the way Bubba had done the day before. I cup my hands to my ears, as if to say, 'I can't hear you!' That sends the level up another fifty decibels. Then I stand up and hit my tee shot. I hit it a bit left into the bunker and Bubba doesn't hit the fairway either.

It's a fun thing to do, but, if you ask Bubba and he replies honestly, he is going to tell you that his heart rate is 185 right now, and if he says anything else, he is lying. His heart rate is absolutely through the roof. Mine is.

There is no way you can tee off on every hole like that. You'd have a cardiac arrest. Your heart couldn't take that. It is intense. You have got 15,000 fans going absolutely barmy. It is awesome, but it is unnerving.

It is the right thing to do to take Bubba on, but purely in terms of hitting the golf shot, it is horrendous. It's very hard to concentrate. I can't equate it to anything else I have ever done. It's like taking someone who is scared of heights up to the top of the Burj Al Arab, to the helipad, and asking them to tee off from up there.

It is bizarre, but it's good.

Look, I know Bubba's going to do it to us again. He's a crowd-pleaser, like me. That's his style.

Does the fact that he went bananas on the first tee the day before, whipping the crowd into a frenzy, have anything to do with him and Webb Simpson giving Paul Lawrie and Peter Hanson a good hiding? I don't know.

But I am not allowing that to happen to me and Justin.

It is not a case of proving a point. It is just me not allowing that to happen on my tee box. I'm not letting anybody do that over me. I don't mind him doing it as well, but I am not going to be intimidated.

It takes a toll, though. I'm walking down the first after I hit the shot and I feel like I need to control my breathing a bit. I need to bring my heart rate back down. It feels like I have been running at full pelt for five minutes and my heart rate is up to 190. And it has got there in twenty seconds.

I feel worse than Luke Donald did when I saw his hands shaking that time at Oakland Hills. I'm sure of it. My hands aren't shaking, but my heart is pounding. It is like a cartoon where you can see someone's chest expanding and contracting. It feels worse than the nerves I had at Oakland Hills. Worse in a good way.

Some American journalists write about those scenes on the first tee as if they are the death of golf. They say respect is leaving the game. They are appalled that players should be encouraging fans to yell while they are taking their tee shots. They say it is indicative of golf moving away from its traditions. They say it is being swamped by a new breed of fan who does not understand the game.

I have some sympathy for that view, which will strike some people as ironic, I'm sure. I'm partly responsible for the rise of that kind of behaviour in golf, I suppose, because of how I get so pumped up when I'm out on the course. I'm all for atmosphere in golf and the crowd getting involved, but there's a line to tread and occasionally things are said too early.

I see what happened with me and Bubba at Medinah on that first tee as a one-off, a product of the unique pressures and passions that the Ryder Cup creates. The fact remains that, if you are concentrating on a shot and someone screams on your backswing, it is off-putting. It has the potential to affect the outcome of a match or a tournament.

The whole gallery screaming is an atmosphere thing. Someone yelling out, 'Get in the hole!' on a 500-yard par five, rather less so. I don't know of any player that has ever got a hole-in-one on a par five. So that is very stupid. That's exactly what it is. It is also really annoying. Shout out something else. 'Hit the fairway!' would be more helpful.

'Get in the hole!' is even more annoying than 'Baba booey!' – whatever that is. Actually, I know what it is because I heard people shouting it so often at golf courses in the States that I made a point of finding out. It originated on Howard Stern's radio show, apparently, and kind of caught on. It has no particular relevance to golf.

I'm all for creating atmosphere, but let's not be stupid about it. Guys are trying to get themselves heard on TV – that's what it is. It's somebody thinking, I am going to go to a golf tournament today and I'm going to shout, 'Me nan wears pants!' It's really not very clever.

Maybe it's symptomatic of a different kind of fan being attracted to the game and, if that's the case, either I need to embrace it and understand it is going to happen, or this new breed of supporter needs to be educated to shout out something golf-related which actually makes sense.

'Mashed potato!' some of them shout. I don't get it.

What has that got to do with golf? It just doesn't sound right. I like loud and up and buzzing, but mashed potato? Baba booey? I don't get it.

The match between me and Justin and Bubba and Webb is loud all the way round. It is a great match. We go one up at the first hole. They peg us back to all square. They have the upper hand from the fifth to the ninth hole, but we get it back to all square on the ninth, go ahead on the tenth and take a two-hole lead on the twelfth.

We get our noses in front and keep them in front. It is tense. It is tight. Foursomes is an awkward game. It is a tricky format to get your rhythm and momentum right. Sometimes, you don't hit a putt for six holes. Your partner rolls it down, it's given, it's given, it's given, it's given and then suddenly you have to hole an eight-footer. Sometimes, it is really quite difficult to get into any flow. That's why it's one of the purest forms of match-play golf.

We hold on to win, 1up. But the jubilation I feel at winning another point is tempered by what I see when I look up at the scoreboard by the eighteenth green. Our match is blue. The rest of the board is red.

Westwood and Donald have been crushed 7&6 by Bradley and Mickelson. That match has been over for a while. Colsaerts and García have just lost 2&1 to Dufner and Zach Johnson. And half an hour later, Rory and GMac go down to Furyk and Snedeker.

So the score at the end of the third session is 8-2 to the USA. It is starting to look like an irretrievable situation. We are not just being beaten; we are being humiliated. I start to think it is slipping away. I realise we have to clean sweep them in the afternoon, just to get back on level terms.

You are looking at the board, always looking at the board, thinking, What's happening? What's happening? Are we able to gain any momentum of any kind? Pride kicks in. It's damage-limitation time. It's all so hectic and frantic. There's so little time to think. You play your match, you concentrate on your match, you get told you are teeing off again in twenty-five minutes, so you'd better have a quick bit of lunch and get going.

Do you need anything? Do you need a quick leg stretch? Do you need any treatment? You have a bite of food, get to your locker. You change your shoes or put a clean shirt on or change your outfit, some fresh socks, have a stretch with the physio to try to loosen you up again quickly, and that's it – you're back off to the tee. There's no real time to go and start hitting balls and doing warm up. You have a few putts and you go.

When I finish the morning match with Justin, it never crosses my mind that I am going to play with Rory in the afternoon fourballs. That hasn't looked like an option during the week. You have a vibe, you have a feeling about who you could potentially play with because you are put out in pairings in practice. Or vice-captains have spoken to you.

I have only played with Justin before at Medinah. But after we beat Bubba and Webb, Olly tells me I am going out with Rory. It's a shock. I don't see it coming. GMac and Rory have always been a partnership, but they have lost a couple of games and Olly wants to give GMac a rest so he is firing for the singles on Sunday.

García has played a lot of golf with Donald. That is a pairing that has done well in the past. They are paired together for this session as well. Rory and I are the last match out against Dufner and Zach Johnson.

By the time we get to the first tee, the first two matches have already turned American red. A thought flashes through my mind, an inevitable thought: If those matches stay red, we are ten-four down.

They stay red. Justin and Frankie Molinari lose five and four to Watson and Simpson. Colsaerts and Lawrie lose narrowly to Dustin Johnson and Matt Kuchar.

I have never partnered Rory in match play before. Sure, he is my mate and I know him and his golf game ridiculously well. I have played enough golf with him to know how he plays, but there are still lots of unknowns. Does he want me to help him read his putts? Do I ask him to help with mine? Justin and I do that, but I know the vibe with Justin. I don't with Rory.

We talk about it as we walk down the first.

'Let's do our thing,' he says, and that's it.

Everybody's different. He wants to do his own thing and that's good. You don't want to put someone off. He might see a putt going in firm and, if I see it going in soft, you have got two different lines.

It is a surprise to both of us that we are playing together. But he is the world number one. He is one of the guys I want to play with, so it's a good surprise. I think it's going to be a great pairing, but it goes flat. It goes flat for a number of holes. I find it very difficult to get into the game.

It is Rory's fourth match. He's tired. That's what you're going to be up against in the Ryder Cup. You are always fighting to stay fresh in your mind. Rory's last two games haven't gone well. That makes it worse.

I'm tired, too, both physically and mentally. I am weary from looking up at the scoreboards and seeing our team losing. It's draining the adrenaline out of my body.

Rory and I can't get anything going. We are 2down after two holes. For the first nine holes we are two under par as a fourball, and that is not good enough. The good shots we are hitting aren't being backed up with good putts. I'm missing putts and he is missing putts and we are struggling to stay in the match.

We talk as we go up the tenth hole, trying to raise our morale. We tell each other we just need a bunker shot to go in, or a long putt, or a chip – something to get some energy going.

Then, it happens. On the thirteenth, a long, tough par three, Rory makes a breakthrough.

It's an awkward tee shot for me. I know I have to go in there with a hybrid, but Rory hits a fantastic three-iron to within about fifteen feet. It is a brilliant shot. It's a ridiculously tough hole to make birdie on but, as we walk down off the tee box, we are talking again about getting some energy going, holing a putt, getting a kick-start.

I come in to have a look at the putt because by this stage we are helping each other out on the greens. I have a little look at his putt from behind. I can tell he feels comfortable with it. That's my cue to sod off and let him get on with the putt. He rolls it right in, off the left edge of the hole, and that's it. That's the spark. We have cut the US lead to one hole. We feel that is our turning point.

I walk to the next tee, feeling good. I tee off on the

fourteenth and, as I begin to walk down the fairway, I notice that Michael Jordan, the great US sports icon, has joined the American supporters inside the ropes. He is staring at me as I walk past, so I give him a cheeky wink and he wags his finger at me, as if to say I'm spoiling everyone's fun.

I'm buzzing now. The adrenaline is pumping again. I begin to think we can do something. Rory has hit it left off the tee. I've hit it in a good spot, down the middle of the fairway. Rory is behind some trees and doesn't hit a good lay-up shot. It's over to me. I hit a great shot into the front bunker – the same spot as Dufner.

Dufner splashes out stiff, so it was a gimme. I have to get up and down for a half. I try to hole it and hit it to about five feet past the hole. Not very clever, but I roll that putt straight in the middle. We are still 1 down.

I've teed off first all the way round, but on the fifteenth tee, I tell Rory I want him to hit first this time. It's an awkward tee shot for me, but it could be perfect for him because he might be able to get it on the green with his three wood, or at least to come to rest in the back bunker. He agrees.

He goes first and hits it in the back bunker. That means I can commit to my line, which is a tougher shot to hit with a driver. I hit it in the back bunker, the same spot as his three wood. Zach hits his tee shot in the water, which means Jason has to lay up.

Zach takes quite a bit of time messing around, getting his drop right. He's not going to be a factor on this hole. Jason hits his second shot to about twelve feet. Rory plays first from the bunker, pin high left and twelve feet. I size up my shot. It's a tricky bunker shot over a ridge which feeds all the way down to the hole.

I see from Rory's shot that the ball isn't breaking left to right, which I had thought it would. So I take a more direct line straight at the pin. I hit it perfectly and it lands on the top of the ridge. It gets down there stiff. Dufner's missed his putt. Mine's a gimme for birdie. They concede the hole and we're level with three to play.

It's game on, now. I can see from the scoreboards that Sergio and Luke are still ahead against Woods and Stricker, even if their lead has shrunk from a healthy four up to a nail-biting one-shot advantage. I know things are still bad, but if we can just win these last two matches then a score of ten-six gives us a glimmer of a chance on Sunday. It's a slim chance, but it's a world away from ten-four.

On the sixteenth, we hit two good shots off the tee. I hit a really high cut with a three hybrid, which goes to about twenty feet. Rory hits his shot to about thirty feet. Zach hits to the back of the green, but Dufner is just inside my shot. He will putt last.

Rory hits his putt five feet past the hole. I ask him if he wants to finish. He says, 'Sure'. He misses it. The crowd oohs and aahs and groans. I tell myself it doesn't matter and that I'll hit my putt the same, anyway. Zach leaves his putt short.

It's my turn. I think the ball's going to break slightly left to right early and then break back a little at the end. I send the putt out to the left and, as soon as I hit it, I know I've hit my line. Whether I have chosen the right line or not,

I am about to find out. It's taken the break and it's still got some pace on it as it drops in the right half of the hole. That's it for me. I'm going bananas.

I turn round to Terry Mundy, my caddy, and Rory with a double-fisted fist-pump. The putter goes up in the air. The crowd is going bananas, too, but Dufner still has to putt. Dufner putts and misses. We are 1up, ahead for the first time in the match. We have turned the match from red to blue in three holes.

I walk off that sixteenth green and Michael Jordan is standing right there and he's looking at me. I look at him and I pump my chest, a fist-on-heart pump. He looks straight at me and starts to shake his head. It's like he's saying, 'You son of a bitch.' He is always part of that American team thing, always there, like a giant, intimidating mascot.

I walk right past him, close, and he gives me a jab in the chest with his fist. It's like a fricking sledgehammer. His fists are not small.

'You'll need to hit me harder than that,' I say.

It is a sign of respect, I suppose. I mean, Christ, it's Michael Jordan. He is one of the biggest legends who has ever played sport. He's fucking with me. That's what he's doing, and I know what he's doing, and that's fine. I respect him. That's what he did in his heyday. He messed with people. He was the best.

I find out before the Ryder Cup at Gleneagles that Jordan has done a television interview about that moment at Medinah and his motivation for jabbing me. He tells the Golf Channel that he started trying to get into my head as far back as 2008 at Valhalla. He tells them he was doing it for his country. But he also says, 'One thing I have learned with Ian Poulter is that you do not mess with him during the Ryder Cup. I have tried and tried,' Jordan says, 'and I just cannot get him.'

In the interview, he says he had been planning to say to me, 'See? You cannot do it every time,' as I walked past him after the sixteenth. Then I holed the putt. Then Jordan says he started to worry about whether I was going to swing the match away from the US. As I watch that interview a couple of years later, I feel it is such a big compliment.

Because, as Jordan stands there by the sixteenth, he is starting to realise how pivotal that match is for the Ryder Cup. He was one of my idols when I was growing up but, when he hits me as I walk past him, suddenly he is a rival. In a way, I'm getting to play against him now. Over my dead body is Michael Jordan going to get the better of me when I am playing my game. On the court he might beat me, not on the course.

We get to the seventeenth tee. Par three. Over water. I hit a seven-iron to eight feet. Rory hits it just left of the green. He's chipping. Zach hits it stiff. Fantastic shot. Pretty much a gimme. It's three feet uphill. It is down to me.

I see Olly while I'm standing on the seventeenth tee. As I hit my shot into that green, Olly comes in. I can tell he's desperate to help. He knows how important these last two matches are. He tells me that, earlier, someone else had the putt I'm faced with now. He says it broke a bit to the left.

'Thanks,' I say. 'I've got it, don't worry.'

He follows us all the way down that hole and sits at the back of the green. Again, I can tell he's itching to come in and have a good look and tell us what he would do. It's natural. That's his job. I walk down there. I remember what he said. It's in my mind as I'm walking.

I'm thinking about what he said about it moving a little left, but I'm wondering whether the other player had pulled it a touch. Had he read it right? Was his ball exactly in the same spot, or a foot to the right or a foot to the left?

Rory chips on and doesn't hole out for birdie. So it's over to me. It's a must-make putt. Mentally, I give Zach his putt. I know he's going to make it. So I tell myself I have to hole it. I walk around the hole and I see a little bit of right to left in it. Just a tiny bit. It's going to move just a fraction. I can see it in the contour of the green.

I stand over it and hit the putt. And I turn round to Terry and Rory as it goes in. They're standing next to each other about thirty feet away and I can see Rory's head start shaking in disbelief.

'You're some boy, you,' Rory says.

Terry has been winding him up on the seventeenth green, saying, 'What's the matter with you? It's Ian – he's going to hole that putt; he's never going to miss that.' I don't think Rory believed him, but it's Terry and his banter, lightening the tension.

I have a massive feeling of pride, but it does not occur to me in that situation, nor would it ever, that I am leading the pair. Who's making the birdies is kind of irrelevant. You're both there to do your job. As long as one of us is making birdie, I don't give a hoot. It was Rory who had got the crucial birdie on the thirteenth. It's about being a team. We are getting the job done together.

Rory keeps shaking his head as we walk towards the eighteenth tee.

'You're taking the piss, aren't you?' he says.

We hear Sergio and Luke have beaten Stricker and Woods. That gives us another massive boost. We have to finish the job off. We both hit decent tee shots down the last. So do the Americans. I hit a lovely approach shot to twelve feet behind the hole. Dufner stiffs it. That's a big shot from Dufner. It's three feet from the cup, slightly uphill. Rory goes in with a wedge, but it spins off the front of the green.

I want Rory to roll his putt in so the game's done and dusted and we've got our point. I'm lying on the ground, trying to look at the line of Rory's putt. I want him to hole it. He doesn't hit it quite hard enough and it comes up short.

I'm fully aware of the situation now. It is plain. It's the last match of the day. It's almost dusk. We need this. We need this to stay in the Ryder Cup. If I drain it, we halve the hole and win the match and go in at ten-six. If I don't, it's all over.

I do my usual thing. I put the ball down, I go to the left and do a 360 around the hole. I walk round the putt and I take a look at it from the side. I can see it's going to go right to left. As I get round the back of the hole, I can see both teams. I can see the captains and the vice-captains, the wives, the entourages, every one of the players from the two teams, all watching, all waiting. I pan around all of them. I see Davis Love. I pan the European team. Maybe it takes a millisecond. It's almost like my eyes are scanning everybody in slow motion.

I feel good about my line. I feel confident it's going to break a little right to left.

'I want to send my team into a frenzy,' I say to myself.

There is no way I can miss that putt. I have to hole it. I visualise the reaction when I hole it. I can sense what it would mean to the team. I can sense what it would mean in momentum and atmosphere and sowing a seed of doubt in the US team. All that stuff processes in my mind in a really short space of time, but it seems like a lifetime.

'Come on, roll this in, because I want to turn to my guys,' I say to myself as I stand over it.

If I can turn to my guys in that state and let them feel it, let them get a bit of joy that they have been starved of for two days, maybe we'll have a chance. This is to stay four points down. No way is this a good day because we have a worse deficit on Saturday night than we had on Friday night. But for some reason, this would feel quite big to us as a team, if we can turn this match around.

I don't take too long. I have a couple of looks, head down, hit the putt. As I hit it, I know. I hit my line and, in my head, as the ball is tracking, I am telling it to break right to left and, in another split second, I know it is going to go straight in the middle. It is probably the most amazing putt I have ever holed. For timing, for what it means to the team, for a million reasons.

I turn to the team and turn to Rory and let the emotion flow. Let both fists go. This is massive. I see the team, every one of them, all sharing the joy of what is happening. It is a big putt. It brings big momentum. The American fans want to go home celebrating another good day. Instead, they melt away from the eighteenth with images of wild European celebrations in their mind.

It's crazy for a couple of minutes on the green. It is as

if we are all square. Dufner and Zach had been 2up with six to play. They had birdied three of those last six and they have still lost. That's the measure of what Rory and I have done.

Everybody on the European team is absolutely pumped. There is a lot of high-fiving and hugging and all that stuff. The television crews are swarming all over us.

Eventually, I walk down the steps, over on to the putting green and down into the locker room. The second I open the locker-room door, I can hear singing. We are 10-6 down but the team room is absolutely bouncing. I have never seen anything like it. They are all singing my name. They are all chanting my name.

I realise then that I have finished with five straight birdies. For what it meant, it may have been the greatest stretch of play in my career. It is unbelievable. It is an amazing experience. Everyone is energised. We are four points down, but it is the most energised team I have ever seen.

I try to take it all in. Something has happened. A change has come. I feel unbelievably elated. I have changed the mood. I have ignited a fire.

CHAPTER 29
You Remind Me of Him

I stay behind in the clubhouse after most of the other players leave for the hotel. I am still there when the team sheet arrives for Olly to enter his singles pairings for the next day. Luke Donald is there, too. Olly asks us what positions we'd like to go out in. Luke is so pumped after his fourballs, he wants to go out first. Olly says that's fine. He puts me out second.

If we are to have any chance at all, we need to get off to a fast start. That is obvious. So the order is heavily front-loaded. It goes Luke, me, Rory, Justin, Paul Lawrie, Colsaerts, GMac, García, Hanson, Westwood, Kaymer, Molinari. Olly sets the rest of the order and hands the sheets in. We go back to the hotel, get some food and study the draw.

There's a team meeting at 7.30 p.m. It is completely different to Friday evening. No bollocking this time. We have a decent chat about the singles pairings and how they look. Luke will play Bubba, I will be up against Webb, Rory will face Keegan, Justin will play Mickelson and Lawrie will have to beat Snedeker. It looks good to me.

I like the match-ups. I can see all that top five winning. Do I really think we can do it? A betting man backs against us. We are still heavy outsiders. Everything has to be perfect. So many things have to go our way. The top of the board has to be blue to sow enough doubt in their minds that we have a realistic chance. They have to start to lose confidence.

I have a little lie-in on Sunday morning because the tee-off times are set a bit later than on the previous two days. I set my own alarm. I never have any problem waking up those mornings. I try to lie in as late as possible to get as much rest as I can, but the second my alarm goes off, I'm up, changed and straight out to the golf course.

Because everyone has staggered tee times on the Sunday, everybody leaves the hotel at different times. There are cars waiting outside the hotel, which is about twenty minutes away from the course. I leave, get to the golf course and have some breakfast. Because I am in the second match on, it's very quiet in the team room.

Some of the other guys begin to arrive. I finish breakfast, have my physio stretch and jump on the exercise bike for five minutes just to warm the legs up and get things moving. Then I go off to the range and hit balls for forty-five minutes or so, get to the putting green and have a few putts.

Rory is the next match after me and it occurs to me that I haven't seen him. I am fifteen minutes away from my tee time and I hear a murmur that he hasn't showed up at the golf course yet. It is half an hour from his tee time.

Half an hour, I think. He's cutting it a bit fine.

I hear someone say they have got hold of him and he is on his way. I don't think that much of it. I think everything will be okay. If there is one player there who does not need to hit a warm-up shot, it is Rory McIlroy. If there is one person on either team who only needs two practice swings before he has to play, it would be him. He swings it naturally. You just have to let him go.

I find out he has arrived as I'm walking to the tee. It turns out he forgot we were on Central Time so he miscalculated his tee time. He has hitched a lift to the course in a police car. I don't see him until I have teed off. As I'm walking down the first, I see him sauntering on to the putting green, chewing on an energy bar. Olly is with him, putting his arm around him and telling him to get the job done.

I am relieved to see him, of course, but by that point my brain has blanked out everything not connected with my own game. That's the only thing I can control. That's the most difficult thing about the whole week. You're in pairs for the first two days and you have got your teammate to talk to and your partner's caddy and you are bouncing around, but now it's just you and your caddy.

I feel horrendously flat at the start of my game against Simpson. I'm exhausted. I have spent a lot of energy in that match on Saturday night, a lot of nervous energy. My body doesn't feel alive yet. I'm struggling. I chip in on the first for birdie, but Webb matches me with a superb fifteen-foot putt.

I struggle for a number of holes. It takes me a while to get into the match. I am 2down through four. Then I birdie five, but Webb comes straight back and I make a silly bogey on six. I know I have to try to get a grip of the match. I can't let it slip now. I know that would ruin everything.

I keep looking up at the scoreboards. This time, I feel

buoyed by what I see. All the matches around me have gone blue. The top five are all blue. What a beautiful sight. I make a lovely birdie on seven to get to within a hole of Webb and tee off first at eight. I hit it to the back edge of the green. When Webb steps up, he hits a full shank.

Here's my chance, I think. Here's my window. I need to take care of this now.

Webb is obviously feeling uncomfortable. He had a bad swing at it and hit a shank and now I need to take advantage. I get it back to all square at the eighth, but then fall behind again at the tenth. When we get to the twelfth, I have another chance to even things up.

I hit a lovely shot into the green, to about seven feet. I am standing over my putt when one of the US spectators shouts out from the back right-hand corner of the green. I have to back off the putt and look at it again. When I hole it, I turn to that side of the green and let them have some medicine. I know that putt is big. I guess that kind of stuff from the fans helps me. It gets me really fired up. I give it the fist-pump and let them know I am right back in it.

We halve the next four holes in par. We are all square with two left to play. The pin is back right at seventeen, awkward to get at. You have to be very aggressive to get anywhere near. I hit my shot just on the back fringe. Webb pulls his tee shot into a bunker behind the green, which leaves him a difficult bunker shot. He hits a lovely shot out of the sand to about seven feet and I leave my putt short in the middle. It's on the right line but I just don't hit it. But then Webb misses his putt and I am 1up with one to play.

I nearly mess it all up on the eighteenth. I hit my drive

way right. It misses the bunkers and bounces on a walkway and runs down quite a way. I have trees in front of me and spectators to my right. The gallery are all there in the Grand Pavilion overlooking the spot where my ball has come to rest.

I create a semi-circle around where I am playing my shot. These big, mature trees are in front of me and the wind is into me and I have got 158 yards to the green. I calculate it's a nine iron to get it up over the tree, but I need the eight iron for distance into the wind to get it there.

If I hit nine iron, I have to aim for the front of the green, land it short and try to up and down it and hope that Webb doesn't make birdie. I discuss it with Terry. I think I can open an eight iron out and hit a big banana slice around the edge of the tree and knock the ball on to the green. He asks me if I can pull it off. What he's really saying is, 'Just go for it.'

I know I have the shot. I don't second-guess it. I look up towards the green. There is a massive flag behind the green and it has gone limp. There is no wind, so that is to my advantage. I pull the eight iron out of the bag, open the face up and hit it, all within a couple of seconds. I don't want the wind to pick up.

I absolutely flush it, a big high-raking cut round the tree to about eight feet. Webb pulls his shot to about forty-five feet. I feel a little more comfortable. He hits a good putt on a good line, but it's too hard. He takes his hat off.

Point secured.

I feel a great flood of relief and elation. I look up at the board and realise it isn't just point secured. We have made an amazing start and my win has actually brought the scores level at 10-10. Luke has beaten Bubba, Paul Lawrie has destroyed Snedeker and Rory has beaten Keegan Bradley.

Justin and Mickelson are coming to the seventeenth with Mickelson 1up, so I do a quick couple of television interviews, jump on a buggy and off we go. I miss the drama. Mickelson nearly chips in on the seventeenth green, which would have won the match, but then Rosie drops the bomb, holing a forty-five footer to win the hole. As Mickelson heads off to the eighteenth tee, he turns to give Justin the thumbs-up. What a great piece of sportsmanship. It is one of the enduring images of this Ryder Cup.

Justin completes a remarkable turnaround by winning the match on the eighteenth to tie the scores up again at 11-11 after Dustin Johnson puts the first point of the day on the board for the US by beating Colsaerts. When Rosie beats Mickelson, I realise this thing might go all the way and that we have a real chance of pulling off a miracle.

I jump back on the buggy and go all the way to the last group where Francesco Molinari is playing Tiger. It's a tight game. I watch it until they reach the fifteenth, and then move ahead to the sixteenth, where Sergio has just secured another point against Jim Furyk. Lee Westwood has beaten Kuchar. Zach Johnson has beaten GMac. We are leading 13-12. We need one more point to retain the trophy.

Sergio is 1down after sixteen, but Furyk has missed putts on the seventeenth and eighteenth, which would have got him at least half a point. The match is there for Furyk to close out and he can't quite do it. It is in his hands, but it slips away. It is another massive point for us. Furyk looks devastated.

I wait at the back of the seventeenth tee. Olly has arrived by then and one of the team helpers has a little mini television. I watch that for a while, then pick up Martin Kaymer's match against Steve Stricker, which is all square as it goes down to the seventeenth green. It is down to this match now. This and Molinari verses Woods, which is also all square.

Martin hits his shot into the seventeenth to about thirty feet. Stricker is inside him. Martin rolls his putt five feet past. Stricker hits his too hard and misses his next putt as well. That leaves Martin with a slippery little putt to put some blue on the board. He holes the putt to go 1up, going up the last. The miracle comes closer.

I am sitting there with Olly at the back of the seventeenth green as Martin addresses the putt that wins the hole. Olly can't watch the putt. He has his head in his hands and his hat is tipped backwards on his head. Martin holes that putt, which guarantees half a point.

We walk up the last, just behind them. Martin hits his second shot on to the green and I pat Olly on the back and say, 'Listen, it's done.' Wrong. Martin rolls his putt seven feet past the hole. I'm yelling, 'Sit down, sit down, sit down!' as it rolls. That gets Olly alarmed. We are too far away to see exactly what is happening.

It is pretty much just me and Olly watching by then. We haven't gone all the way to the eighteenth green because, if Martin wins that match, a half for Molinari wins the Ryder Cup outright. Olly's mindset is very much that he wants to be a winning captain. Just retaining it isn't going to be enough for him.

Eventually, Martin stands over a seven-foot putt to retain the Ryder Cup, to complete the Miracle of Medinah. I can't decide whether to watch on TV or watch in real time. He holes that putt and I let out a massive sigh of relief.

I hug Olly. As joyful and emotional it is, it is just a relief that Martin has holed that putt. It would have been heart-breaking to have got so close and failed right at the last.

We have pulled it off. Somehow, we have pulled it off. I can't quite take it in. I look over at Olly again. He is very emotional.

'You have no idea what this means to me,' he says.

After a minute or so, his mind switches back to the score. He wants something out of that last match between Molinari and Tiger. He goes over and speaks to Frankie and tells him he has a chance to win the hole, halve the match and win the Ryder Cup.

Olly wants to finish the match off properly, and he gets his wish. On the eighteenth green, Tiger makes a huge gesture and concedes Frankie's birdie putt, which means the match is halved and we have won fourteen and half to thirteen and a half.

And then the party begins. Everybody is joyful, but the joy is mixed with disbelief. We are all jumping around, and hugging and high-fiving, congratulating Kaymer.

'We've done it!' we keep shouting. 'We've done it!'

It is the most wonderful moment of my career.

Somehow, we have pulled it off. This is a hell of a steal.

At one point, I find myself looking at Seve's silhouette on my left arm. I think of the strength we have gained from all the imagery of him that was with us that week. Others are the same. 'As soon as I came off the eighteenth green,' Justin tells a television crew, 'my first thought has been to Seve. I had a glance down and looked at my left sleeve, and the kind of stuff we did today, that's the kind of stuff he would have done. He's been an inspiration for this team all week long.'

Everyone goes bananas for quite a while. The American fans seem to disappear pretty quickly. The floodgates open and they all run away, which I suppose is understandable. The next hour is crazy. There is champagne being sprayed everywhere and people running round with European flags.

I get in the locker room. The music is playing, even the locker-room attendants are singing, the bartenders from the team room are joining in, everybody is ordering drinks and downing champagne. We are drinking and singing and bouncing around.

We get back to the stage for the closing ceremony and one team feels like they have had the Ryder Cup ripped out of their hands and the other team is the one that stole it. What do you say to them? A few of them take it really badly. You can see that. It is painful. You can only be respectful, say, 'Hard luck,' and, 'It was a great match.'

Eventually, we go back to the hotel. We aren't invited in their team room. In fact, we are asked to stay away. I guess emotions are still too raw. It is a shame because it has become a tradition over the past few years. But I get it. I get that they're upset.

Davis Love comes into our team room. He is very dignified. In fact, he is brilliant. He comes in and chats to us all. A few of the American caddies come in and have a couple of drinks, but there is no get-together. I don't know who is particularly wound up because we never see them. We are just told that a few of them have taken it badly and it would be better if we don't go in there. So we don't.

It doesn't matter to me. I understand their emotions. And anyway, I am just wrapped up in the joy of celebrating with my own team. I have got time left in the game of golf, but to help that comeback, to be part of that Miracle of Medinah – how can it get any better than that? If sporting fairy tales are written down, how can they get any better?

I thought Celtic Manor was pretty good, but Medinah is unbelievable. I enjoy that week more than any other week that I have ever played golf. It is the most emotional I have ever been on a golf course. It gives me memories I will always, always cherish.

As the celebrations wear on, I get a clearer and clearer picture of what Olly had been alluding to when he said I could have no idea of how much it all meant to him. Actually, I begin to get a pretty decent idea.

'All men die, but not all men live,' he says at his closing-ceremony speech. 'You made me feel alive again this week.'

It means everything for him to take that trophy back home to Spain. Whether he will take it to where Seve has been laid to rest, I don't know, but I can now sense what it means.

I can see all the stress and emotion of the week come out in Olly now. Somehow, his team has managed to get him across the line. Westwood is sitting close to him in the locker room and we give Olly a hug and he breaks down. He is crying, but crying with joy.

Before the party moves on, Olly pulls me to one side. He mentions Seve a couple of times and then he pays me the greatest compliment I could ever imagine.

'You remind me of him,' he says.

CHAPTER 30
The Postman Always Rings Twice

A few months after Medinah, I win the WGC-HSBC Champions at Mission Hills in China. I come from way back to beat Ernie Els, Phil Mickelson, Jason Dufner and Scott Piercy by two shots. It's a big win and I keep the roll going through 2013. I have a good run at The Open at Muirfield, tying for third. At the end of the season, I push Henrik Stenson all the way in the Race to Dubai but I can't quite catch him.

Things are looking good and I'm full of optimism for 2014 but then I pick up a series of niggling injuries. I get a labrum tear in my left shoulder at the start of the year when I'm throwing heavy weights around in the gym. I start to get over that, then I lock up my lower back and just as I am almost recovered from that I jar my wrist at the Scottish Open in July.

The injuries dominate my season. I do well in the first round of the USPGA at Valhalla in August but then fade away. I'm close to qualifying automatically for the 2014 Ryder Cup at Gleneagles despite all the injuries but I don't quite make it. I'm still hopeful that I'm going to be selected as one of the wild card picks of the captain, Paul McGinley. I talk to Paul. He never guarantees that I'm a lock for the team but I know I'm going to be in the frame.

Stephen Gallacher, Lee Westwood and Luke Donald are also in contention and four into three doesn't go. Because of the quality of the other guys, I have some uncertainty in my mind but not much. I am confident I am going to make it. I hope my record in previous Ryder Cups, and especially at Medinah, will count for something.

Paul calls me the day before the official press conference to tell me the news. I am at home in Orlando.

'You're coming,' he says. 'Get yourself ready and I'll see you in a couple of weeks.'

Gallacher and Westwood make it, too. I feel very optimistic about our chances, partly because I have always been close to Paul and I know how much work and preparation he has put into his captaincy. I have played for him in the Seve Trophy and he was a great captain then. He has always been very methodical and statistic-orientated and I have always been impressed with his management style. When it first becomes clear he is a candidate to be captain at Gleneagles, I am vocal in my support for him.

I am the first of the players to arrive at Gleneagles. I want to soak up as much of the atmosphere as possible, just like I had at Celtic Manor in 2010. I arrive at the hotel on Sunday morning. I have a look at the team room. Paul has done a great job with it.

There are a lot of pictures on the wall that have been enhanced with graphic design. There is an image of Justin Rose just after he has holed that putt against Mickelson on the seventeenth at Medinah. In the picture, Justin has his hands outstretched and there are shock waves coming from them and rippling over the crowd.

There is a picture of me fist-pumping. And it has been

changed so that I am holding a heart in my hand and squeezing it. As I'm squeezing it, a mass of European stars are bursting out of that heart. There is a lot of imagery like that. There are quotations from Bob Torrance and Seve Ballesteros on the walls that enforce the idea that these are the happiest days of our lives as players. In the locker room, there is an emotive picture of Seve as a young kid.

In another room, there is picture of a scroll that is a history of the Ryder Cup and a list of its winners and losers. It shows the USA had dominated the competition for a long, long time and that they are still way ahead of us in the win-loss ratio.

They've won it twenty-five times against Europe's thirteen.

It's clearly something Paul wants to make a point about. We are aware of the dangers of complacency. Everyone's talking about how we are favourites and how the Americans have a weak team, how there's no Tiger, how they've messed up by not picking Billy Horschel, the FedExCup winner, as one of their wild cards.

I don't think it is in the nature of anyone in the European team at Gleneagles to be complacent but I understand why Paul is highlighting the danger. You can't afford a single man in the side to think the job is already done. I look at that scroll of the past winners and see there is still way too much American red, white and blue on it.

Complacency is one of the main things that Sir Alex Ferguson talks about when he comes in to the team room to talk to us on Tuesday night. Paul's had this planned for more than a year and it goes down well, not just because players like Rory and GMac are big Manchester United fans.

Sir Alex says complacency is one of the biggest dangers in sport and that the way he urged his players to guard against it was through complete concentration. He talks about some of the big matches he took charge of and how mistakes only came from complacency in one form or another. It might be because one player switches off for a couple of seconds at a corner or even a throw-in. That's all it takes for the opposition to make inroads.

He talks about the team, too. He talks about the importance of how the team must take precedence over the individual and about how if anyone ever threatened that at United, then he would not stand for it. No matter how good the player was, if he threatened team spirit, Sir Alex would move him on.

The role of Ryder Cup captain is a manager's role and Paul McGinley makes an analogy between the dominance of Manchester United and our team at Gleneagles. He says the reason why Ferguson was so successful was because he managed his team better than anyone else.

Paul says that sport is about the players going out and delivering, but the manager has to make them comfortable enough to give their best. Paul has studied Sir Alex carefully and I think Sir Alex is impressed. He tells me he knows Paul is going to do a good job.

Rory says later that he is in awe of Sir Alex. He says that when he was speaking, he was looking at him like he was in a trance. But Sir Alex gets a bit of stick, too. Mainly from the caddies later on when he speaks to them. Lee Westwood's caddy, Billy Foster, is a Leeds fan and he lets him know he isn't happy about all the Leeds players that Ferguson took to Old Trafford, particularly Eric Cantona.

Ferguson gets a bit of grief from Thomas Bjørn, too, because Thomas is a big Liverpool fan. He takes it all well. Arsenal are playing Southampton in the Capital One Cup that evening and I am checking the score from time to time. When the final score comes in, I mention it to him.

'You'll be pleased to know Arsenal have just lost,' I say.

'You won't be getting any sympathy from me,' he smiles.

As well as the images I have mentioned, there are some slogans on the walls of our team room and these relate to Paul's admiration for Sir Alex, too. One of them says: 'Wave after wave after wave'.

It's to encapsulate the idea of how Sir Alex wanted his Manchester United teams to play. Wave after wave after wave of attack. No let up. No respite for the opposition. Paul wants to reproduce that in our team and as the competition unfolds, I think he does.

The way he juggles the line-up and the pairings has guys champing at the bit to play. He has twelve players and he wants to keep them fresh and hungry and with points to prove. I think he does that an awful lot better than the American skipper, Tom Watson, who asks seven of his players to play thirty-six holes on Saturday.

McGinley only asks Justin and Rory to play in all five sessions and that is because they are probably the strongest and fittest players in the team. McGinley judges that perfectly. Everyone else is fresh and raring to go, so when each of us gets our chance, we are ready to tear into the Americans. Wave after wave after wave.

The build-up to the event is a little quieter than it has

been before, although with an event as huge as the Ryder Cup, these things are relative. We want to keep it that way anyway. We are the favourites. There is no point in us rattling anybody's cage or getting any of the opposition fired up.

Off the course, the Americans make the running. Tom Watson says that his team will be targeting me and Rory. I take that as a massive compliment. It doesn't bother me at all. I feel flattered by it. I know that's going to be the case anyway. The Americans have never made any secret about how much they relish the idea of beating me in the Ryder Cup.

When Mickelson does his press conference at the course on Wednesday, he makes a crack about Rory and GMac, who have been sucked into a legal case concerning a management company. Rory and GMac are close friends. There is no issue between them at all, but lawyers are involved and Phil tries to make a point about how well the American team get on and suggests their team spirit, which is so often questioned and will be again by the time they fly home, is actually better than ours.

'Well, not only are we able to play together,' Phil says, 'we also don't litigate against each other and that's a real plus, I feel, heading into this week.'

It is noted. Let's put it that way. It's a dig. It's pre-meditated. We all know that.

There is no way that remark is off the cuff. Phil thinks he's doing his bit for his team and that it will unnerve Rory and GMac so he throws it out there and it gets everybody talking.

Rory and GMac handle it well. They don't get involved

publicly. They don't need to. But we go to the gala dinner at the Kelvingrove Art Gallery and Museum in Glasgow that night and when Rory bumps into Phil, he makes sure he mentions the fact Phil had been cleared over some insider trading issues recently. He says something along the lines of 'at least I'm not wanted by the FBI'.

That's the right way to do it. Have a joke with the guy face to face. It's funny then. It would have been funny if Phil had said what he said face to face, too, rather than it coming out through the media at a press conference. It's not something that winds any of us up particularly. No one's bitter towards Phil for it. It's part of the week.

I feel a bit more pressure going into this Ryder Cup than I have before. It's not anything to do with the Americans banging on about targeting me. That kind of pressure pleases me. But I've not been in the best of form and that is a worry.

I'm still trying to get over those niggly little injuries and however positive I am, those things start to get you down a bit after a while. I'm not overly concerned but I'm aware of the expectations on me and I desperately want to perform.

On the eve of the competition, Paul McGinley makes an inspiring speech. By that stage, I'm already full of admiration for the way he is handling the captaincy. It's not about him. It's about the team. He is respectful of the captaincy in that he has put a hell of a lot of effort into it. He has been thorough. In fact, he has been meticulous.

He is up against Tom Watson, don't forget, a man who is an icon of the game. This is a David and Goliath story. This is about Paul being up against a man who was his hero when he was a player, a man who is known as one of golf's great statesmen.

After we get back from the Opening Ceremony on Thursday evening, Paul stands in front of us all in the team room and begins to speak.

'I am not going to tell any of you how to play golf this week,' he says. 'I was never the player that every one of you guys has become. You know what to do. I just want to make sure that you have everything you need to be able to go out there and do your job properly. And more than anything else, I trust you guys. I trust you implicitly.'

I find his speech moving. There are a lot of men who would not have been able to say what he said. There are a lot of men who would want to emphasise their role and their importance and who would not be able to stop themselves telling someone else how to play the game.

What he says fills me with confidence. He is telling all of us what great players we are. He is building us up. Most of all, he is telling us that he trusts us. I find it very motivating. I look around and sense that everyone else feels the same. The mood is great.

Paul doesn't have a big ego. During the week, he talks to the press about the template of European success that he wants to follow. It comes down to this: if it ain't broke, don't fix it. Paul doesn't want to make any big changes to what we have been doing in the past few years. He wants to make it even better, certainly, but he knows we have a winning formula.

When it comes to the first morning, I know I'm going to go out in the fourballs with either Justin or Stephen Gallacher, the Scottish rookie. McGinley decides that I should partner Stephen. He feels my experience can help him through his nerves and get the best out of him. He wants GMac to do the same for Victor Dubuisson in the afternoon.

I try my best. Maybe I get him too pumped. Maybe I make him nervous. Maybe he's just trying too hard because it's a home Ryder Cup for him and he wants to play well so, so badly. I should mention here that I don't exactly rip the course up myself in our match against the American rookies Jordan Spieth and Patrick Reed.

I don't play well and between us, we just never get anything going. Jordan and Patrick are incredibly motivated, too. Jordan says later that he was desperate to get the first shot at me and that some of his teammates came up to him to say how jealous they are. They're taking this targeting thing seriously.

I find it hard taking on the responsibility of helping a rookie. I'm nervous, too. I know how much it means to Stephen and I want to win for him as much as for myself and the team. But it just never happens. We miss putts we should drain and Jordan and Patrick play well.

We get humped 5&4. It's my heaviest ever loss in the Ryder Cup, worse than the 4&3 beating I took in my first ever match when I played with Darren Clarke against Tiger Woods and Chris Riley at Oakland Hills. I hate losing. Absolutely hate it. Especially to a pair of rookies.

I'm desperately disappointed but through it all I'm aware how hard it must be for Stephen to take. He's waited a long time for his chance to play Ryder Cup and I feel I've let him down in a way. I tell him about how Darren and I lost to Woods and Riley and how I felt then. I tell him things can turn around.

I'm devastated to have lost but I get over it quickly. There's no other option if you want to help the team. I already know I'm going to be sitting out in the afternoon. That's always been the plan and I've got no problem with that. I was never expecting to play five games.

We're down at the end of the fourballs but the guys turn things around brilliantly in the afternoon foursomes and win three of the four matches, halving the other. Jamie Donaldson and Lee Westwood get things off to a great start by beating Jim Furyk and Matt Kuchar, Justin and Henrik Stenson win for the second time in the day by beating Hunter Mahan and Zach Johnson and GMac and Victor play superbly to beat Mickelson and Keegan Bradley.

That turns out to be a massive win for us. Phil and Keegan are a really important pair for the USA but for reasons that will later become apparent we won't see them again in this Ryder Cup. By the end of the day, we hold a 5-3 lead.

The mood in the team room that evening is good. We feel we have hit them with wave after wave, just as we had hoped. And in the end, the waves have swamped them. We know we have finished the day on a real high. Now we just need to keep up the pressure.

There is only one negative. At the press conference after the foursomes, it emerges that Nick Faldo has been heavily critical of Sergio García. He has said on television that Sergio had a bad attitude when he played under Nick in the 2008 Ryder Cup at Valhalla and that he was 'useless' there.

Sergio puts a brave face on it but the rest of the guys are fuming. I find out about it when they get back. I'm shocked that he's said it. I think it's highly disrespectful. It's a cheap shot and it's the worst possible timing.

It makes me laugh. Faldo is talking about someone being useless at the 2008 Ryder Cup. That's the Ryder Cup where he was captain. That's the Ryder Cup where the Europe team suffered a heavy defeat. That's the only Ryder Cup we've lost in the last fifteen years. And he was captain. So who's useless? I think Faldo might need to have a little look in the mirror.

I have always got on great with Faldo in the past and I have a great deal of respect for everything he has achieved but this feels like sour grapes. It feels like a guy who is still bitter that he lost in 2008. He was someone that I looked up to but I just don't get where he was coming from with what he said about Sergio.

I'm sorry but Faldo has lost a lot of respect from players because of what he said. There were plenty of things a lot of the players were unhappy with at Valhalla, but none of us criticised him. I think he may find that begins to change now.

The next morning, I go out with Rory in the fourballs against Rickie Fowler and Jimmy Walker. I feel very comfortable. Rory is an even better player now than when I partnered him on the Saturday afternoon at Medinah and he is coming off an unbelievable summer where he's won two Majors and established himself as the world number one again.

We know each other's games now and when the match begins, we gel well. We're having fun. We're helping each other out. We know when to intervene and when not to. It all feels good but it also develops into an extremely tough match and I notice that all around us the boards are turning American red.

We are playing well but then Rickie holes a bunker shot at the tenth, Rory and I both miss birdie opportunities and the momentum shifts. I see my old buddy Michael Jordan standing at the back of the twelfth green but he doesn't follow us this time or attempt to catch my eye or jab me. He stays where he is when we move on to the thirteenth.

Rickie and Jimmy are flying now and by the time we get to the fifteenth, we are 1down. Then Rickie stiffs his approach to within four feet and suddenly we are looking at being 2down with three to play. That is not a good scenario.

Rory is somewhere to the left of the green and I have hit a wedge shot out of the rough that has finished up about fifty yards from the pin, just short of the bunker that guards the right side of the putting surface. I know we are staring down the barrel.

For the first time in this Ryder Cup, it feels as if the competition is swinging decisively towards the USA. They are up or all square in all the games and suddenly they have all the momentum. It feels like it is vital that Rory and I rescue something from our match to give us something to cling on to going into the afternoon.

I'm aware I haven't contributed as much as I would like to have done. Rory's playing well and I'm backing him up but I have been struggling a little bit. I haven't had any moments that have really fired my confidence and made me feel the way I did at Medinah. All that stuff about the postman and how I always deliver is starting to sound a bit hollow.

The shot I'm facing is not an easy one by any means but it could be worse. I know that if I get it right, it is going to land on a downslope and run down towards the pin. So I try to visualise the second half of what is going to happen as a putt. I gauge the line and try to concentrate on chipping the ball on to the green so that it hits that line.

When I play the chip and see where it lands, I know it has a chance. It rolls and rolls and it starts to curl towards the hole. I know it's in a long time before it drops and when it disappears, I let it all go. All the frustration of losing on the first morning, all the relief of dragging Rory and me back into our match and of helping the team comes pouring out.

I get the double fist-pump going. I beat my chest. I'm totally exhilarated. Rory goes mad, too. We stand together by the side of the green as Fowler sizes up his putt and I feel grateful that I've got my mojo going again. Fowler sinks his putt. We are still 1 down.

But it's great to have that feeling again. It's great to hear the roars when the big screens show a replay of my chip shot. It's great to feel the energy spreading round the course. Those are the kind of moments that make the Ryder Cup my drug. They're magic moments.

A television interviewer says to me later that the postman finally showed up on the sixteenth and delivered. Better late than never.

'Second-class post,' I tell him.

We go to the sixteenth and now I am full of confidence. I drain a twelve-foot putt that wins us the hole and moves us back to all square. Cue more fist-pumping. I'm starting to feel like I'm invincible again. I think fleetingly about the afternoon. I'm hoping I'm going to be going out with Justin but I know the decision had to be made half an hour earlier, about the time we were going down fifteen. I don't think about it for long.

We can't push ourselves into the lead on the seventeenth and it looks as if we might be in a bit of trouble on the eighteenth but then Rory plays a magnificent chip shot out of the light rough at the side of the green that he nearly holes. Fowler has an eagle putt to win it but it slides by and the match finishes all square. It isn't a win but it feels like an important half.

I feel pleased that I've been able to make a contribution but I know instinctively that I have been left out of the afternoon foursomes. I see Terry, my caddy, standing by the side of the green and I know that if I was going straight back out, he would already be on his way back up to the clubhouse, preparing for the next round.

At that point, Des Smyth, one of Paul's assistants comes over to me on the green and puts his arm around me. He tells me I am being rested and asks if there's anything I need. I'm fine. I'm disappointed because I was looking forward to playing with Justin, but Paul has decided to pair him with Martin Kaymer instead.

Later in the day, Paul comes to find me. He apologises to me for leaving me out. He tells me that if I had made that chip shot at the fifteenth five minutes earlier, I would have been playing. But Paul had to make the decision while we were on the fifteenth tee and I hadn't begun to fire then. He had to make his choice and he went with Martin.

I tell him he doesn't need to apologise to me and I mean it. I wanted to play and Martin wanted to play and when Paul made the judgment call, he made the right call. I hadn't shown him enough when he took the decision.

Our team isn't about people getting pissed off with the captain's decision anyway. It never has been. Not while I've been playing. I know that GMac was desperate to play on Saturday morning but I never once saw him looking annoyed when he was left out. Everyone buys into the team ethic. It's one of the reasons why we win.

It's difficult for anyone to quibble with the choices Paul made anyway. They are all spectacularly successful. We totally dominate the afternoon session again. We win three matches and halve the other again. We turn things around completely. By the end of the second day, we have a 10-6 lead.

Ecstatic as we are, quite a few of us are surprised by Tom Watson's decision-making during Saturday's play. Most of all, I'm astonished that he does not play Mickelson and Bradley. I mean, he does not play them at all. He doesn't just leave them out of one session. He leaves them out of both sessions. It completely baffles me.

Watson says later that Phil was texting him, begging him for the chance to play. I also find it slightly odd that he should make that public. But it is not as strange as leaving two players like that out of your team altogether. Most of us in the European team are astonished when we see the Saturday morning pairings and their names are not there.

It gave us a real boost, to be honest. Phil makes an awful lot of birdies. Sure, he makes some mistakes, too, but generally he makes more birdies than mistakes. He doesn't usually stay flat for long. We feel it is a big advantage that he appears to have been exiled from the team.

I am almost equally mystified by the absence of Keegan. He is one of the most passionate, talented players the US team has, he has a brilliant partnership with Phil, he's fit, he's healthy and he's playing great. But he's not there in the line-up. I find it utterly bizarre.

It gives us a double boost really, because it tells us that there are problems in the US team room. There have to be. It's the only explanation for leaving out two players like that. And if there are problems in the team room, then you're in trouble. It's not healthy.

Watson's choices also mean that seven of his players play thirty-six holes on Saturday. I find it hard to see the sense in that. Some of them look shattered in the afternoon and Paul's strategy really starts to pay off. We're fresh. We keep coming at them. Wave after wave after wave.

We talk about complacency again on Saturday night. Lee Westwood, who has passed the Ryder Cup points total of Seve Ballesteros that day, gets up in the team room and makes a speech. He reminds us that 10-6 was the score at the same stage of the competition at Medinah. Only that time, the USA were leading us. We turned it round, Lee said, and so could they.

Paul plays us three motivational videos. One of them is a kind of compilation of some of our best moments as individuals and as a team. Another shows the Americans celebrating at key moments when they have had great victories. It's a good reminder of what could happen if we allow ourselves to think we have already won.

Paul puts me out ninth in the singles. I'm drawn against Webb Simpson who I played and beat at the same stage at Medinah. I'm pumped up for it and I know he will be, too. He'll want revenge for what happened the last time and he's another one who did not hit a ball on Saturday so will want to prove a point to Watson.

We know that they will go out strong. Watson puts his form players, Spieth and Reed, at the top of the order and they go out against GMac and Stenson. By the time I get out to the tee to start my match, things don't look great. We're just about okay but there's enough red on the board for it to be a concern.

One of the exceptions to that is Rory, who is blowing Rickie Fowler away with some breathtaking golf. He puts the first point of the day on the board for either team to extend our lead to 11-6 and gradually some of the other boys get their reward for hanging tough and start to turn their matches around. GMac is crucial and he comes back from behind against Spieth to put another point on the board.

I'm well into my own battle with Simpson by then. I don't make the best start and I go 1 down on the first but I fight back and the match swings back and forth. I am 2 up after nine holes but Webb wins the tenth and then chips in at the thirteenth to stop my advantage getting wider again.

I'm looking at the board. We needed four points at the start of the day to retain the trophy. Rory and GMac have won and Martin Kaymer has beaten Bubba Watson. Justin has halved his match with Hunter Mahan and so we are half a point away from retaining the trophy and a point away from winning the competition again outright.

I'm in a struggle with Webb. I'm not really thinking that it might be me who holes the winning putt but I am thinking that whatever I can contribute might be important all of a sudden. I'm thinking that the team might need something from me to get us over the line.

But one match behind me, Jamie Donaldson is destroying Keegan Bradley. So as Webb and I are walking down the sixteenth, we hear roars coming from the fifteenth where Jamie has just played that magnificent wedge shot to seal his 4&3 victory and win the Ryder Cup. All around us, the crowd starts going bananas.

It is a strange feeling being out on the course in the middle of a match when that happens. I had experienced it at Valhalla but I was on a losing team then. This is different. There is a great sense of elation and relief and you can feel your body relaxing. You want to be with your mates celebrating but you know you have to finish your match and do your job.

I find it hard to concentrate and Webb goes 1up at the seventeenth. Then my pride kicks in. I don't need to get half a point for my team any more but I need to get half a point for myself. I have never lost a Ryder Cup singles match and I don't want to start now. I want to keep my unbeaten record.

I play the eighteenth beautifully. Webb has to hit out of a fairway bunker and I'm in control. My third shot rolls down for a gimme so Webb has to make his birdie putt to win the match. He misses. I have my half and my unbeaten record and I can start to celebrate with the rest of the lads.

I go back to the seventeenth where Paul is following the last match, Victor Dubuisson against Zach Johnson. I find

Paul and hug him and congratulate him. I'm full of admiration for the job he's done. He deserves every bit of praise that is coming his way.

It is different to Medinah. Not quite as wild. Not quite as raucous. It's bound to be different. At Medinah we won when nobody expected to win. At Gleneagles, the final day is about making sure we do our job. We are favourites and favourites are expected to win from a 10-6 overnight position. We do what is expected of us.

The celebrations afterwards reflect that. We have a really lovely evening in the hotel. I have my picture taken outside with Katie and the Ryder Cup. That feels special. We grab a quick snack after the closing ceremony and I wander into the US team room for a bit and chat with a few of their guys.

That feels good, too. There is none of the acrimony and upset that there was in Medinah. The US lads are happy to talk this time. I have a chat with Jordan Spieth and tell him how impressive he was. He says all the other US players wanted to play me on that first day.

By then, the Americans have started to implode publicly. Mickelson has voiced his opinion on where it all went wrong at the press conference and Tom Watson has argued with him. It all comes out in the wash. Maybe the Americans should look more closely at how we win. A bit later, I ask Paul if it's okay if I take the Ryder Cup into the hotel bar. A few of the other players are in there with a lot of our supporters. I march in with it, holding the trophy aloft, singing 'Ole, Ole, Ole'. The place goes mad and it quickly turns into selfie paradise. Everybody wants a picture with the trophy.

I get to bed about 4 a.m., have a couple of hours' sleep and then head off to Edinburgh Airport to get a flight to Gatwick where we'll get on a plane back to Orlando. I'm waiting for the flight in Edinburgh when Michael Jordan comes over.

'Congratulations,' he says. 'You did it again.'

'I didn't see you out on the course this time,' I say.

'I was there,' he says, 'but I stayed out of your way. I didn't want to give you any inspiration. I saw you helped to turn the tide at the right time, though.'

I tell him it's about time we had a game of golf.

'You got cash?' he asks.

I pull out a small wad of notes from my pocket but he shakes his head.

'That is not going to be enough,' he says.

It makes me laugh. In a way, it sums up his philosophy and mine. No limits.

INDEX

Index

Acknowledgements

This book, and my whole story actually, would not have been possible without the support and encouragement of many people. Some are named in this book, and some are not – you know who you are!

I would like to specifically thank and acknowledge:

My parents for supporting me and always believing in me;

Paul Dunkley for sponsoring me many years ago, always mentoring, teaching and helping me grow;

R. J. Nemer, for understanding how to represent and manage me, and never losing your patience;

Ollie Holt for helping to get my thoughts organized and on paper;

Richard Milner for making the book real, and the entire team at Quercus for their efforts.

And everyone else along the way – it's been a hell of a journey. I can't wait for the next chapters of my life to unfold.